400 Best
Sandwich
Recipes

400 Best Sandwich Recipes

From Classics & Burgers to Wraps & Condiments

Alison Lewis

Robert
ROSE

Dedicated to my three children: Alec, Leigh and Zachary

400 Best Sandwich Recipes
Text copyright © 2011 Alison Lewis
Photographs copyright © 2011 Robert Rose Inc.
Cover and text design copyright © 2011 Robert Rose Inc.

For complete cataloguing information, see page 349.

Disclaimer
The recipes in this book have been carefully tested by our kitchen and our tasters. To the best of our knowledge, they are safe and nutritious for ordinary use and users. For those people with food or other allergies, or who have special food requirements or health issues, please read the suggested contents of each recipe carefully and determine whether or not they may create a problem for you. All recipes are used at the risk of the consumer.

We cannot be responsible for any hazards, loss or damage that may occur as a result of any recipe use.

For those with special needs, allergies, requirements or health problems, in the event of any doubt, please contact your medical adviser prior to the use of any recipe.

Design and Production: Kevin Cockburn/PageWave Graphics Inc.
Editor: Carol Sherman
Copy Editor: Karen Campbell-Sheviak
Recipe Editor: Jennifer MacKenzie
Indexer: Gillian Watts
Photography: Colin Erricson
Associate Photographer: Matt Johannsson
Food Styling: Kathryn Robertson
Prop Styling: Charlene Erricson

We acknowledge the financial support of the Government of Canada through the Book Publishing Industry Development Program (BPIDP) for our publishing activities.

Published by Robert Rose Inc.
120 Eglinton Avenue East, Suite 800, Toronto, Ontario, Canada M4P 1E2
Tel: (416) 322-6552 Fax: (416) 322-6936
www.robertrose.ca

Printed and bound in Canada

1 2 3 4 5 6 7 8 9 MP 19 18 17 16 15 14 13 12 11

Contents

Acknowledgments

I have so many people to thank. I will start with my agent, Lisa Ekus, and all of her incredible staff at the Lisa Ekus Group. I thank Lisa for introducing me to Bob Dees, president of Robert Rose Books, and I appreciate him for believing in me and taking a chance on me. Thanks to my editor, Carol Sherman, for all of her diligent and endless hours of work. Thanks to Jennifer MacKenzie and Karen Campbell-Sheviak for editing and proofing my recipes and offering helpful suggestions. Thanks to everyone at PageWave Graphics, including designer Kevin Cockburn for making such a beautiful book and photographer Colin Erricson for the fabulous photographs.

Special thanks to Nancy Bynon for all of her help. I met her toward the end of my book journey, but she was an angel from above, offering advice and wonderful ideas and putting in incredible hours of recipe testing. I also thank my assistant, Alatia Butler, for all of her optimism and wonderful help with this project as well as so many others. Special thanks to my Birmingham recipe editor, Kate Nicholson, for all of her help. It has been so fun to work with Kate again. I also want to thank my graphic designer, Mandy Lamb Meredith, for all her hard work and artistic talent.

A huge thanks goes out to all the people who tested recipes for me out of the goodness of their hearts, including Caroline Downing, Ted and Catherine Pewitt and Carrie McMahon. Also, thanks for all the wonderful creative ideas from my friends: Lisa Goldstein, Keil Gross, Heidi Bloomston and Stephanie Smith. Additionally, thanks so much to my niece, Meredith Asman, and my good friend Amy Stein, who helped with initial research for this project. I also thank my parents, Alvin and Audrey Rich, my sisters, Natalie and Julie, and my brother, Craig, for their support.

Most of all I have to thank Jon Lewis for his endless help from start to finish with this book as well as with the kids during my crazy six months working on this project. I owe you more than words can say. Also to my three children, Alec, Leigh and Zachary, who helped me from start to finish on this project, helping me test recipes and grocery shop, offering ideas and tasting almost every sandwich in this book. You are three great critics, and you are going to be so talented in whatever you do. You all are what life is all about, and I love you more than anything.

Introduction

Coming up with an idea for a cookbook is a lot more difficult than one might think. You never know how it might happen, but for me, it was a rainy day in the car. I have to attribute this book idea to my youngest son, Zachary, who is 9. I had been talking to my agent Lisa Ekus and publisher Bob Dees for several months. I had several conversations discussing hundreds of cookbook ideas with Bob, and he asked me for another phone meeting on a Friday, the day before spring break. I was in the car on the way to the beach and it was pouring rain. I had my three kids in the backseat, and I was definitely struggling to pull ideas out of my head. We talked through a few ideas that I came up with off the top of my head, and finally, Zachary blurts out, "What about sandwiches?" Bob asked me, "What did he say?" When I told him, "Sandwiches," he said, "That sounds interesting." He told me to enjoy my trip, and we would talk the very next week. Within two weeks, Bob told me he wanted a very comprehensive book on sandwich recipes filled with wraps, grilled cheese, regional, international etc. I had two weeks to show him a proposed Table of Contents and recipe title list, and the rest is history.

Working on this book was amazingly fun. It was an incredibly tight deadline, but sandwich recipes are so versatile, fun, and, of course, perfect for kids. They offer you a chance to be creative and to offer so much variety, tradition and memories. Sandwiches are great for every meal of the day and for entertaining. From breakfast to dessert and from classic to international, there's something for everyone in this book.

Tips for Making Great Sandwiches

Sandwiches are more versatile than ever. You can serve them hot, cold, grilled, fried, rolled, open-faced or with a knife and a fork. Here are some of my tips for making the best sandwich ever.

1. Use only the freshest ingredients from start to finish — meat, produce, bread and condiments.
2. Use firm textured breads. These will hold fillings better.
3. Toast bread for sandwiches that have saucy or warm fillings.
4. Don't make sandwiches with moist fillings in advance or the bread gets soggy.
5. Use a serrated or sharp knife to cut a sandwich neatly.
6. Avoid freezing sandwiches with eggs, mayonnaise, sour cream, lettuce or tomato. This will produce poor results when thawing and reheating.

Sandwich Basics

Top-quality ingredients are the basics for good cooking, and this holds true for sandwiches.

Breads

Great breads make great sandwiches. Your options are limitless. You can use freshly baked breads or any of your favorite store-bought or bakery breads. Whether you choose sourdough bread, Italian bread, rye, pumpernickel or ciabatta, there are so many incredible easy-to-find breads and new artisanal breads to try. Whole grains provide more fiber and can feel more satisfying when used in sandwiches such as Almond Butter, Honey and Banana (page 56). Pita works great in so many sandwiches such as Lamb Gyros (page 260) or Shawarma Sandwich (page 245). Most varieties of pita bread are low in fat. Flour tortillas create the perfect wraps such as in Classic Spinach Salad Wraps (page 188), Veggie and Goat Cheese Wraps (page 187) and an entire chapter filled with tortillas starting on page 186. Each of the recipes state which breads to choose, but feel free to substitute any of your favorites.

Most breads stay fresh for 5 to 7 days at room temperature if they are wrapped airtight, except for French or Italian breads, which usually only last about 2 days. To freeze bread, double wrap and place in an airtight container and freeze for up to 3 months.

Meats and Seafood

Choose the best meat or fish when building a sandwich. You can make fabulous sandwiches with meats from the deli, or ones that are grilled, baked or roasted. You will find an array of recipes in this book with meats including beef, poultry, pork and turkey. There's also fish and seafood ones.

Cheeses

I like to use a variety of cheeses on sandwiches because cheese can be a key component of a great sandwich. Cheeses can be sliced, shredded, grated, shaved, spread or crumbled. Creamy cheese, such as Brie, adds great texture and has a mild flavor. Goat cheese pairs well with almost any combination. Varieties of Cheddar as well as Italian cheeses are readily available and add depth to sandwiches.

To store firm, semifirm and semisoft cheese, wrap tightly in a plastic bag or foil. Store in the refrigerator's cheese compartment for up to several weeks. Soft cheeses should be tightly wrapped but only last about 2 days. Cheeses such as Cheddar, Swiss and Monterey Jack are easier to grate when they are cold. There are more than 90 recipes in the Grilled Cheese sandwich chapter (page 75).

Sandwich Toppings

Toppings for sandwiches add texture, flavor and crunch.

Vegetables

Vegetables such as cucumbers, lettuces, sprouts, mushrooms, onions and tomatoes add huge flavor, texture and depth to sandwiches. For lettuces, I like romaine, Bibb and iceberg if I want a softer topping — perfect for Lobster Rolls with Creamy Dijon Sauce (page 284), Vegetable Piadine (page 243) or Easy Tostadas (page 236). Arugula or radicchio adds pepperiness to sandwiches such as Grilled Roast Beef and Stilton (page 84) and Tomato Tea Sandwiches with Arugula and Basil (page 42). Spinach adds color and, of course, nutrition to Grilled Ham, Goat Cheese and Figs (page 84). Onions offer great flavor and variety from sweet onions to caramelized onions in Dijon Peppercorn Wraps (page 308) and Grilled Gruyère and Caramelized Onions (page 88). I also love to roast vegetables such as bell peppers, zucchini and tomatoes as a sandwich topper. They add terrific flavor, color and texture.

Fruits

Fruits are a great sandwich component. I love using red and green apples in sandwiches such as Grilled Brie, Apple and Thyme (page 95). They add crunch and taste wonderful with cheese. Melons go great with prosciutto and ham such as in Prosciutto and Melon Grilled Cheese (page 117). Strawberries pair well with cream cheese, mascarpone cheese, goat cheese and feta as seen in the Strawberry Cream Cheese Sandwich (page 252), and in the dessert sandwich, Strawberry and Mascarpone Sandwich (page 340).

Dried fruits also add crunch and texture to sandwiches and go well when using preserves as a spread. Avocados add creaminess, color and awesome flavor to all types of burgers and sandwiches. I like using Hass avocados because they are smaller and have deeper flavor. Tomatoes add flavor, juiciness and color to any sandwich and pair well with so many meats and cheese.

Condiments

Condiments have become popular and trendy. From aïolis, pestos and spreads to mustards, mayonnaise and salsas, there's something for everyone. The Condiment chapter starting on page 309 has an array of great condiment recipes. Some of my favorites are Chipotle Aïoli (page 311), which is used on the Burgers with Grilled Onion and Smoked Cheddar (page 146), and Peach Ginger Chutney (page 335) served on Grilled Brie with Chutney (page 94).

Think Seasonally

When making sandwiches, use the best fresh produce that each season has to offer.

- **Fall:** Autumn favorites include mushrooms, fresh herbs, apples, nuts and pears.
- **Winter:** Enjoy greens, apples, pears, citrus fruits and fresh pineapple.
- **Spring:** Try asparagus, fresh herbs and strawberries.
- **Summer:** Arugula leaves, tomatoes, corn, peaches, nectarines and fresh herbs.

Sandwich Shortcuts

When creating recipes, I try to get the best result possible but save time as well. Here are some great shortcut tips:

1. Gather all of your ingredients before you begin.
2. I like to purchase chicken cutlets or thinly sliced pork loin chops because they are thinner and cook faster.
3. I purchase fresh or frozen shrimp that has already been peeled and deveined.
4. I use rotisserie chicken a lot! When recipes call for chopped cooked chicken, I usually use rotisserie purchased at the grocery store. The lemon pepper rotisserie chicken is my favorite.
5. I love to grill. It's quick and easy and when the weather is bad, I use the grill pan on the stove.
6. Panini makers and slow cookers are a lifesaver.
7. I use precut carrots, sliced mushrooms and bagged, washed greens whenever I can to save time.
8. I make very organized grocery lists and even try to list my ingredients in order of the way the store is organized.
9. When I purchase hamburger meat (beef or turkey), I buy extra to freeze.
10. When I grill steak, salmon or chicken, I grill extra for a main-dish salad the next day.
11. I like to get my kids involved because it provides help in the kitchen, and they get excited about the meal.

Making Ahead and Storing Sandwiches

The beauty of many cold sandwiches is that they can be made ahead and eaten later unless the recipe states to "serve immediately." To store sandwiches, cover in plastic wrap and store in the refrigerator for up to 4 hours. Wraps that don't contain eggs, fish or greens can be covered and refrigerated for up to 24 hours or frozen for up to 1 week. Remove from the refrigerator 15 minutes before eating them.

To reheat sandwiches, cook in a microwave on High for 1 to 2 minutes or uncover and bake on a small baking sheet at 350°F (180°C) for 15 minutes. If the sandwiches are frozen, let thaw in the refrigerator and then microwave or bake.

Low-Fat Advice

Use lean cuts of beef, fish and white meat poultry. Use fillings that add little or no fat such as lettuce, cucumbers and tomatoes. Use nonstick sauté pans to cut down on the amount of oil needed and just spray lightly with cooking spray. Use reduced-fat tortillas, breads or cheese or leaner deli meats. I substitute reduced-fat mayonnaise and cream cheese for regular more often than not. Grainy mustards, chutney and low-fat yogurts make great toppings without adding much fat. I also like to use flavorful ingredients such as sun-dried tomatoes and capers for robust results. My all-time favorite healthy sandwich toppers are arugula, tomatoes, pears, sprouts, radishes, cucumbers, apples, mangos, grilled onions and sweet peppers.

More Tips

Burger Tips

- Choose your beef wisely. I like using ground sirloin or lean ground beef when making burgers with beef.
- Don't overwork the meat when making patties. The less handling the better because the more you compress, the tougher the burger will be.
- When forming the patty, make an indent with your thumb in the middle. This ensures it plumps nicely. Flatten the patty before placing on the grill, and do not press down on the patty while it's cooking.
- Only flip the burgers once.
- Start with a clean, well-oiled heated grill.
- Melt the cheese properly. Trap the heat by closing the grill over the burger. If making them in a skillet, place a metal bowl over the burger to melt the cheese.
- Look for the best sandwich buns you can find.
- Salt is essential to a great-tasting burger.

Wrapping Wraps

My kids get a little frustrated wrapping tortillas. The first step to wrapping is to warm the tortilla slightly to loosen the oil so it won't break or tear. You can either warm it in the microwave on High for 10 seconds, over the stove on medium heat for about 15 seconds or wrap tortillas in foil and bake in a preheated 350°F (180°C) oven for about 4 minutes.

To wrap tortillas, fold the right and left ends of the tortilla over the filling, toward the center. Fold the bottom edges of the tortilla toward the center and gently roll up. Try not to overfill tortillas.

Panini Tips

- Using a good panini maker makes a difference. You can also cook panini in a heavy skillet and press down with a metal spatula for the top.
- Have a good metal spatula on hand for easy turning and to help ensure that ingredients don't fall out of the sandwich and the bread stays intact.
- It's helpful to have all the ingredients assembled ahead of time.
- When using a panini grill, large skillet or grill, make sure it's hot enough before you use it.
- Try not to pack too many ingredients in a sandwich so that they don't fall out.
- Use your favorite combinations, have fun and be creative.

Grilled Cheese Tips

- Spread softened butter on the bread instead of adding it to the pan. This will keep the butter from burning.
- Use grated cheese, shredded or thinly sliced cheese for quicker melting.
- Slice and grate the cheese when it's cold, but cheese melts better when it's brought to room temperature.
- The more cheese, the better the result.
- If the cheese hasn't melted by the time the bread is golden, turn off the heat, and let stand, covered, until cheese melts.
- Use your favorite bread and don't slice it too thick.

Breakfast

Open-Faced Nectarine and Chèvre Sandwich

In the heat in summer, my friend Caroline makes these open-faced sandwiches. They're fabulous not only for breakfast but also for an appetizer or dessert.

4	slices white bread (½-inch/ 1 cm thick slices), toasted	4
4 oz	goat cheese, at room temperature	125 g
3	medium nectarines, thinly sliced (see Tip, below)	3
4 tsp	liquid honey	20 mL
¼ cup	chopped pecans, toasted (see Tip, right)	60 mL

Tip: Don't worry about removing the skin from the nectarines. It gives it more texture.

1. Place bread slices on a work surface. Spread each slice with goat cheese. Arrange nectarine slices on top and drizzle with honey. Sprinkle with pecans and serve open-faced.

Variations

I love to also make this with fresh peaches and plums.

Substitute your favorite bread, such as multigrain, whole wheat or English muffins, for the white bread.

Tip: To toast pecans: Spread nuts in a single layer on a baking sheet. Bake in a preheated 350°F (180°C) oven, stirring occasionally, for 10 to 15 minutes.

Eggs Benedict Biscuit Sandwich

This is a classic breakfast or brunch item, but I like it served on a hot biscuit. It's so good and slightly more Southern!

4	slices Canadian bacon	4
4	baked biscuits, warmed and split	4
4	poached eggs (page 16)	4
	Hollandaise sauce (page 16)	
¼ tsp	freshly ground black pepper	1 mL

Tip: When poaching eggs, use a measuring cup with a handle to slide the egg into the simmering water. This makes it easier not to break the egg.

1. In a large nonstick skillet over medium heat, fry bacon, turning once, until crisp. Drain on paper towels.

2. Place biscuits on a work surface. Place bacon slices on each biscuit and top with poached egg. Drizzle with hollandaise and sprinkle with pepper.

Variations

Smoked Salmon Benedict: Substitute 4 oz (125 g) smoked salmon for the Canadian bacon. Substitute 2 English muffin halves for the biscuits.

Crab Benedict: Substitute 6 oz (175 g) fresh or canned crabmeat for the Canadian bacon and 2 English muffin halves for the biscuits.

Breakfast Tacos

Serves 6

When I made these the first time, my youngest son, Zachary, said, "Tacos for breakfast?" He ate the entire thing.

8	slices bacon	8
1 tbsp	vegetable oil	15 mL
2 cups	cooked hash browns (see Tip, below)	500 mL
2	green onions, white parts and a bit of green, chopped	2
4	large eggs, lightly beaten	4
1/2 tsp	chipotle seasoning	2 mL
1/2 tsp	salt	2 mL
4	8-inch (20 cm) flour tortillas, warmed (see Tip, page 23)	4
	Sour cream, optional	
	Southwestern Corn Salsa (page 334) or store-bought, optional	

Tip: I used frozen hash browns for this recipe, but you can also use 1 large potato, cut into cubes.

1. In a large nonstick skillet over medium heat, fry bacon until crisp. Drain on paper towels. Let cool and then crumble. Set aside.

2. In same skillet, heat oil over medium heat. Sauté hash browns for 10 to 12 minutes or until cooked through. In the last 5 minutes of cooking the hash browns, add green onions and sauté until tender.

3. In a large bowl, combine eggs, chipotle seasoning and salt. Pour over potato mixture in skillet and cook over medium heat, stirring gently, until eggs are set. Stir in bacon.

4. Place tortillas on a work surface. Divide egg mixture equally among tortillas. Fold both ends over filling and top with sour cream or salsa, if using. Roll up and serve immediately.

Variation

Substitute 1/2 tsp (2 mL) chili powder or taco seasoning for the chipotle seasoning.

Eggs Sardou Sandwich

Serves 4

This is a great play on eggs Benedict filled with spinach and artichokes. Eggs Sardou is named for Victorien Sardou, a famous French dramatist. The specialty is famous in New Orleans served at Antoine's or Brennan's restaurants.

2 tsp	butter or margarine, melted	10 mL
1 tbsp	chopped green onions, white parts with a bit of green	15 mL
1	package (8 to 10 oz/250 to 300 g) package frozen spinach, thawed and well drained	1
¾ cup	artichokes, drained and chopped	175 mL
¾ cup	sour cream	175 mL
¼ cup	freshly grated Parmesan cheese	60 mL
2 tbsp	milk	30 mL
¼ tsp	salt	1 mL
	Freshly ground black pepper	
4	large eggs	4

Hollandaise Sauce

2	egg yolks	2
1 tbsp	freshly squeezed lemon juice	15 mL
8 tbsp	butter or margarine, divided	120 mL
⅛ tsp	salt	0.5 mL
⅛ tsp	hot pepper flakes	0.5 mL
2	English muffins, split and toasted	2

Tip: If you don't have time to make the Hollandaise Sauce, just sprinkle with shredded mozzarella cheese and broil until cheese melts. Or, there is a dry package Hollandaise mix you can purchase at the grocery store.

- **Dutch oven**
- **Double broiler**
- **Instant-read thermometer**

1. In a Dutch oven, melt butter over medium-low heat. Sauté green onions for 3 minutes or until tender. Add spinach, artichokes, sour cream, Parmesan, milk, salt, and pepper to taste, stirring constantly, until thoroughly heated.

2. *To poach eggs:* Lightly grease a large saucepan. Add water to depth of 2 inches (5 cm). Bring to a boil. Reduce heat and maintain a simmer. Using a measuring cup with a handle, slide in eggs, one at time, into the simmering water. (This makes it easier not to break the egg.) Simmer for 5 minutes or until desired doneness. Remove eggs with a slotted spoon and trim edges, if desired.

3. *Hollandaise Sauce:* On top of a double boiler over medium heat, gradually add egg yolks and lemon juice, stirring constantly. Add 3 tbsp (45 mL) of the butter and melt over hot (not boiling water), stirring constantly with a wire whisk, until butter is melted.

4. Add 3 tbsp (45 mL) butter to egg mixture, stirring constantly. As egg thickens, stir in remaining butter. Sauté until mixture is thickened and temperature reaches 160°F (71°C). Season with salt and hot pepper flakes.

5. Place English muffins on a work surface. Spoon spinach mixture over muffin halves. Top with poached egg and Hollandaise. Serve immediately.

Huevos Rancheros Wraps

Serves 4

The first time I ever had huevos rancheros was in Boulder, Colorado, when I was in college. I ate them every Saturday morning while I was living there. I love making these still today.

4	large eggs	4
¼ tsp	salt	1 mL
¼ tsp	freshly ground black pepper	1 mL
1 tbsp	butter or margarine	15 mL
1	can (14 to 19 oz/398 to 540 mL) black beans, rinsed and drained	1
1	small tomato, sliced	1
⅓ cup	sliced black olives	75 mL
2 tbsp	chopped red onion	30 mL
1 cup	salsa or Pico de Gallo (page 328) or store-bought	250 mL
4	8-inch (20 cm) flour tortillas, warmed (see Tip, page 23)	4
1 cup	shredded Cheddar cheese	250 mL
2	avocados, thinly sliced	2
2 tbsp	chopped fresh cilantro (see Tips, right)	30 mL

1. In a bowl, whisk together eggs, salt and pepper.

2. In a medium skillet, melt butter over medium heat. Sauté eggs for 3 to 4 minutes or until scrambled. Set aside.

3. In a large nonstick skillet over low heat, combine beans, tomato, olives and red onion. Stir in salsa and sauté for 5 to 10 minutes or until heated and slightly thickened.

4. Place tortillas on a work surface. Divide egg mixture equally in center of each tortilla. Arrange cheese, avocados and cilantro equally over top. Fold both ends over filling then roll up tortilla. Serve immediately.

Tips: Cilantro, also called Chinese parsley or coriander in its dried form, has a pungent flavor and fragrance and is used in many cuisines. Choose bunches with leaves that are bright and vibrant with no sign of wilting.

Don't forget to drain and rinse canned beans to get rid of excess salt.

Fried Egg Sandwich

We make the classic Fried Egg Sandwich on the weekends or when we're on vacation at the beach. The kids love them served on white or cinnamon-raisin bread.

8	slices white bread (½-inch/ 1 cm thick slices)	8
¼ cup	butter, softened	60 mL
4	large eggs	4
¼ tsp	salt	1 mL
¼ tsp	freshly ground black pepper	1 mL
4	slices cooked ham or bacon, optional	4

1. Place bread slices on a work surface. Spread butter equally over each side of bread slices.

2. Heat a large skillet over medium heat. Add 4 bread slices, buttered side down. Top with egg and sprinkle with salt and pepper. Top with ham or bacon, if using, and cook for about 3 minutes or until edges of egg begin to firm and ham is lightly browned.

3. Using a spatula, flip bread with egg and cook for 30 seconds. Flip again and top egg with remaining bread slice. Flip sandwich and cook 2 minutes more or until bread is toasted. Serve immediately.

Variation

Use 4 slices cinnamon-raisin bread instead of the white bread.

Egg, Avocado and Sprout Wraps

This vegetarian wrap is out of this world and it is so easy to prepare with very few ingredients.

1 tbsp	butter	15 mL
6	large eggs, lightly beaten	6
4 oz	cream cheese, softened	125 g
3 tbsp	salsa or Pico De Gallo (page 328) or store-bought	45 mL
4	8-inch (20 cm) white or whole wheat flour tortillas, warmed (see Tip, page 23)	4
1	avocado, thinly sliced	1
½ cup	alfalfa sprouts (see Tips, page 22)	125 mL

1. In a medium skillet, melt butter over medium heat. Sauté eggs until scrambled. Keep warm.

2. In a small bowl, stir together cream cheese and salsa. Place tortillas on a work surface. Spread mixture equally in center of each tortilla. Top with scrambled eggs, avocado and sprouts. Fold both ends over filling and roll up tortillas. Serve immediately.

Variations

Reduced-fat cream cheese works fabulously in this recipe. You can also use egg whites instead of whole eggs.

Cook 4 slices of bacon and add to wrap.

Scrambled Egg Panini

Serves 4

My kids love making panini sandwiches for breakfast. This is always a crowd pleaser and an easy go-to recipe.

4	large eggs, lightly beaten	4
1 tbsp	milk	15 mL
1/4 tsp	salt	1 mL
1/4 tsp	freshly ground black pepper	1 mL
6 tbsp	butter, divided	90 mL
8	slices whole wheat bread (1/2-inch/1 cm thick slices)	8
4	slices bacon, cooked	4
1/4 cup	shredded Cheddar cheese	60 mL

Tip: Check the stamped date on the package of bacon to make sure it's fresh.

• **Preheat panini grill or large skillet**

1. In a medium bowl, combine eggs, milk, salt and pepper.

2. In a skillet, melt 1 tbsp (15 mL) of the butter over medium heat. Sauté egg mixture until scrambled. Set aside egg mixture and wipe skillet clean.

3. Place bread slices on a work surface. Spread remaining butter equally over bread slices. Place bread slices, buttered side down, on preheated panini grill or in a skillet over medium heat. Top with scrambled eggs, bacon, cheese and remaining bread slice. Cook, turning once if using a skillet, for 3 to 5 minutes per side or until browned and cheese is melted. Serve immediately.

Variations

Scrambled Egg and Fontina Panini: Add 1 cup (250 mL) shredded Fontina cheese to the egg mixture and proceed as directed.

Wild Mushroom Cheddar Panini: Sauté 1 1/2 cups (375 mL) chopped wild mushrooms in 1 tbsp (15 mL) butter before adding eggs. Remove from skillet. Cook eggs until scrambled. Add mushrooms and proceed as directed.

To make this lighter, use 2 eggs and 3 egg whites. Omit the bacon and use 4 thinly sliced tomatoes instead.

Overnight Stuffed French Toast

Serves 10 to 12

I have been making versions of this recipe for years. It's often requested by my niece, Jamie, and is great for brunches and get-togethers.

1	loaf (1 lb/500 g) French bread, cut into cubes (8 cups/2 L)	1
1	package (8 oz/250 g) cream cheese, cut into pieces	250 g
6	large eggs	6
4 cups	milk	1 L
1/2 cup	granulated sugar	125 mL
1/4 cup	butter or margarine, melted	60 mL
1/4 cup	pure maple syrup (approx.)	60 mL
	Confectioner's (icing) sugar, optional	
	Fresh berries or sliced bananas, optional	

Tip: This can be made up to 8 hours ahead. Just assemble all ingredients, cover and refrigerate. Remove from refrigerator and let stand for 30 minutes at room temperature before baking as directed.

- **Preheat oven to 350°F (180°C)**
- **13- by 9-inch (33 by 23 cm) baking dish, lightly greased**

1. Arrange half of bread cubes in prepared baking dish. Place cream cheese over top and cover evenly with remaining bread cubes.

2. In a large bowl, whisk together eggs, milk, sugar, butter and maple syrup. Pour over bread mixture, pressing bread cubes to absorb egg mixture.

3. Cover and bake in preheated oven for 30 minutes. Uncover and bake for 30 minutes more or until lightly browned and set. Let stand for 5 minutes before serving. Cut into thin slices. Place berries on half the slices and then top with another slice. Drizzle with maple syrup and dust with confectioner's sugar, if desired.

Variations

Stuffed Banana French Toast. Add 2 cups (500 mL) sliced bananas after cream cheese in the recipe. Proceed as directed.

Strawberry French Toast: Add 1 cup (250 mL) sliced strawberries after cream cheese. To make a sauce, stir together 2 cups (500 mL) sliced strawberries and one 10-oz (300 g) jar strawberry preserves in a saucepan over low heat until warm. Serve over French toast.

Garlic-Herb Bagel Sandwiches

Serves 4

We love any kind of flavored cream cheese. This one is full of green onions, basil, parsley and garlic. It's great spread on top of a warm crusty bagel.

1 tbsp	butter	15 mL
4	large eggs, lightly beaten	4
1	package (8 oz/250 g) cream cheese, softened	1
3	green onions, white parts and a bit of green, chopped	3
1 tbsp	chopped fresh basil	15 mL
1 tbsp	chopped fresh parsley	15 mL
1	clove garlic, chopped	1
$1/8$ tsp	sea salt, optional	0.5 mL
4	sesame, multigrain or other type bagels, split and toasted	4
4 oz	smoked salmon	125 g

- **Food processor**

1. In a medium skillet, heat butter over medium heat. Sauté eggs until scrambled. Set aside.

2. In a food processor, pulse cream cheese, green onions, basil, parsley, garlic, and sea salt, if using, until combined.

3. Place bagels on a work surface. Spread cream cheese mixture equally over bagels. Top with scrambled eggs and smoked salmon. Serve immediately.

Tips: Make sure your cream cheese is softened before using in this recipe.

If you don't have a food processor, mix well in a large mixing bowl.

Albacore Tuna and Hard-Boiled Egg Sandwich

Serves 4

This is a healthy and hearty fresh breakfast sandwich. When I make these for breakfast, we don't eat again until dinnertime.

2	cans (each 6 oz/170 g) tuna, packed in water, drained (see Tips, below)	2
2 tbsp	Homemade Mayonnaise (page 321) or store-bought	30 mL
1 tsp	grated lemon zest	5 mL
1 tbsp	freshly squeezed lemon juice	15 mL
1/4 tsp	freshly ground black pepper	1 mL
4	English muffins, split and toasted	4
2	hard-boiled eggs, sliced (see Tips, right)	2
3/4 cup	thinly sliced cucumber	175 mL
1/2 cup	mixed salad greens (see Tips, right)	125 mL
1/3 cup	alfalfa sprouts (see Tips, below)	75 mL

Tips: I like to purchase tuna packed in water as I think it tastes great and has less fat.

When purchasing sprouts, select crisp-looking sprouts and avoid sprouts that look dark or smell musty. Refrigerate sprouts immediately when you get home and wash thoroughly before consumption.

1. In a medium bowl, combine tuna, mayonnaise, lemon zest, lemon juice and pepper. Cover and refrigerate for at least 30 minutes to allow mixture to chill and flavors to develop.

2. Place English muffins on a work surface. Spread tuna equally over muffin halves. Layer with egg, cucumber, lettuce and sprouts. Serve immediately.

Variation

Reduced fat-mayonnaise or nonfat Greek yogurt also works great in this tuna mixture instead of the regular mayonnaise.

Tips: To hard-boil eggs: Place eggs in a single layer in a saucepan and cover with at least 1 inch (2.5 cm) of water. Cover and bring to a boil, then remove from the heat and let stand for 15 minutes for hard-boiled. Drain the eggs and run them under cool running water.

For the lettuces, I like a mixture of arugula, Boston and Bibb or spring mix lettuces.

Spinach and Mushroom Scramble Wraps

Serves 4

Fresh spinach, mushrooms and Havarti create the perfect mixture in this breakfast wrap.

1 tbsp	butter	15 mL
6	large eggs, lightly beaten	6
1 tbsp	olive oil	15 mL
½ cup	diced red bell pepper (about 1 small)	125 mL
2 tbsp	diced onion	30 mL
8 oz	sliced mushrooms	250 g
5 oz	baby spinach	150 g
¼ tsp	salt	1 mL
¼ tsp	freshly ground black pepper	1 mL
4	8-inch (20 cm) flour tortillas, warmed (see Tip, right)	4
4	thin slices Havarti cheese	4

1. In a large skillet, melt butter over medium heat. Sauté eggs until scrambled. Set aside and wipe skillet clean.

2. In skillet, heat oil over medium heat. Sauté bell pepper and onion for 3 minutes or until tender. Add mushrooms, spinach, salt and pepper and sauté for 4 minutes or until spinach is wilted.

3. Place tortillas on a work surface. Layer eggs and spinach mixture equally in center of each tortilla. Top with cheese. Fold both ends over filling then roll up. Serve immediately.

Tip: To warm tortillas: Place tortillas in the microwave on High for 10 seconds or warm over medium heat in a skillet for about 15 seconds.

BLT Breakfast Sandwich

Serves 4

Bacon, lettuce and tomato sandwiches take on new life for breakfast or even for dinner.

1 tbsp	butter	15 mL
4	large eggs, lightly beaten	4
4	sourdough English muffins, split and toasted	4
1/4 cup	Homemade Mayonnaise (page 321) or store-bought	60 mL
4	lettuce leaves	4
4	slices tomato	4
4	slices bacon, cooked	4
1/4 tsp	salt	1 mL
1/4 tsp	freshly ground black pepper	1 mL
4	thin slices Swiss cheese	4

Tip: Purchase Swiss cheese already-sliced to save time in the kitchen.

- **Preheat broiler with rack set 3 to 5 inches (7.5 to 12.5 cm) from heat**

1. In a medium skillet, melt butter over medium heat. Sauté eggs until scrambled. Keep warm.

2. Place English muffins on a work surface. Spread mayonnaise on one side of muffins. Top with lettuce, tomato, bacon and eggs. Sprinkle with salt and pepper and top with cheese.

3. Place open-faced sandwiches on a baking sheet and broil for 2 minutes or until bread is slightly toasted and cheese is melted. Serve immediately.

Variation

Light BLT Breakfast Sandwiches: Substitute 4 egg whites for the eggs, 4 oz (125 g) turkey bacon for regular bacon, 1/4 cup (60 mL) reduced-fat mayonnaise for regular mayonnaise and whole wheat English muffins.

Bacon, Mushroom and Swiss Croissant

Serves 6

I make a casserole similar to this, which is very popular. When I made this into a breakfast sandwich, everyone begged for the recipe.

1 tbsp	butter	15 mL
6	large eggs, lightly beaten	6
8 oz	sliced mushrooms (see Tips, below)	250 g
6	5-inch (12.5 cm) croissants, split	6
4 oz	baby Swiss cheese, cut into thin slices	125 g
6	slices bacon, cooked	6
2 tbsp	chopped fresh chives, optional	30 mL

Tips: When purchasing mushrooms, avoid ones that look shriveled or have bruises. Be sure not to wash them until you are ready to cook them and don't let them sit in water.

If you can find day-old croissants at your local store, they work great in this dish as well.

- **Preheat broiler with rack set 3 to 5 inches (7.5 to 12.5 cm) from heat**

1. In a large nonstick skillet, melt butter over medium heat. Sauté eggs and mushrooms for 3 minutes or until eggs are scrambled. Place croissants on a work surface. Top each croissant half equally with egg mixture, Swiss cheese and bacon.

2. Place open-faced croissant halves on a broiler pan and broil for 2 minutes or until croissant is slightly toasted and cheese is melted. Garnish with chives, if using.

Variation

Ham and Cheese Croissants: Substitute $1/4$ cup (60 mL) diced cooked ham for the bacon and 4 slices Cheddar or American cheese for the baby Swiss cheese.

Mini Broccoli Quiche Sandwich

Serves 12

These are not only low carbohydrate but also delicious. My daughter, who does not like broccoli, loved these.

1	package (14 oz/400 g) frozen chopped broccoli, thawed	1
1 cup	shredded Cheddar cheese	250 mL
1 cup	shredded Swiss cheese	250 mL
1	egg white	1
1	egg	1
1	can (10 oz/284 mL) reduced-fat cream of mushroom soup	1
¼ tsp	freshly ground black pepper	1 mL
6	sourdough English muffins, split and toasted	6

Tips: Make sure you grease your muffin pans well so they don't stick to the pan. I like to use cooking spray.

Store these sandwiches in the refrigerator for up to 3 days. These make a great snack as well.

- **Preheat oven to 350°F (180°C)**
- **12-cup muffin pan, lightly greased**

1. In a large bowl, combine broccoli, Cheddar cheese, Swiss cheese, egg white, egg, soup and pepper.

2. Fill prepared muffin cups equally with broccoli mixture.

3. Bake in preheated oven for 30 to 35 minutes or until golden brown on top. Let cool for 15 minutes. Using a knife, remove from pan and serve open-faced over English muffin halves.

Variation

Spinach-Artichoke Quiche Sandwiches: Substitute 1 package (16 oz/500 g) frozen spinach for the broccoli. Add 1 can (14 oz/398 mL) artichoke hearts, drained and quartered, and mix as directed in Step 1.

Cheese Danishes

Serves 18

These Cheese Danishes are beyond incredible and, almost, dangerous because you can't eat just one. These look so professional and are great to serve for company or for a brunch.

1	package (8 oz/250 g) cream cheese, softened	1
½ cup	granulated sugar	125 mL
2	eggs, lightly beaten	2
6 tbsp	ricotta cheese	90 mL
1 tbsp	grated orange zest	15 mL
1 tsp	vanilla extract	5 mL
¼ tsp	salt	1 mL
1	box (18 oz/540 g) puff pastry, thawed (see Tip, below)	1
1	large egg, lightly beaten	1
¾ cup	confectioner's (icing) sugar, sifted	175 mL

Tip: Don't leave puff pastry out too long after it has been thawed. It gets difficult to work with and the danishes will not come out as pretty.

- **Preheat oven to 375°F (190°C)**
- **Baking sheet, lined with parchment paper**

1. In a bowl, using an electric mixer on low speed, combine cream cheese and sugar. Add eggs, ricotta, orange zest, vanilla and salt and mix well.

2. Unfold puff pastry sheets on a lightly floured surface. Roll out to an 14- by 11-inch (35 by 27.5 cm) rectangle. Cut each sheet into 9 squares with a sharp knife. Place 1 tbsp (15 mL) of the filling into middle of each square. Brush border of pastry with egg wash and fold two opposite corners to the center, brushing overlapping corners firmly. Brush top with remaining egg wash.

3. Place squares on prepared baking sheet. Bake in preheated oven for 12 to 15 minutes or until golden brown. Sprinkle with confectioner's sugar. Serve warm.

Scrambled Eggs and Smoked Salmon Sandwich

Serves 4

If you like smoked salmon for breakfast, you will love this sandwich. This makes a great "breakfast for dinner" recipe.

6	large eggs	6
2 tbsp	milk	30 mL
½ tsp	salt	2 mL
¼ tsp	freshly ground black pepper	1 mL
2 tbsp	butter	30 mL
4 oz	sliced smoked salmon, chopped	125 g
2 tbsp	chopped fresh chives	30 mL
4	bagels, split and toasted	4
	Fresh chopped chives or dill, optional	

Tip: Store bagels in plastic bags and not paper bags. They may be softened up by toasting or microwaving for a few minutes.

1. In a small bowl, beat together eggs, milk, salt and pepper. Set aside.

2. In a large skillet, melt butter over medium-low heat. Sauté eggs for 4 minutes, stirring frequently to scrape bottom and sides of pan. Add salmon and 2 tbsp (30 mL) chives and sauté for 2 minutes or until heated through. Serve egg mixture equally on bagel halves, open-faced, and top with chives, if using.

Variation

Smoked Salmon and Cream Cheese Sandwiches: Omit the eggs and milk and spread ¼ cup (60 mL) cream cheese on toasted bagel halves. Top with 4 oz (125 g) smoked salmon, ½ cup (125 mL) chopped red onion and ¼ cup (60 mL) capers. Garnish with fresh chives.

Breakfast Sausage Quesadillas

These breakfast quesadillas are great for a weekend hearty breakfast when you have company in town or just want something special and a little different.

12 oz	pork sausage (see Tip, below)	375 g
1 tbsp	butter	15 mL
10	large eggs, beaten	10
1½ cups	shredded Pepper Jack cheese	375 mL
¼ tsp	salt	1 mL
⅛ tsp	freshly ground black pepper	0.5 mL
6	8-inch (20 cm) flour tortillas, warmed (see Tip, page 23)	6

Toppings, optional

Salsa
Sour cream
Avocado
Green onions

Tip: If you use reduced-fat sausage, there is no need to drain. Then, you can omit the butter and use the same skillet. This reduces fat and cleanup.

1. In a large nonstick skillet coated with cooking spray, cook sausage over medium-high heat for 10 minutes or until sausage crumbles and is no longer pink. Drain and pat dry with paper towels. Set aside.

2. In a large skillet, melt butter over medium heat. Sauté eggs for 3 minutes, stirring frequently to scrape bottom and sides of pan. Stir in sausage, cheese, salt and pepper and sauté for 2 minutes or until cheese is melted.

3. Place tortillas on a work surface. Spoon sausage mixture equally over each tortilla. Fold in half, pressing gently to seal.

4. In a large skillet, coated with cooking spray over medium heat, brown tortillas, in batches, for 3 minutes per side or until lightly browned and cheese is melted. Top with desired toppings.

Variation

If you like less spicy flavor, use Monterey Jack cheese instead of Pepper Jack.

Vegetable Cream Cheese Sandwiches

Serves 8

I love to make flavored cream cheese because I use the leftover cream cheese to spread on crackers for the rest of the week for lunchtime and snacks.

2	packages (each 8 oz/250 g) cream cheese, softened	2
¼ cup	finely chopped carrots	60 mL
¼ cup	finely chopped celery	60 mL
3 tbsp	finely chopped radish	45 mL
2 tbsp	finely chopped green onions	30 mL
2 tbsp	finely chopped pimento-stuffed olives	30 mL
⅛ tsp	hot pepper sauce	0.5 mL
8	bagels, split and toasted (see Tip, right)	8
2	tomatoes, thinly sliced	2
	Fresh basil leaves, optional	

1. In a bowl, using an electric mixer on low speed, combine cream cheese, carrots, celery, radish, green onions, olives and hot pepper sauce until blended.

2. Place bagels on a work surface. Spread cream cheese mixture equally over each bagel half. Layer with tomatoes, and basil, if using, and serve open-faced.

Tip: Be careful slicing bagels. To slice, place bagels on a flat surface. Place your hand on top of it and use a serrated knife to cut the bagel crosswise halfway through.

Country Ham and Biscuits

Serves 12

Being from the South, I had to include a recipe for Country Ham and Biscuits. You can't go wrong with these.

½ cup	raspberry preserves or jam	125 mL
2 tbsp	Dijon mustard	30 mL
12	baked biscuits, warmed and split (see Tip, below)	12
1 lb	thinly sliced country ham	500 g

Tip: I like to use frozen biscuits and bake right before making these. They taste really fresh and homemade.

1. In a small bowl, combine preserves and mustard. Set aside.

2. Place biscuits on a work surface.

3. In a large nonstick skillet over medium-high heat, brown ham for 2 minutes per side. Fill each biscuit bottom equally with ham and top with preserve mixture. Press top gently over each bottom and serve immediately.

Variation

Substitute ½ cup (125 mL) fig preserves for the raspberry preserves and proceed as directed.

Appetizers

Tomato, Avocado and Boursin

This twist on Caprese salad is a wonderfully fresh and flavorful light appetizer with Boursin cheese.

1/3 cup	olive oil	75 mL
1/4 cup	balsamic vinegar	60 mL
1 tbsp	Dijon mustard	15 mL
1	clove garlic, minced	1
1 tbsp	liquid honey	15 mL
4	medium tomatoes, thinly sliced	4
1	package (5.2 oz/148 g) Boursin cheese with garlic and herbs (see Tip, right)	1
2	avocados	2
3/4 cup	chopped fresh basil	175 mL

- **Large serving platter**

1. In a small bowl, whisk together olive oil, balsamic vinegar, Dijon, garlic and honey. Set aside.

2. Place half of tomato slices on a large serving platter. Spread each slice with 2 tsp (10 mL) of the cheese. Thinly slice avocados. Top cheese with avocados, remaining tomatoes and basil. Drizzle with balsamic dressing and serve immediately.

Variation

Feel free to substitute fresh mozzarella for the Boursin in this recipe.

Tip: Boursin is all-natural Gournay cheese that comes in flavored varieties and is a soft spreadable cheese that is creamy and mild. It is perfect for entertaining.

Peach-Glazed Hot Roast Beef Sandwich

These individual mini sandwiches combine the sweetness of peach preserves with tangy coarse-grain mustard. They make great party pick-up food.

12	mini hamburger buns, split	12
1/2 cup	peach preserves or jam	125 mL
1/2 cup	coarse-grain mustard	125 mL
12 oz	thinly sliced deli roast beef	375 g
4 oz	Muenster cheese, cut into 12 small slices	125 g

Tip: These can be made ahead of time. Just prepare, wrap in foil and refrigerate for up to to 8 hours. When ready to serve, bake in preheated oven as directed.

- **Preheat oven to 325°F (160°C)**

1. Place buns on a large baking sheet. Spread preserves and mustard evenly over bottom half of bun. Arrange roast beef and cheese over mustard. Cover with top half. Wrap in foil.

2. Bake in preheated oven for 20 to 25 minutes or until cheese is melted.

Variation

Apricot-Glazed Turkey Sandwiches: Substitute 1/2 cup (125 mL) apricot preserves for the peach preserves, 12 oz (375 g) smoked turkey for the roast beef and 4 oz (125 g) Havarti for the Muenster and proceed as directed.

Coconut Shrimp Tea Sandwich

Makes 16 appetizer servings

These coconut shrimp are oven-fried instead of deep-fried, and they have a light crunchy texture and coconut flavor. My kids can't eat these fast enough.

1½ lbs	large shrimp, peeled and deveined (see Tips, below)	750 g
½ cup	sweetened flaked coconut	125 mL
½ cup	panko bread crumbs (see Tips, below)	125 mL
½ tsp	sea salt	2 mL
⅛ tsp	hot pepper flakes	0.5 mL
½ cup	all-purpose flour	125 mL
2	eggs, lightly beaten	2
½ cup	honey mustard	125 mL
16	slices cocktail bread (see Tips, page 44)	16
	Watercress or spinach leaves	

Tips: When choosing shrimp, look for ones that are firm, moist and translucent.

Panko bread crumbs are Japanese-style bread crumbs that are made from breads without crusts. They add an airier, crisper texture than most other bread crumbs. You can find them in the grocery store where bread crumbs are sold.

- **Preheat oven to 400°F (200°C)**
- **Large baking sheet, greased**

1. Rinse shrimp in cold water. Drain on paper towels until dry.

2. In a large bowl, combine coconut, panko bread crumbs, salt and hot pepper flakes. Place flour on a plate and eggs in a bowl. Dip shrimp in flour, then into eggs. Dredge in coconut mixture.

3. Place shrimp on large prepared baking sheet. Bake in preheated oven, turning after 10 minutes, for 20 minutes or until shrimp are pink and opaque.

4. Place bread slices on a work surface. Spread honey mustard equally over bread slices. Arrange watercress and then shrimp on top and serve open-faced.

Variation

Coconut Chicken Tea Sandwich: Omit the shrimp and use 1¼ lbs (625 g) chicken cutlets, cut into 1-inch (2.5 cm) slices in Step 2. Bake for 10 minutes or until chicken is no longer pink inside. Proceed with Step 4.

Prosciutto, Mozzarella and Basil Mini Panini

Serves 8 or 4 main dish servings

I love serving mini panini sandwiches as an appetizer. This combination of prosciutto, tomato and basil is full of Italian flair, which guests always love.

8	slices Italian bread (½-inch/ 1 cm thick slices)	8
¼ cup	Basil Pesto (page 329) or store-bought	60 mL
4 oz	thinly sliced prosciutto (see Tip, below)	125 g
4	slices mozzarella cheese	4
4	tomatoes, thinly sliced	4
½ cup	chopped fresh basil	125 mL
½ cup	olive oil	125 mL

Tips: When purchasing prosciutto, look for golden pink, moist-looking meat.

Serve these with Prosecco or Pinot Grigio.

- **Panini grill or large nonstick skillet**
- **Preheat panini grill to medium-high, if using**

1. Place 4 bread slices on a work surface. Spread each with 1 tbsp (15 mL) of the pesto. Layer prosciutto, cheese, tomatoes and basil over pesto and top with remaining bread slices. Brush outsides of bread slices with olive oil.

2. Place sandwiches on preheated panini grill or a large skillet over medium-high, and cook, turning once if using a skillet, for 3 to 4 minutes or until golden brown and cheese is melted. Cut into thirds and serve immediately.

Variation

Substitute regular or turkey bacon for the prosciutto.

Bacon, Figs and Brie Crostini

Makes 12

Two of my favorite ingredients are bacon and Brie. How can you go wrong with this appetizer?

12	baguette slices (about ½ inch/1 cm thick)	12
½ cup	olive oil	125 mL
½ cup	fig preserves or jam	125 mL
8	slices bacon, cooked (see Tip, below)	8
8	dried figs, finely chopped	8
4 oz	Brie, thinly sliced	125 g

Tip: To microwave bacon, place side by side on a microwave-safe plate with a double-layer of paper towels and cook on High for 5 minutes or until done.

- **Preheat oven to 350°F (180°C)**
- **Preheat broiler**
- **Large baking sheet, lightly greased**

1. Brush one side of baguette slices evenly with olive oil and place, oiled side down, on prepared baking sheet. Bake in preheated oven for 3 to 5 minutes or until lightly browned.

2. Spread 1 tbsp (15 mL) of the fig preserves evenly over each crostini. Arrange bacon, figs and Brie over preserves. Broil in preheated broiler for 2 minutes or until Brie is slightly melted. Serve immediately.

Italian Tuna Crostini

Serves 8 to 10

This special appetizer is worth the price of the Italian tuna, which has a great combination of health benefits and taste. When people say they want to follow the Mediterranean diet or prefer a healthy appetizer, I suggest this.

8	baguette slices (about ½ inch/1 cm thick)	8
1½ cups	fresh arugula leaves	375 mL
1	jar (7 oz/210 g) Italian tuna (see Tip, right)	1
3	plum (Roma) tomatoes, thinly sliced	3
½ tsp	freshly ground black pepper	2 mL

Tip: Roma tomatoes, also called plum tomatoes, have fewer seeds and are great for sandwiches, salads and sauces.

- **Preheat oven to 350°F (180°C)**
- **Large baking sheet, lightly greased**

1. Arrange baguette slices on prepared baking sheet. Bake in preheated oven for 5 minutes or until lightly toasted.

2. Arrange arugula, tuna and tomatoes over bread slices. Sprinkle with pepper and serve immediately.

Tip: I prefer jars of Callipo tuna, available online or at specialty stores. You can also use the canned variety instead. You'll need about one-and-a-half 5 oz (142 g) cans in place of the jar. If you can't find Italian tuna, use 7 oz (210 g) good-quality water-packed tuna and combine with 3 tbsp (45 mL) white wine vinegar and ¼ tsp (1 mL) freshly ground black pepper.

Pear, Pecan and Gorgonzola Crostini

Serves 8 to 10

I love to make crostini appetizers during autumn. Pecans, pears and Gorgonzola are some of my favorite fall ingredients, creating an awesome crostini.

8 to 10	baguette slices (about ½ inch/1 cm thick)	8 to 10
4 oz	cream cheese, softened	125 g
¼ cup	crumbled Gorgonzola cheese	60 mL
1½ cups	thinly sliced pear (about 2 medium) (see Tip, right)	375 mL
4 tbsp	liquid honey (see Tip, below)	60 mL
½ cup	chopped pecans, toasted (see Tip, page 14)	125 mL

Tip: Store honey in a cool place away from direct sunlight in a tightly covered container. It is not necessary to refrigerate.

- **Preheat oven to 350°F (180°C)**
- **Preheat broiler with rack 4 inches (10 cm) from heat**

1. Arrange baguette slices on a large baking sheet. Bake in preheated oven for 5 minutes or until lightly toasted.

2. In a small bowl, combine cream cheese and Gorgonzola. Spread bread slices evenly with 1 tbsp (15 mL) of the Gorgonzola mixture. Top with pear slices. Drizzle with honey and sprinkle with pecans.

3. Broil crostini for 1 to 2 minutes or until pears are tender and cheese is slightly melted. Serve immediately.

Tip: When purchasing pears, look for ones that are fragrant and have no blemishes. I store mine in the refrigerator in a plastic bag.

Smoked Salmon and Dill Crostini

Serves 8 to 10

We eat a lot of smoked salmon at my house because the kids love it. I serve these as an appetizer for a light start to a party. They're also great to serve at a brunch.

8 to 10	baguette slices (about ½ inch/1 cm thick)	8 to 10
1½ cups	store-bought smoked salmon spread	375 mL
½ cup	drained capers, rinsed	125 mL
½ cup	chopped fresh dill	125 mL
¼ cup	finely chopped red onion, optional	60 mL

- **Preheat oven to 350°F (180°C)**

1. Arrange baguette slices on a large baking sheet. Bake in preheated oven for 5 minutes or until lightly toasted. Spread slices with salmon spread and top equally with capers, dill and red onion, if using.

Tip: Smoked salmon can stay in the refrigerator for up to 2 weeks if it hasn't been opened or in the freezer for up to 3 months.

Roasted Red Pepper and Goat Cheese Crostini

Serves 8 to 10

This appetizer is always popular with guests. Serve leftovers with crackers and fresh vegetables for a wonderful dip.

8 to 10	baguette slices (about ½ inch/1 cm thick)	8 to 10
4 oz	cream cheese, softened	125 g
4 oz	crumbled goat cheese	125 g
¼ cup	mayonnaise	60 mL
2	cloves garlic, coarsely chopped	2
½ cup	roasted red peppers (see Tips, right)	125 mL
2 tbsp	chopped fresh basil (approx.)	30 mL

Varieties of toppings for crostini appetizers are endless. Here are some of my favorites from the Condiment Chapter.

- Basil Pesto (page 329)
- Caponata Spread (page 320)
- Cherry Tomato Relish (page 322)
- Guacamole (page 336)
- Hummus (page 313)
- Mango-Avocado Relish (page 323)
- Peach Salsa (page 335)
- Red Pepper Hummus (page 314)
- Tapenade (page 315)

- **Preheat oven to 350°F (180°C)**
- **Food processor or blender**

1. Arrange baguette slices on a large baking sheet. Bake in preheated oven for 5 minutes or until lightly toasted.

2. In a food processor or blender, pulse cream cheese, goat cheese, mayonnaise, garlic, roasted peppers and basil until combined. Spread roasted pepper mixture on crostini and garnish with additional basil.

Tips: I use reduced-fat cream cheese and reduced-fat mayonnaise instead of regular, and it still produces a delicious spread.

You can find roasted red peppers in a jar in the grocery where pickles and olives are sold.

Tomato, Fresh Herbs and Feta Crostini

Make this appetizer in the spring or summer when herbs are abundant. The flavor is wonderful. It's really pretty to serve these crostini on a platter.

½ cup	crumbled feta cheese	125 mL
½ cup	olive oil	125 mL
2 tbsp	chopped fresh basil (see Tips, right)	30 mL
2 tbsp	chopped Italian flat-leaf parsley	30 mL
2	cloves garlic, minced	2
½ tsp	freshly ground black pepper	2 mL
8 to 10	baguette slices (about ½ inch/1 cm thick)	8 to 10
5	plum (Roma) tomatoes, thinly sliced (see Tips, right)	5

• **Preheat oven to 350°F (180°C)**

1. In a small bowl, combine feta, basil, and parsley. Set aside.

2. In a separate bowl, stir together olive oil, garlic and pepper. Brush oil mixture equally over each bread slice. Place on a large baking sheet. Bake in preheated oven for 5 minutes or until lightly toasted. Remove from oven and top with tomato slices. Spoon basil mixture on top of each tomato slice. Serve immediately.

Tips: Don't forget to wash basil thoroughly before using. I dry mine by blotting with paper towels.

If you can't find plum tomatoes, use 3 medium ripe tomatoes, thinly sliced, instead.

Miniature Crab Cake Sandwich

Serves 24

Everyone is always impressed when I serve crab cakes as an appetizer. I like to make these on New Year's Eve to start the night off right.

1 lb	cooked lump crabmeat, drained	500 g
½ cup	panko bread crumbs (see Tips, page 33)	125 mL
2 tbsp	Homemade Mayonnaise (page 321) or store-bought	30 mL
2 tbsp	chopped Italian flat-leaf parsley	30 mL
1½ tsp	Cajun seasoning (see Tips, right)	7 mL
1 tsp	grated lemon zest	5 mL
¼ cup	olive oil	60 mL
24	mini hamburger buns, split	24
1½ cups	chopped lettuce leaves	375 mL
	Tartar Sauce (page 333) or store-bought	

1. In a large bowl, combine crabmeat, panko, mayonnaise, parsley, Cajun seasoning and lemon zest. Shape mixture into 1-inch (5 cm) patties.

2. In a large skillet, heat oil over medium-high heat. Cook crab cakes for 4 minutes per side or until crab cakes are golden.

3. Place buns on a work surface. Line bottom halves of buns with lettuce, crab cakes and tartar sauce. Cover with top half. Serve immediately.

Tips: I like using a microplane for zesting lemons and limes, which can be found at most cooking stores. Turn the lemon as you zest, so you only remove the yellow part and not the white pith, which is bitter.

If you can't find Cajun seasoning, use ½ tsp (2 mL) each cayenne pepper, salt and chili powder.

Mini Southwest Sliders

Everyone loves Mexican and mini hamburgers, so these are always a hit with adults and children. This makes a great neighborhood party appetizer.

8 oz	Monterey Jack cheese	250 g
2 lbs	lean ground beef	1 kg
½ cup	panko bread crumbs (see Tips, page 33)	125 mL
1	large egg, lightly beaten	1
1 cup	diced tomatoes with green chiles, drained (see Tips, right)	250 mL
2 tbsp	chopped fresh cilantro	30 mL
¼ tsp	sea salt	1 mL
24	mini hamburger buns, split and toasted	24
2 cups	Pico de Gallo (page 328) or store-bought	500 mL

Toppings, optional

	Avocado
	Shredded lettuce
	Sour cream

- **Preheat greased grill or grill pan to medium-high heat**

1. Cut cheese into 24 thin slices, about 1-inch (2.5 cm) square. Set aside.

2. In a medium bowl, combine beef, panko, egg, tomatoes, cilantro and salt. Shape mixture into 1-inch (2.5 cm) patties.

3. Place patties in a grill basket or on a grill rack and grill, turning once, for 4 to 5 minutes per side or until no longer pink inside. Top with cheese and grill for 2 minutes or until cheese is melted.

4. Place buns on a work surface. Spread 1 tbsp (15 mL) of the salsa on bottom halves of buns and top with patties. Garnish with desired toppings and cover with top half. Serve immediately.

Tips: You can find jars of diced tomatoes with green chiles in Latin American stores.

Store fresh cilantro in the refrigerator, wrapped loosely in paper towels sealed in a plastic bag, for up to 5 days.

Olive Cream Cheese Sandwich

These sandwiches are an old Southern traditional known as a "tea sandwich," which I had growing up (although the only tea we ever had was iced tea). This recipe works great for an appetizer.

1	package (8 oz/250 g) cream cheese, softened	1
1 tbsp	Greek yogurt	15 mL
¾ cup	finely chopped pimiento-stuffed olives	175 mL
1 tbsp	chopped fresh shallots, optional (see Tip, right)	15 mL
8	slices bread (each ½ inch/ 1 cm thick), toasted and crusts removed	8

Tip: Feel free to substitute reduced-fat cream cheese and nonfat Greek yogurt for the regular full-fat versions.

1. In a bowl, stir together cream cheese, yogurt, olives and shallots, if using.

2. Place bread slices on a work surface. Spread cream cheese mixture on bread slices, pressing together gently. Cut into triangles.

Variations

Greek yogurt works great in this recipe, but use sour cream if you don't have yogurt on hand.

If you like less olive taste, use only ½ cup (125 mL) olives.

Substitute 16 mini pita bread rounds for the bread in this recipe.

Tip: Shallots are a member of the onion family and have a mild onion-garlic flavor. Store them for up to 1 month in the refrigerator and use before they begin to sprout.

Tomato Tea Sandwich with Arugula and Basil

Serves 20

These sandwiches showcase the freshness of the arugula and basil, creating a pretty spring or summer appetizer.

1	package (7 oz/210 g) package whole-wheat mini pitas (see Tips, right)	1
½ cup	olive oil	125 mL
1 cup	fresh arugula leaves	250 mL
20	cherry tomatoes, halved	20
4 oz	Havarti cheese, cut into ½-inch (1 cm) cubes (see Tips, right)	125 g
¾ cup	balsamic vinegar	175 mL
2 tsp	freshly ground black pepper	10 mL

- **Preheat oven to 350°F (180°C)**

1. Lightly brush pita rounds evenly with olive oil. Place on a large baking sheet. Bake in preheated oven for 3 to 5 minutes or until lightly browned. Remove from oven.

2. Layer arugula, cherry tomatoes and cheese over each pita round. Drizzle with balsamic vinegar and sprinkle with pepper. Serve immediately.

Tips: Mini pitas are great for making mini tea sandwiches, mini pizzas and mini grilled cheese. Toast and serve with a side salad.

Havarti is a semisoft cheese made in Denmark and made of cow's milk. It is wonderful on sandwiches, salads, in desserts and on top of vegetables.

Mini Lemon-Chicken Salad Sandwich

Serves 4

Lemon zest and juice add wonderful flavor to this chicken salad. I love to make these for appetizers on a Sunday game day or afternoon porch party.

1¼ cups	chopped cooked chicken	300 mL
2 tbsp	diced celery	30 mL
1 tbsp	chopped walnuts, toasted (see Tip, right)	15 mL
3 tbsp	chopped fresh basil, divided	45 mL
1 tsp	grated lemon zest	5 mL
3 tbsp	mayonnaise	45 mL
2 tbsp	Greek yogurt	30 mL
1 tsp	freshly squeezed lemon juice	5 mL
¼ tsp	freshly ground black pepper	1 mL
⅛ tsp	salt	0.5 mL
8	baguette slices, cut into ½ inch (1 cm) thick slices	8

Tip: I love to use Greek yogurt in the place of sour cream. It adds creamy texture and flavors to this dish.

- **Preheat oven to 350°F (180°C)**

1. In a medium bowl, combine chicken, celery, walnuts, 1 tbsp (15 mL) of the basil, lemon zest, mayonnaise, yogurt, lemon juice, pepper and salt. Refrigerate for at least 30 minutes to allow flavors to blend.

2. Arrange baguette slices on a large baking sheet. Bake in preheated oven for 5 minutes or until lightly toasted. Arrange chicken salad on top of crostini slices and top with remaining chopped basil.

Variation

Mini Tarragon Chicken Sandwich: Substitute 3 tbsp (45 mL) fresh tarragon for the basil in this recipe.

Tip: Walnuts are 99 percent oil and have a great nutty taste. They add great crunch to salads, sandwiches and appetizers. To toast walnuts: Place in an ungreased skillet over medium heat, stirring frequently, for 5 to 7 minutes or until golden brown.

Mini Cucumber Sandwich

I like to serve these for appetizers before a light lunch or dinner. Fresh dill and lemon zest flavor the cream cheese mixture, which pairs so nicely with freshly sliced cucumbers.

1	package (8 oz/250 g) cream cheese, softened	1
2 tbsp	Homemade Mayonnaise (page 321) or store-bought	30 mL
2 tbsp	chopped fresh dill (see Tips, right)	30 mL
1 tbsp	grated lemon zest	15 mL
1/4 tsp	hot pepper sauce	1 mL
1/8 tsp	sea salt	0.5 mL
1/8 tsp	freshly ground black pepper	0.5 mL
24	slices cocktail bread (see Tips, right)	24
2 cups	thinly sliced cucumbers (about 1 large)	500 mL
	Fresh dill sprigs, optional	

Tip: Feel free to substitute reduced-fat cream cheese and mayonnaise for the regular versions.

1. In a medium bowl, combine cream cheese, mayonnaise, dill, lemon zest, hot pepper sauce, salt and pepper until smooth.

2. Place bread slices on a work surface. Spread cream cheese mixture over bread slices. Top each with a cucumber slice and garnish with fresh dill, if using.

Variation

Turkey Cucumber Sandwich: Add 8 oz (250 g) turkey and layer on cream cheese mixture and then top with cucumber slice.

Tips: Dill is a mild herb with a lemony taste. I love using fresh dill, and it's simple to cut with a knife or kitchen scissors.

Cocktail bread is small loaves of bread about 2 inches (5 cm) square and sliced about 1/4-inch (0.5 cm) thick. They are often found in the deli section at supermarkets, at delis and cheese shops and at specialty stores. There are many varieties available, including rye and pumpernickel.

Apricot, Walnut and Blue Cheese Sandwich

My kids love apricot and walnuts, and believe it or not, blue cheese. I threw this mixture together one day, and everyone loved it.

½ cup	chopped walnuts, toasted (see Tip, page 43)	125 mL
2 tbsp	finely chopped dried apricots	30 mL
1	package (8 oz/250 g) cream cheese, softened	1
4 oz	crumbled blue cheese (see Tip, right)	125 g
8	slices whole-grain bread (each ½ inch/1 cm thick), toasted	8
½ cup	baby spinach leaves	125 mL
¼ cup	apricot preserves or jam	60 mL

1. In a small bowl, stir together walnuts, apricots, cream cheese and blue cheese.

2. Place bread slices on a work surface. Spread cream cheese mixture equally on one side of 4 bread slices. Top with spinach leaves. Spread apricot preserves on remaining bread slices and press slices together gently. Slice in half and serve immediately.

Variation

When in season, peaches are a great substitute for the dried apricots in this recipe.

Tip: Purchase already crumbled blue cheese in the cheese section of your grocery store.

Mini Veggie Hoagies

Serves 10 to 12

These mini hoagies are so good. My kids ate them and were asking for more, which is always a good sign for vegetarian recipes.

2 tbsp	Kalamata and Black Olive Pesto (page 332)	30 mL
2 tbsp	Homemade Mayonnaise (page 321) or store-bought	30 mL
2 cups	diced tomatoes (about 2 medium)	500 mL
1 cup	diced green bell pepper (about 1 medium)	250 mL
1 cup	diced portobello mushrooms (see Tip, below)	250 mL
1 cup	diced cucumber	250 mL
1 cup	shredded mozzarella cheese	250 mL
2 tbsp	diced red onion	30 mL
4	hoagie buns, split horizontally	4
4	large lettuce leaves	4

Tips: Mushrooms stay fresh longer if they have air circulating around them so they can breathe. Avoid storing them in a tightly closed plastic bag but place in a paper bag instead.

Feel free to substitute button mushrooms for the portobello.

- **Preheat oven to 350°F (180°C)**

1. In a small bowl, combine pesto and mayonnaise, stirring well.

2. In a separate medium bowl, combine tomatoes, bell pepper, mushrooms, cucumbers, mozzarella and red onion, mixing well.

3. Place hoagie buns on a work surface. Spread bottom halves of buns with pesto mixture. Arrange lettuce leaves over pesto. Arrange tomato mixture over lettuce. Cover with top half.

4. Wrap sandwiches tightly in foil and bake in preheated oven for 5 minutes. Open foil and broil for 5 minutes more. Cut each hoagie into 3 slices to make mini sandwiches.

Variation

If you don't have the homemade pesto on hand, spread 2 tbsp (30 mL) of store-bought pesto on top of bread and add 1/2 cup (125 mL) chopped black olives to the vegetable mixture.

Black Bean Quesadillas

*This is the perfect vegetarian hearty appetizer
filled with black beans, bell peppers and spices.*

1 tbsp	olive oil	15 mL
1 cup	sliced mushrooms	250 mL
1 cup	chopped red onion (about 1 medium)	250 mL
½ cup	diced red bell pepper	125 mL
½ cup	diced yellow bell pepper	125 mL
1	can (14 to 19 oz/398 to 540 mL) black beans, rinsed and drained	1
½ cup	chopped tomatoes	125 mL
¼ cup	salsa	60 mL
2 tbsp	sliced black olives	30 mL
¼ tsp	ground cumin	1 mL
4	8-inch (20 cm) flour tortillas	4
1 cup	shredded Pepper Jack or Monterey Jack cheese	250 mL

Toppings, optional

	Sour cream
	Salsa or Pico de Gallo (page 328) or store-bought
	Chopped green onions

1. In a large skillet, heat oil over medium heat. Sauté mushrooms, red onion and red and yellow bell peppers for 5 minutes or until tender. Add beans, tomatoes, salsa, olives and cumin. Sauté for 2 minutes or until heated through. Remove from pan.

2. In same skillet, heat tortillas over medium heat. Spread bean mixture equally over center of each tortilla. Top each with ¼ cup (60 mL) of the cheese. Fold tortilla over and cook for 2 minutes or until lightly browned and cheese is melted. Repeat with remaining quesadillas. Cut each quesadilla into 6 wedges and garnish with desired toppings.

Variation

Chicken and Black Bean Quesadillas: Add 1½ cups (375 mL) cooked chicken for a heartier appetizer or main dish quesadilla.

Tip: To make ahead, chop bell peppers, red onions and mushrooms and refrigerate in a tightly sealed container for up to 8 hours.

Mini Hot Roast Beef Sandwich

Serves 8

Dijon mustard, vinegar and parsley provide a wonderful light base for these roast beef sandwiches.

1/4 cup	Dijon mustard	60 mL
2 tbsp	white wine vinegar	30 mL
2 tbsp	olive oil	30 mL
2 tbsp	finely chopped fresh parsley	30 mL
2 tbsp	diced red onion	30 mL
8	mini hamburger buns, split	8
12 oz	thinly sliced deli roast beef	375 g
1	avocado, thinly sliced	1
4	slices Monterey Jack cheese	4

Tip: If you're pressed for time, omit parsley and vinegar and just use 1/4 cup (60 mL) Dijon mustard.

- **Preheat broiler**

1. In a small bowl, combine Dijon, vinegar, olive oil, parsley and red onion. Set aside.

2. Place buns on a large baking sheet. Brush bottom halves of buns with mustard mixture. Arrange roast beef, avocado and cheese over top. Leave buns open-faced and broil on high for 2 minutes or until sandwiches are warm and cheese is melted. Cover with top halves and serve immediately.

Variation

Mini Turkey Swiss Sandwich: Substitute 4 oz (125 g) Swiss cheese slices for the Monterey Jack cheese and 12 oz (375 g) sliced turkey or ham for the roast beef.

Mini Pastrami Reuben

Serves 16

These are a classic family favorite, especially during football season. Feel free to halve this recipe or double it depending on the size of your crowd.

16	slices cocktail bread (see Tips, page 44)	16
1 cup	deli mustard	250 mL
1 lb	thinly sliced pastrami	500 g
1 1/2 cups	sauerkraut, rinsed and well-drained	375 g
8	slices Swiss cheese, cut into 4 small pieces	8

- **Preheat oven to 375°F (190°C)**

1. Place half of bread slices on a large baking sheet. Spread mustard on bread slices. Arrange pastrami, sauerkraut and cheese on top and top with remaining bread slice.

2. Bake in preheated oven for 5 minutes or until bread is golden and cheese is melted. Serve immediately.

Variation

Add 1 cup (250 mL) Thousand Island salad dressing and omit the mustard.

Lunch Box

Smoked Turkey Hummus Wrap

Serves 4

I eat these sandwiches at least once a week because they are light, fresh and high in protein.

4	8-inch (20 cm) white or whole wheat flour tortillas	4
1 cup	Hummus (page 313) or store-bought	250 mL
8 oz	thinly sliced smoked turkey	250 g
1	medium cucumber, peeled and thinly sliced	1
2	ripe tomatoes, thinly sliced	2
3/4 cup	alfalfa sprouts (see Tip, right)	175 mL
1/4 tsp	freshly ground black pepper	1 mL

1. Place tortillas on a work surface. Spread 1/4 cup (60 mL) hummus over each tortilla. Arrange turkey, cucumber, tomatoes and sprouts equally in the center. Sprinkle with pepper. Fold both ends over filling. Roll up and serve.

Tip: When purchasing sprouts, choose crisp sprouts with the buds attached.

Fresh Basil and Red Pepper Tuna

Serves 4

Fresh basil, red pepper and lemon juice make this no ordinary tuna salad. I love it because it has no mayonnaise and has a clean, fresh flavor.

2	cans (each 6 oz/170 g) tuna, packed in water, drained	2
1/4 cup	chopped red bell pepper	60 mL
2 tbsp	chopped fresh basil	30 mL
2 tbsp	white wine vinegar	30 mL
2 tbsp	olive oil	30 mL
1 tbsp	freshly squeezed lemon juice (see Tip, right)	15 mL
1/4 tsp	sea salt	1 mL
1/4 tsp	freshly ground black pepper	1 mL
4	slices hearty wheat bread (1-inch/2.5 cm thick slices)	4
4	romaine lettuce leaves	4
4	tomatoes, thinly sliced	4

1. In a small bowl, combine tuna, bell pepper, basil, vinegar, olive oil, lemon juice, salt and pepper.

2. Place bread slices on a work surface. Arrange tuna mixture equally on each bread slice. Top with lettuce and tomato. Serve immediately.

Tip: When juicing lemons, start with lemons that are at room temperature. Roll them over the counter back and forth, pressing with your palm, before juicing.

Chicken Caesar Salad Sandwich

Serves 4

Since my kids love Caesar salad, I thought this would make a great sandwich. These are a great adult and kid pleaser.

½ cup	Homemade Mayonnaise (page 321) or store-bought	125 mL
¾ cup	freshly grated Parmesan cheese	175 mL
2	cloves garlic, minced	2
⅓ cup	chopped fresh parsley	75 mL
1½ tsp	Dijon mustard	7 mL
1 tsp	grated lemon zest	5 mL
2 tbsp	freshly squeezed lemon juice	30 mL
1	large ciabatta bread, cut into 4 wedges, split	1
2 cups	thinly sliced cooked chicken (see Tip, right)	500 mL
4	romaine lettuce leaves	4

Toppings, optional

	Tomatoes, sliced
	Red onion, sliced

1. In a medium bowl, combine mayonnaise, Parmesan, garlic, parsley, mustard, lemon zest and lemon juice.

2. Place bread slices on a work surface. Spread mayonnaise mixture equally over cut sides of each bread wedge. Top equally with chicken, lettuce, desired toppings and remaining bread. Serve immediately.

Tip: I used rotisserie chicken for the chicken in this recipe, and it saves me a lot of time and effort.

Lunch Box Sushi

Serves 4 to 6

I came up with this idea because sushi for lunch is often requested at my house. These came out great, and I love using shrimp instead of crabmeat in this recipe.

1 tsp	wasabi powder	5 mL
2 tbsp	soy sauce	30 mL
2 cups	cooked sushi short-grain rice, cooled	500 mL
2 tbsp	chopped green onions	30 mL
1 tsp	Homemade Mayonnaise (page 321) or store-bought	5 mL
1/8 tsp	hot pepper flakes	0.5 mL
6	10-inch (25 cm) white or whole wheat tortillas	6
6	sheets nori	6
1 1/2 lbs	peeled cooked shrimp, chopped	750 g
1 cup	chopped avocado	250 mL
1 cup	finely chopped cucumber	250 mL
1/3 cup	soy sauce	75 mL

1. In a small bowl, combine wasabi and 1 tsp (5 mL) water. Add 2 tbsp (30 mL) soy sauce and mix well.

2. In a medium bowl, combine rice, wasabi mixture, green onions, mayonnaise and hot pepper flakes.

3. Line each tortilla with nori. Arrange rice mixture equally in center of each wrap. Add shrimp, avocado and cucumber. Fold both ends over filling. Roll up and serve with soy sauce.

Variation

You can use flavored tortillas in this recipe and imitation crab instead of shrimp.

Tip: Prepare your rice the day before. I like to prepare my sushi rice with seasoned vinegar and toasted sesame seeds.

Sandwich on a Stick

Serves 4 to 6

My kids love when I make anything on a skewer. Sometimes using the same ingredients in a different way makes all of the difference.

4	slices white or wheat bread (1-inch/2.5 cm slices), cubed	4
4 oz	Cheddar or mozzarella cheese, cut into 8 cubes	125 g
4 oz	sliced turkey or ham, cut into 8 slices, about 1 inch (2.5 cm) thick	125 g
1 cup	chopped lettuce leaves	250 mL
1 cup	grape tomatoes (see Tip, right)	250 mL
½ cup	small dill pickles	125 mL
½ cup	pitted black or green olives	125 mL
¾ cup	deli or regular mustard	175 mL

- **Eight 8-inch (20 cm) bamboo skewers, soaked in water for 30 minutes**

1. Thread skewers with bread cubes, cheese, turkey, lettuce, tomatoes, pickles and olives. Serve with mustard for dipping.

Variation

Feel free to substitute any of your favorite meats, cheese or toppings for this recipe.

Tip: Grape tomatoes are similar to plum tomatoes but are bite size. Store tomatoes at room temperature away from sunlight and use within a few days.

Turkey-Pesto Roll-Up

Serves 4

Because we love pesto, these wraps are always a hit. I love this recipe for lunch on the go.

4	8-inch (20 cm) white or whole wheat flour tortillas, warmed (see Tip, page 23)	4
¼ cup	Basil Pesto (page 329) or store-bought	60 mL
1 lb	sliced smoked turkey	500 g
4	slices provolone cheese	4
1 cup	mixed lettuce leaves	250 mL
2	avocados, sliced (see Tip, right)	2
1	large tomato, thinly sliced, optional	1

1. Place tortillas on a work surface. Spread 1 tbsp (15 mL) of the pesto over each tortilla. Arrange turkey, cheese, lettuce, avocados, and tomato, if using, in the center. Fold both ends over filling. Roll up and serve.

Variation

Feel free to substitute any of your favorite flavored tortillas, such as tomato-basil.

Tip: Store unripe avocados at room temperature and ripe ones in the refrigerator for up to 1 week.

Chicken Salad Pita Pockets

Serves 4 to 6

Pita bread is great for lunchtime sandwiches. This chicken salad, filled with grapes, walnuts and fresh dill, is one of my family's favorites.

2½ cups	chopped cooked chicken	625 mL
1/2 cup	reduced-fat mayonnaise	125 mL
1 cup	sliced red grapes	250 mL
1/3 cup	diced celery	75 mL
1/4 cup	chopped walnuts, toasted (see Tips, right)	60 mL
1 tbsp	chopped fresh dill	15 mL
4	6- to 8-inch (15 to 20 cm) pitas with pockets (see Tips, right)	4
	Leaf lettuce, optional	

1. In a medium bowl, combine chicken, mayonnaise, grapes, celery, walnuts and dill. Cover and refrigerate for at least 30 minutes.

2. Place pitas on a work surface. Line pita halves with lettuce, if using. Fill each pita equally with chicken salad.

Tips: Store pita bread in a plastic bag at room temperature and use within one week. Pita is usually sold near the bakery or in the bread section of most grocery stores.

Toasting nuts intensifies their flavor. To toast walnuts: Toast in an ungreased skillet over medium heat, stirring frequently, for 5 to 7 minutes or until golden brown.

Turkey, Apple and Brie Sandwich

Serves 4

I love making crusty sandwiches with turkey, Granny Smith apples and Brie. Tart apples pair great with the creaminess of Brie.

8	slices multigrain bread (1-inch/2.5 cm thick slices)	8
1/4 cup	Dijon or deli mustard	60 mL
8 oz	thinly sliced cracked pepper turkey	250 g
6 oz	Brie, thinly sliced	175 g
2	large Granny Smith apples, thinly sliced (see Tip, right)	2

1. Place bread slices on a work surface. Spread deli mustard equally on half of bread slices. Arrange turkey, Brie slices and apple slices over mustard. Cover with remaining bread slices and serve.

Variation

Substitute 1/4 cup (60 mL) mayonnaise or prepared mustard for the Dijon mustard.

Tip: Store fresh apples in a cool, dark place or refrigerate in a plastic bag. They keep longer if they don't touch each other during storage.

Garden Tuna Checkerboard Sandwich

Serves 4

It's fun to mix and match different types of bread to jazz up lunch sandwiches. This recipe gives classic tuna a twist using fresh lemon juice, white wine vinegar and patterned bread slices.

2	cans (each 6 oz/170 g) tuna, packed in water, drained	2
3 tbsp	white wine vinegar	45 mL
1 tbsp	olive oil	15 mL
1 tsp	freshly squeezed lemon juice	5 mL
1/4 tsp	freshly ground black pepper	1 mL
2	slices whole wheat bread (1-inch/2.5 cm thick slices)	2
2	slices white bread (1-inch/2.5 cm thick slices)	2
1/2 cup	mixed salad greens (see Tips, right)	125 mL
1/3 cup	alfalfa sprouts, optional	75 mL

1. In a medium bowl, combine tuna, vinegar, oil, lemon juice and pepper.

2. Place whole wheat and white bread slices on a work surface. Spread tuna equally over half of the bread slices. Top equally with lettuce and sprouts, if using. Cover whole wheat and white with remaining bread slices.

3. Cut each sandwich into 4 squares and arrange in a checkerboard pattern.

Variation

Use any of your favorite breads or stuffing to make checkerboard sandwiches. Kids love them!

Tips: Once canned tuna is opened, refrigerate it and use within 2 days.

For the mixed greens, I like to use arugula, Boston and Bibb or spring mix lettuces.

Tomato, Cucumber and Feta Roll-Up

Serves 4

This is a variation of a cucumber tomato salad that I make often. This makes a great wrap sandwich — perfect for a quick, healthy lunch.

2	large tomatoes, thinly sliced	2
1	large cucumber, thinly sliced (see Tips, right)	1
2	green onions, white and green parts, chopped	2
1/3 cup	crumbled feta cheese	75 mL
2 tbsp	chopped Italian flat-leaf parsley	30 mL
3 tbsp	white wine vinegar	45 mL
2 tbsp	olive oil	30 mL
1/8 tsp	sea salt	0.5 mL
1/8 tsp	freshly ground black pepper	0.5 mL
4	6-inch (15 cm) white or whole wheat tortillas	4

1. In a large bowl, combine tomatoes, cucumber, green onions, feta, parsley, vinegar, olive oil, salt and pepper.

2. Place tortillas on a work surface. Arrange tomato mixture in center of each tortilla. Fold both ends over filling. Roll up and serve.

Tips: I like to buy English, or seedless, cucumbers as they are very tender and have excellent flavor. Store unwashed cucumbers in a plastic bag in the refrigerator for up to 10 days. Once they are cut, store in a plastic bag and use within a few days.

Refrigerate tortillas in a plastic bag for up to 1 week. Freeze for up to 3 months.

Almond Butter, Honey and Banana Sandwich

Serves 4

This has to be my favorite lunchtime sandwich of all time. My favorite almond butter is the self-grind kind but I like all of the all-natural varieties, which can be found at specialty grocery stores or health food stores.

8	slices whole wheat bread (1/2-inch/1 cm slices)	8
1/2 cup	almond butter	125 mL
1/4 cup	liquid honey	60 mL
2	large bananas, sliced lengthwise (see Tip, right)	2

1. Place bread slices on a work surface. Spread 1 tbsp (15 mL) of the almond butter over each bread slice. Top 4 slices equally with honey and bananas. Cover with remaining bread, pressing together.

Tip: When choosing bananas, look for plump, evenly colored yellow bananas that have no bruises. Store on the counter and do not refrigerate because that will stop the ripening process.

Trio Hoagie

Serves 2

My running friend, Caroline, is very creative. She gave me this idea and called it the "wreck" sandwich.

2	hoagie rolls, split and warmed	2
2 tbsp	deli mustard	30 mL
4 oz	sliced roasted or smoked turkey	125 g
4 oz	sliced deli roast beef	125 g
4 oz	sliced salami (see Tip, right)	125 g
4	slices Swiss cheese	4
1/2 cup	lettuce leaves	125 mL

1. Place hoagies on a work surface. Spread one side of each roll with 1 tbsp (15 mL) of the mustard. Arrange turkey, roast beef, salami, cheese and lettuce over mustard. Top with remaining bread half. Serve immediately or wrap and store in the refrigerator for up to 2 hours.

Variation

Use multigrain, rye, pumpernickel or pita instead of hoagie roll, if desired.

Tip: When choosing salami, I prefer the small Italian salami slices.

Roast Beef and Pepper Jack Sandwich

Serves 4

If you're in the mood for a different lunch sandwich, try this combination with zesty hummus and a kick from Pepper Jack cheese.

4	8-inch (20 cm) pita pockets	4
3/4 cup	Hummus (page 313) or store-bought	175 mL
8 oz	thinly sliced roast beef	250 g
3/4 cup	thinly sliced red and green bell peppers	125 mL
1/2 cup	chopped romaine lettuce leaves	125 mL
4 oz	Pepper Jack cheese, cut into 4 slices	125 g

1. Place pita pockets on a work surface. Spread hummus equally inside each pita pocket. Stuff each pocket equally with roast beef, bell peppers, lettuce and Pepper Jack cheese. Serve immediately or wrap tightly in plastic wrap or foil and refrigerate for up to 8 hours.

Variation

For a vegetarian version, omit roast beef and add 2 sliced avocados. I also like to add yellow bell peppers, button mushrooms and sprouts for added crunch, color and flavor.

Ham, Turkey and Muenster Sandwich

Serves 4

This easy ham sandwich is the perfect lunchtime pleaser. This is also wonderful to make when you have leftover ham or turkey from the holidays.

8	slices multigrain bread (1-inch/2.5 cm thick slices)	8
¼ cup	Dijon or deli mustard	60 mL
4 oz	thinly sliced Black Forest ham	125 g
4 oz	thinly sliced cracked pepper turkey	125 g
6 oz	Muenster cheese, cut into 4 thin slices	175 g
1 cup	watercress (see Tip, right)	250 mL
2	avocados, thinly sliced	2

1. Place bread slices on a work surface. Spread deli mustard equally on 4 bread slices. Arrange ham, turkey, cheese, watercress and avocados equally over mustard. Cover with remaining bread slices, pressing gently together.

Variation

If you don't have watercress leaves on hand, substitute any of your favorite lettuce.

Tip: Watercress is a member of the mustard family and it has crisp, dark green leaves with a slightly peppery flavor. Store in a plastic bag in the refrigerator for up to 2 days. Wash thoroughly before using.

Salami and Cheese Sandwich

Serves 4

This is my daughter's favorite sandwich to take to school for lunch, so I had to be sure to include it.

8	slices multigrain bread (1-inch/2.5 cm thick slices)	8
¼ cup	Homemade Mayonnaise (page 321) or store-bought	60 mL
8 oz	thinly sliced salami (see Tip, page 57)	250 g
4	slices mozzarella cheese	4
1 cup	romaine lettuce leaves	250 mL

Tip: When storing or including in a lunch box, wrap tightly in foil for better freshness.

1. Place bread slices on a work surface. Spread mayonnaise equally on half of the bread slices. Arrange salami, cheese and lettuce equally over mayonnaise. Cover with remaining bread slices, pressing gently together.

Variations

Feel free to substitute mustard for the mayonnaise in this recipe.

Substitute your favorite cheese and bread as well as mustard for the mayonnaise to create your own creative, simple sandwich.

Classics

Classic Tuna Sandwich

Serves 4

When I was pregnant with my first child, I ate this almost every day. Now my son loves this version, too.

2	cans (each 6 oz/170 g) tuna, drained (see Tip, below)	2
¼ cup	finely chopped celery	60 mL
⅓ cup	Homemade Mayonnaise (page 321) or store-bought	75 mL
¼ tsp	salt	1 mL
¼ tsp	freshly ground black pepper	1 mL
8	slices whole wheat or white bread (½-inch/1 cm thick slices)	8
4	lettuce leaves	4
4	small tomatoes, thinly sliced	4

Tip: Be sure to always drain the liquid from the canned tuna.

1. In a large bowl, combine tuna, celery, mayonnaise, salt and pepper. Cover and chill in the refrigerator for at least 30 minutes or for up to 1 day for flavors to blend.

2. Place bread slices on a work surface. Arrange lettuce, tuna and tomatoes over half of bread and cover with remaining bread slice.

Variations

Classic Tuna with a Twist: Add 1 tbsp (15 mL) pickle relish and 1 tsp (5 mL) grated lemon zest in Step 1. Proceed as directed.

Greek-Style Tuna: Omit celery. Add ¼ cup (60 mL) finely chopped red bell pepper, ¼ cup (60 mL) finely chopped green bell pepper, 2 tsp (10 mL) freshly squeezed lemon juice and ¼ cup (60 mL) chopped black olives in Step 1. Proceed as directed.

All-Natural Peanut Butter and Jelly Sandwich

Serves 4

This was my all-time favorite sandwich when I was growing up and still is. I was always partial to strawberry rather than grape jelly.

8	slices whole wheat or white bread (1/2-inch/1 cm thick slices)	8
1/2 cup	all-natural peanut butter (see Tip, below)	125 mL
1/4 cup	strawberry preserves or jam	60 mL

Tip: When purchasing all-natural peanut butter, look for brands that have little to no added fat or sugar.

1. Place bread slices on a work surface. Spread 1 tbsp (15 mL) of the peanut butter on one side of each bread slice. Spread preserves equally on the peanut butter on 4 slices. Cover with remaining bread slices and press together gently.

Variations

Substitute 4 cinnamon-raisin bread slices for the whole wheat or white bread.

Substitute 1/2 cup (125 mL) almond butter or hazelnut butter for the peanut butter and 1/4 cup (60 mL) seedless raspberry preserves for the strawberry.

Classic BLT Sandwich

Serves 4

I have to admit that these are my kids' favorite classic sandwiches. My daughter calls hers "BL" because she doesn't like tomatoes on hers.

8	white bread slices (1/2-inch/ 1 cm thick slices), toasted	8
1/2 cup	Homemade Mayonnaise (page 321) or store-bought	125 mL
8	slices bacon, cooked (see Tip, right)	8
8	iceberg lettuce leaves	8
8	slices ripe tomatoes	8

1. Place toasted bread slices on a work surface. Spread 1 tbsp (15 mL) of the mayonnaise on one side of each slice. Arrange bacon, lettuce and tomatoes on 4 of the slices. Cover each with remaining slice of bread and press together gently.

Tip: Use your favorite bread for this recipe and feel free to substitute turkey bacon or any of your favorite bacon.

Salmon BLT Sandwich

Serves 4

We eat salmon almost once a week at my house. This is a great way to serve it for a change of pace.

8 tbsp	Homemade Mayonnaise (page 321) or store-bought	120 mL
1 tbsp	chopped shallot	15 mL
1 tsp	freshly squeezed lemon juice	5 mL
1/4 tsp	finely chopped fresh dill	1 mL
4	pieces skinless salmon fillet, each about 6 oz (175 g)	4
1 tbsp	olive oil	15 mL
1/2 tsp	sea salt	2 mL
1/2 tsp	hot pepper flakes	2 mL
4	hamburger buns, split and toasted	4
4	leaves green lettuce	4
8	slices bacon, cooked	8
8	slices ripe tomatoes	8

- **Preheat barbecue grill to medium-high, lightly greased**

1. In a small bowl, combine mayonnaise, shallot, lemon juice and dill. Set aside.

2. Brush salmon fillets with olive oil and sprinkle with salt and hot pepper flakes. Grill for 4 minutes per side for medium or until desired degree of doneness.

3. Place hamburger buns on a work surface. Spread mayonnaise mixture equally on each split side of buns. Arrange lettuce, salmon, bacon and tomatoes on bottom of bun and cover with top half. Serve immediately.

Variation

You can also bake the salmon on a rimmed baking sheet, lined with parchment paper, in the oven at 400°F (200°C) for 8 to 10 minutes for medium or until desired degree of doneness.

Tip: If you're cooking bacon over the stove, be sure to keep a close eye on it and turn it often.

Homemade Sloppy Joes

Serves 4

I first had Sloppy Joes at day camp when I was in elementary school. Apparently schools in the South still have them on their school lunch menu. This is a classic version that's a hit at my house.

1 lb	lean ground beef	500 g
¼ cup	chopped onion	60 mL
¼ cup	chopped green bell pepper	60 mL
1	clove garlic, minced	1
1 cup	tomato sauce	250 mL
1 tbsp	tomato paste	15 mL
1 tbsp	Worcestershire sauce	15 mL
2 tsp	brown sugar	10 mL
⅛ tsp	hot pepper sauce	0.5 mL
	Salt and freshly ground black pepper	
4	crusty rolls, split and toasted	4

Toppings, optional

	Tomato slices
	Pickles
	Lettuce

1. In a large skillet over medium heat, sauté beef, onion, bell pepper and garlic for 5 minutes or until beef is browned. Stir in tomato sauce, tomato paste, Worcestershire sauce, brown sugar and hot sauce. Reduce heat and simmer, stirring occasionally, for 10 to 15 minutes or until slightly thickened. Season with salt and pepper to taste and serve in buns. Garnish with tomatoes, pickles and lettuce, as desired.

Variations

Chipotle Turkey Sloppy Joes: Substitute 1 lb (500 g) ground turkey for the ground beef and add ¼ to ½ tsp (1 to 2 mL) chipotle powder.

Southwestern-Style Sloppy Joes: Omit brown sugar. Add ¼ tsp (1 mL) chili powder, ¼ tsp (1 mL) ground cumin and 1 cup (250 mL) salsa instead of the tomato sauce. Top with sour cream, jalapeños and avocados.

Italian Sub Sandwich

Serves 4

I love making my own sub sandwiches at home. They are better and fresher than the restaurants, and, of course, less expensive.

1/4 cup	red wine vinegar	60 mL
1 tbsp	olive oil	15 mL
1	clove garlic, minced	1
1/2 tsp	dried oregano	2 mL
1/2 tsp	salt	2 mL
4	6-inch (15 cm) sub rolls	4
4 oz	thinly sliced peppered turkey	125 g
4 oz	thinly sliced Italian salami	125 g
4	slices mozzarella cheese	4
2 cups	torn romaine lettuce	500 mL
1	medium tomato, thinly sliced	1
1/3 cup	sliced roasted banana peppers (see Tip, right)	75 mL

1. In a small bowl, combine vinegar, olive oil, garlic, oregano and salt.

2. Place bread on a work surface and slice in half horizontally lengthwise. Brush both cut sides with half of vinegar mixture. Arrange turkey, salami and mozzarella over bottom half. Arrange lettuce, tomato and banana peppers over the other half. Drizzle with remaining vinegar mixture and sandwich bread halves together. Serve immediately.

Tip: When making sandwiches ahead of time, keep tomatoes and banana peppers in a separate bag and don't put dressing on them until ready to serve.

Classic Turkey and Swiss Sandwich

Serves 4

I make this sandwich probably more than anything else in this entire book. I prefer cracked pepper turkey.

8	slices Italian bread (½-inch/1 cm thick slices)	8
½ cup	deli mustard	125 mL
8 oz	sliced deli turkey	250 g
4	slices Swiss cheese	4
4	lettuce leaves	4
1	tomato, thinly sliced	1

1. Place bread slices on a work surface. Spread mustard equally over bread slices. Arrange turkey, Swiss cheese, lettuce and tomato equally on 4 of the slices. Cover with remaining bread and press together gently.

Tip: Once mustard is opened, store in the refrigerator for up to 1 year or unopened for up to 2 years.

Hot Ham and Swiss Cheese Sandwich

Serves 16

You can't go wrong with these ingredients served on a warm croissant. These are a hit for all get-togethers or parties.

⅓ cup	Homemade Mayonnaise (page 321) or store-bought	75 mL
2 tbsp	Dijon mustard	30 mL
1 tbsp	poppy seeds	15 mL
¼ tsp	Worcestershire sauce	1 mL
16	croissants, split	16
12 oz	thinly sliced Black Forest ham	375 g
12 oz	thinly sliced baby Swiss cheese	375 g

- **Preheat oven to 325°F (160°C)**

1. In a small bowl, combine mayonnaise, Dijon, poppy seeds and Worcestershire.

2. Place croissants, crust side down, on a work surface. Spread mayonnaise mixture equally over bottom halves. Arrange ham and cheese over mayonnaise. Cover with top halves. Wrap sandwiches individually in foil and place on a baking sheet. Bake in preheated oven for 30 minutes or until cheese is melted.

Tip: You can make these up to 1 day ahead, but do not add mayonnaise mixture until just before baking.

Grilled Fish Sandwich

Serves 4

Since we live so close to the gulf, we always crave grilled fish sandwiches like the grilled fish sandwiches served at Caliza restaurant in Alys Beach, Florida.

4	skinless fish fillets, such as grouper, snapper or cod, each about ¾ inch (2 cm) thick (about 2 lbs/1 kg total)	4
1 tsp	lemon pepper	5 mL
1 tsp	sea salt	5 mL
¼ cup	freshly squeezed lemon juice	60 mL
4	whole wheat buns, split and toasted	4

Toppings, optional

	Cocktail or Tartar Sauce (page 326 and 333) or store-bought
	Lettuce
	Tomato slices
	Red onion slices

- **Preheat barbecue grill to medium, lightly greased**
- **Grill rack or basket**

1. Place fish in a shallow dish. Sprinkle with lemon pepper and salt and drizzle with lemon juice.

2. Grill on grill rack or basket, covered, for 8 minutes per side or until fish flakes easily when tested with a fork.

3. Place buns on a work surface. Place fish on buns and add cocktail sauce, lettuce, tomatoes and onions, as desired.

Tip: Grill fish over medium or medium low-heat. Fish cooks quickly, and you don't want it to overcook.

French Dip Sandwich

I love sandwiches with dips. This is a wonderful version of a Classic French Dip that's very popular with my friends.

1 tbsp	olive oil	15 mL
½ cup	diced onion	125 mL
½ cup	diced celery	125 mL
½ cup	diced carrot	125 mL
2 tbsp	tomato paste	30 mL
2 cups	reduced-sodium beef broth	500 mL
1 cup	reduced-sodium chicken broth	250 mL
4	6-inch (15 cm) French baguettes, cut in half lengthwise and toasted	4
1 lb	sliced roast beef	500 g

Tip: When making French dip, use crusty, dense bread that can withstand dipping in liquid.

1. In a large skillet, heat oil over medium heat. Sauté onion, celery and carrot for 3 minutes or until tender. Add tomato paste and sauté for 1 minute. Add beef and chicken broths. Bring to a boil. Reduce heat to medium and simmer until reduced by half, about 15 minutes. Keep warm.

2. Place baguettes, crust side down, on a work surface. Arrange roast beef on bottom half of bread. Cover with top half. Serve with hot broth for dipping.

Variations

Turkey French Dip: Substitute turkey for roast beef.

French Dip Panini: Add 4 slices Swiss cheese on top of beef. Brush each bread slice with 1 tsp (5 mL) of French dip, sandwich together and place sandwiches on panini grill or skillet and cook until golden brown, 3 to 4 minutes. Serve immediately.

Tip: I use reduced-sodium prepared chicken and beef broth instead of regular. To me, it has enough salt.

Monte Cristo Sandwich

Serves 4

This sandwich is the American version of the French sandwich croque monsieur. Every time I make these at my house, it's a home run.

8	white bread slices (½-inch/ 1 cm thick slices)	8
¼ cup	Dijon or honey mustard	60 mL
4	slices Swiss cheese, each about 1 oz (30 g)	4
4 oz	thinly sliced smoked ham	125 g
4 oz	thinly sliced roasted turkey	125 g
2	eggs, lightly beaten	2
¼ cup	milk	60 mL
2 tbsp	butter or margarine	30 mL
	Confectioner's (icing) sugar, optional	
	Raspberry jam, optional	
	Fresh fruit, optional	

1. Place bread slices on a work surface. Spread 4 bread slices equally with mustard. Arrange cheese, ham and turkey over mustard and cover with remaining bread slices.

2. In a shallow dish, combine eggs and milk. Dip both sides of each sandwich in milk mixture.

3. In a large nonstick skillet, melt butter over medium heat. In batches as necessary, cook sandwiches about 3 minutes per side or until golden brown. Dust with confectioner's sugar, if using, and serve with raspberry jam and fresh fruit, if using.

Tip: To make these sandwiches healthier, use 4 egg whites, lean ham, turkey, skim milk and omit confectioner's sugar. Use whole wheat bread instead of white bread.

Best-Ever Pimiento Cheese Sandwich

Serves 4 to 6

I keep pimiento cheese in my house all of the time. I love trying new versions of this classic favorite.

1/4 cup	Homemade Mayonnaise (page 321) or store-bought	60 mL
1 1/2 tsp	freshly squeezed lemon juice	7 mL
1 tsp	Worcestershire sauce	5 mL
1	jar (4 1/2 oz/128 mL) diced pimientos, drained	1
1/8 tsp	cayenne pepper	0.5 mL
8 oz	extra-sharp (aged) Cheddar cheese, finely shredded	250 g
8	white bread slices (1/2-inch/ 1 cm thick slices), toasted	8

Toppings, optional

	Lettuce
	Tomato slices

1. In a medium bowl, stir together mayonnaise, lemon juice, Worcestershire sauce, pimientos and cayenne. Stir in cheese. Cover and refrigerate for at least 30 minutes before serving or for up to 8 hours to allow flavors to blend and mixture to chill slightly.

2. Place toasted bread slices on a work surface. Spread pimiento cheese over half of bread slices. Garnish with toppings, as desired, and top with remaining bread.

Variation

Chipotle Pimiento Cheese: Stir 1/2 tsp (2 mL) chipotle powder into mixture in Step 1 and proceed as directed.

Tip: For best results, shred your own cheese rather than buying the pre-shredded type in a bag. My favorite is Wisconsin Cheddar.

Tarragon Chicken Salad Sandwich

Serves 4

There's a great French bakery in my town that has delicious Tarragon Chicken Salad. This version is so easy to make, especially when you start with rotisserie chicken.

3 tbsp	Homemade Mayonnaise (page 321) or store-bought	45 mL
2 tbsp	sour cream	30 mL
1 tbsp	freshly squeezed lemon juice	15 mL
1/4 tsp	fresh ground black pepper	1 mL
2 1/2 cups	chopped cooked chicken (see Tips, right)	625 mL
1/2 cup	diced celery	125 mL
2 tbsp	finely chopped tarragon (see Tips, right)	30 mL
8	slices multigrain bread (1/2-inch/1 cm thick slices)	8

Toppings, optional

	Lettuce
	Tomato slices

1. In a large bowl, stir together mayonnaise, sour cream, lemon juice and pepper. Add chicken, celery and tarragon, tossing gently to coat.

2. Place bread on a work surface. Spread chicken mixture equally over 4 bread slices and top with lettuce and tomatoes, if desired. Top with remaining bread slices and press together gently.

Tips: One deli-roasted chicken usually yields about 3 cups (750 mL) or 1 1/2 lbs (750 g) shredded chicken once the skin and bones are removed.

Kitchen shears are great for cutting small amounts of herbs. I use mine all the time when I'm using fresh herbs.

Chicken Waldorf Sandwich

Serves 4

This recipe is a twist on Waldorf salad. It's perfect to serve during the fall at the peak of apple and pecan season.

3 tbsp	Homemade Mayonnaise (page 321) or store-bought	45 mL
3 tbsp	low-fat apple-flavored or vanilla yogurt	45 mL
1 tbsp	freshly squeezed lemon juice (see Tips, right)	15 mL
2½ cups	chopped cooked chicken (see Tips, page 70)	625 mL
½ cup	chopped apples (see Tips, right)	125 mL
½ cup	diced celery	125 mL
½ cup	chopped pecans, toasted	125 mL
⅓ cup	dried cranberries or cherries	75 mL
8	slices whole wheat bread (½-inch/1 cm thick slices)	8
4	lettuce leaves	4

1. In a large bowl, stir together mayonnaise, yogurt and lemon juice. Add chicken, apples, celery, pecans and cranberries. Mix well. Cover and refrigerate for at least 30 minutes or for up to 2 days to allow flavors to blend and mixture to chill slightly.

2. Place bread slices on a work surface. Arrange lettuce over 4 of bread slices. Spread chicken salad equally over lettuce and cover with remaining bread.

Tips: I used Gala or Braeburn apples in this recipe but any sweet-tart apple will do. There's no need to peel them — the skin adds color and nutrition.

When purchasing lemons, look for ones that are plump, firm and heavy for their size.

Classic Egg Salad Sandwich

Serves 4

We make a lot of egg salad at my house. The kids love it, and it's such a breeze. Here's my version of the classic.

8	large eggs (see Tip, below)	8
	Cold water	
	Ice cubes	
1 tbsp	Homemade Mayonnaise (page 321) or store-bought	15 mL
1 tbsp	Dijon mustard	15 mL
	Salt and freshly ground pepper	
8	slices white bread (1/2-inch/1 cm thick slices)	8

Toppings, optional

	Lettuce
	Tomato slices

Tip: When purchasing eggs, always open and check the eggs in the container looking for broken egg shells as well as the date of expiration.

1. Place eggs in a large saucepan and add enough cold water to cover. Bring to a boil over high heat. Remove pan from heat. Cover and let stand for 15 minutes. Fill a medium bowl with 1 quart (1 L) of cold water and ice cubes and transfer eggs to chill for 5 minutes. Peel off shells and finely dice eggs.

2. In a bowl, combine eggs, mayonnaise and Dijon. Season with salt and pepper to taste. Cover and refrigerate for at least 30 minutes or for up to 2 days to allow flavors to blend and mixture to chill slightly.

3. Place bread slices on a work surface. Divide egg salad equally among 4 bread slices. Garnish with lettuce and tomatoes, as desired, and cover with remaining bread.

Variation

Lower-Fat Egg Salad: Use only the whites from 16 hard-cooked eggs. Discard yolks and add $1/3$ cup (75 mL) finely chopped celery and 2 tbsp (30 mL) chopped fresh chives to Step 2 with reduced-fat mayonnaise and Dijon.

Egg Salad with Smoked Paprika

Serves 4

I love using smoked paprika in dishes. The hint of smoked flavor works wonderfully in this egg salad recipe.

8	large eggs (see Tip, page 72)	8
	Cold water	
	Ice cubes	
2 tbsp	Homemade Mayonnaise (page 321) or store-bought	30 mL
2 tbsp	minced chives	30 mL
1/2 tsp	smoked paprika	2 mL
1/4 tsp	sea salt	1 mL
1/4 tsp	freshly ground black pepper	1 mL
8	slices sourdough bread (1/2-inch/1 cm thick slices)	8
2 cups	watercress leaves	500 mL

Toppings, optional

	Avocado slices
	Tomato slices

Tip: I love to use any leftover chives in many dishes, from appetizers to soups, and as a garnish.

1. Place eggs in a large saucepan and add enough cold water to cover. Bring to a boil over high heat. Remove pan from heat. Cover and let stand for 15 minutes. Fill a medium bowl with 1 quart (1 L) of cold water and ice cubes and transfer eggs to chill for 5 minutes. Peel off shells and finely dice eggs.

2. In a medium bowl, combine eggs, mayonnaise, chives, smoked paprika, salt and pepper. Cover and refrigerate for at least 30 minutes or for up to 2 days to allow flavors to blend and mixture to chill slightly.

3. Lightly toast bread and place on a work surface. Divide egg salad equally among 4 bread slices. Top with watercress, avocados and tomatoes, if desired, and cover with remaining bread.

Variation

Egg Salad Pancetta Club: Add 8 slices pancetta. Cook pancetta in a large skillet over medium-low heat, turning occasionally, for 10 minutes or until crisp. Drain and top each sandwich with 2 slices pancetta, watercress and desired toppings.

Classic Club Sandwich

Serves 4

My favorite club sandwich is at the Pine Tree Country Club in Birmingham, Alabama, where I live. They have been making it the same way since I was a child.

12	slices white bread ($\frac{1}{2}$-inch/ 1 cm thick slices), toasted	12
$\frac{1}{2}$ cup	Homemade Mayonnaise (page 321) or store-bought	125 mL
8 oz	sliced turkey	250 g
2	small tomatoes, sliced	2
8	slices Swiss cheese	8
8	slices bacon, cooked	8
4	lettuce leaves	4

Tip: Deli or roasted turkey can be stored in the refrigerator for up to 4 days.

1. Place bread slices on a work surface. Spread mayonnaise on one side of 8 bread slices. Arrange turkey, tomato and Swiss cheese over mayonnaise on each slice. Stack 2 slices together, keeping toppings up, then place 2 slices of bacon and the lettuce on top of cheese. Cover with remaining top halves and press together gently. Slice into quarters. Secure with toothpicks to hold the stacks together.

Variation

Updated Club Sandwich: Use $\frac{1}{2}$ cup (125 mL) aïoli instead of mayonnaise. Substitute 4 watercress leaves for each lettuce leaf, 8 slices applewood smoked bacon, for bacon, 8 oz (250 g) peppered turkey for turkey and 8 slices pepper Jack cheese for Swiss.

Grilled Cheese
Sandwiches

continued on next page

Grilled Guacomento

Serves 4

This idea of blending guacamole and pimiento cheese came from my friend, Kiel, and when she told me about it, I was so excited to make it. When I made these, everyone asked, "Why didn't I think of that?"

8	slices whole wheat bread (1/2-inch/1 cm thick slices)	8
1/4 cup	butter or margarine, softened	60 mL
1/2 cup	Guacamole (page 336) or store-bought	125 mL
1 cup	fresh spinach leaves	250 mL
2	tomatoes, thinly sliced	2
1/2 cup	Pimiento Cheese (page 114) or store-bought	125 mL

- **Panini grill or large skillet**
- **Preheat panini grill to medium, if using**

1. Brush one side of each bread slice with butter. Place on a work surface, buttered side down. Spread guacamole equally on bread slices. Top 4 bread slices equally with spinach, tomatoes and pimiento cheese. Cover with remaining bread slices, buttered side up, and press together gently.

2. Place sandwiches on preheated panini grill or in a large skillet over medium heat and cook, turning once if using a skillet, for 3 to 4 minutes or until golden brown and cheese is melted. Serve immediately.

Grilled Cheese and Peach-Ginger Chutney

Serves 4

The ginger in the chutney adds a boost of flavor and punch. This is great to serve for a summertime lunch.

8	slices multigrain bread (1/2-inch/1 cm thick slices)	8
1/4 cup	butter or margarine, softened	60 mL
1/4 cup	liquid honey	60 mL
12 oz	thinly sliced turkey	375 g
2	peaches, thinly sliced (see Tip, page 78)	2
4 oz	Muenster cheese, cut into 4 slices	125 g
1 cup	Peach-Ginger Chutney (page 335)	250 mL

- **Panini grill or large skillet**
- **Preheat panini grill to medium, if using**

1. Brush one side of each bread slice with butter. Place on a work surface, buttered side down. Spread 4 bread slices equally with honey. Top with turkey, peach slices, cheese and Peach-Ginger Chutney. Cover with remaining bread slices, buttered side up, and press together gently.

2. Place sandwiches on preheated panini grill or in a large skillet over medium heat and cook, turning once if using a skillet, for 3 to 4 minutes or until golden brown and cheese is melted. Serve immediately.

Grilled Peaches, Mozzarella and Peach Salsa

Serves 4

This summertime favorite is perfect in July or August when peaches are at their peak. Feel free to substitute turkey, roast beef or prosciutto for the ham, or omit the deli meat altogether.

8	slices sourdough bread (½-inch/1 cm thick slices)	8
2 tbsp	butter or margarine, softened	30 mL
¼ cup	liquid honey	60 mL
12 oz	thinly sliced ham	375 g
1 cup	thinly sliced peaches (see Tip, below)	250 mL
8	mozzarella cheese slices	8
1 cup	Peach Salsa (page 335)	250 mL

Tip: Choose peaches that are fragrant and give slightly to palm pressure. Store ripe peaches in a plastic bag for up to 5 days. Store unripe fruit at room temperature.

- **Panini grill or large skillet**
- **Preheat panini grill to medium, if using**

1. Brush one side of each bread slice with butter. Place on a work surface, buttered side down. Spread 4 bread slices equally with honey. Top with ham, peaches, cheese and Peach Salsa. Cover with remaining bread slices, buttered side up, and press together gently.

2. Place sandwiches on preheated panini grill or in a large skillet over medium heat and cook, turning once if using a skillet, for 3 to 4 minutes or until golden brown and cheese is melted. Serve immediately.

Variation

Goat cheese also works great instead of the mozzarella.

Grilled Sun-Dried Tomato Pesto and Vegetables

Serves 4

If you like sun-dried tomatoes as much as I do, you will love this vegetarian combination.

8	slices whole wheat bread (½-inch/1 cm thick slices)	8
2 tbsp	butter or margarine, softened	30 mL
¼ cup	Sun-Dried Tomato Pesto (page 330)	60 mL
1 cup	thinly sliced cucumber	250 mL
1 cup	thinly sliced tomatoes	250 mL
1 cup	dry-packed sun-dried tomatoes (see Tip, below)	250 mL
4 oz	Asiago cheese, thinly sliced	125 g

Tip: I like to use the dry-packed sun-dried tomatoes because they are lower in fat, and this sandwich already has big tomato flavor from the pesto. You can usually find them where the other sun-dried tomatoes are sold in the grocery store.

- **Panini grill or large skillet**
- **Preheat panini grill to medium, if using**

1. Brush one side of each bread slice with butter. Place on a work surface, buttered side down. Spread 4 bread slices equally with pesto. Top with cucumbers, tomatoes, sun-dried tomatoes and cheese. Cover with remaining bread slices, buttered side up, and press together gently.

2. Place sandwiches on preheated panini grill or in a large skillet over medium heat and cook, turning once if using a skillet, for 3 to 4 minutes or until golden brown and cheese is melted. Serve immediately.

Variations

Use Italian or sourdough bread instead of whole wheat.

This also works great by substituting Basil Pesto (page 329) for the Sun-Dried Tomato Pesto.

Grilled Zucchini with Cilantro Pesto

Serves 4

I love the fresh cilantro paired with the zucchini and squash in this vegetarian delight. Cooking the zucchini and cilantro like this also makes a great side dish to serve with pork, chicken or seafood.

2 tbsp	olive oil	30 mL
2	medium zucchini, unpeeled and cut into $1/4$-inch (0.5 cm) round slices	2
1	medium yellow squash (zucchini), unpeeled and cut into $1/2$-inch (1 cm) round slices	1
$1/2$	small onion, thinly sliced	$1/2$
$1/4$ tsp	salt	1 mL
$1/4$ tsp	freshly ground black pepper	1 ml
2 tbsp	freshly squeezed lemon juice	30 mL
8	slices whole wheat bread ($1/2$-inch/1 cm thick slices)	8
$1/4$ cup	butter or margarine, softened	60 mL
$1/4$ cup	Cilantro Pesto (page 330) (see Tips, right)	60 mL
4	slices Monterey Jack or Pepper Jack cheese	4

- **Panini grill or large skillet**
- **Preheat panini grill to medium, if using**

1. In a large skillet, heat oil over medium heat. Sauté zucchini, squash and onion for 5 to 7 minutes or until tender. Sprinkle with salt and pepper. Drizzle with lemon juice.

2. Brush one side of each bread slice with butter. Place on a work surface, buttered side down. Spread 4 bread slices equally with Cilantro Pesto. Top equally with vegetables and cheese. Cover with remaining bread slices, buttered side up, and press together gently.

3. Place sandwiches on preheated panini grill or in a large skillet over medium heat and cook, turning once if using a skillet, for 3 to 4 minutes or until golden brown and cheese is melted. Serve immediately

Tips: Store pesto in an airtight container in the refrigerator for up to 1 week or freeze for up to 6 months.

You could also use store-bought pesto here. Just add 2 tbsp (30 mL) cilantro and process in a food processor until smooth.

Grilled Cheese and Cherry Tomato Relish

Serves 4

Cherry tomatoes are the star of this grilled cheese sandwich filled with Italian flair.

8	slices Italian bread (½-inch/1 cm thick slices)	8
¼ cup	butter or margarine, softened	60 mL
¼ cup	Basil Pesto (page 329) or store-bought	60 mL
4	slices mozzarella cheese	4
½ cup	freshly grated Parmesan cheese (see Tip, right)	125 mL
1 cup	fresh spinach leaves	250 mL
1⅓ cups	Cherry Tomato Relish (page 322)	325 mL

- **Panini grill or large skillet**
- **Preheat panini grill to medium, if using**

1. Brush one side of each bread slice with butter. Place on a work surface, buttered side down. Spread 4 bread slices equally with Basil Pesto. Top equally with mozzarella and Parmesan cheeses, spinach and Cherry Tomato Relish. Cover with remaining bread slices, buttered side up, and press together gently.

2. Place sandwiches on preheated panini grill or in a large skillet over medium heat and cook, turning once if using a skillet, for 3 to 4 minutes or until golden brown and cheese is melted. Serve immediately.

Tip: Grate a large chuck of Parmesan and then refrigerate it in an airtight container to use as needed. If you're short on time, purchase already grated Parmesan.

Grilled Feta and Turkey

Serves 4

This Greek-style grilled cheese is very unique. Feel free to substitute ham, roast beef or any deli meats for the turkey in this recipe.

8	slices Italian bread (½-inch/ 1 cm thick slices)	8
¼ cup	butter or margarine, softened	60 mL
¼ cup	Red Pepper Hummus (page 314) or store-bought	60 mL
12 oz	thinly sliced deli turkey	375 g
4	slices provolone cheese	4
4 oz	crumbled feta cheese (see Tips, page 107)	125 g
1 cup	fresh spinach leaves	250 mL

- **Panini grill or large skillet**
- **Preheat panini grill to medium, if using**

1. Brush one side of each bread slice with butter. Place on a work surface, buttered side down. Spread 4 bread slices equally with Red Pepper Hummus. Top equally with turkey, provolone, feta and spinach. Cover with remaining bread slices, buttered side up, and press together gently.

2. Place sandwiches on preheated panini grill or in a large skillet over medium heat and cook, turning once if using a skillet, for 3 to 4 minutes or until golden brown and cheese is melted. Serve immediately.

Smoked Salmon Pesto Grilled Cheese

Serves 4

This grilled cheese is perfect served with a summer tomato soup or a chopped vegetable salad.

8	slices Italian or multigrain bread (½-inch/1 cm thick slices)	8
¼ cup	butter or margarine, softened	60 mL
¼ cup	Basil Pesto (page 329) or store-bought	60 mL
12 oz	thinly sliced smoked salmon	375 g
2	tomatoes, thinly sliced (see Tips, page 97)	2
4	slices mozzarella cheese	4

- **Panini grill or large skillet**
- **Preheat panini grill to medium, if using**

1. Brush one side of each bread slice with butter. Place on a work surface, buttered side down. Spread 4 bread slices equally Basil Pesto. Top equally with smoked salmon, sliced tomatoes and cheese. Cover with remaining bread slices, buttered side up, and press together gently.

2. Place sandwiches on preheated panini grill or in a large skillet over medium heat and cook, turning once if using a skillet, for 3 to 4 minutes or until golden brown and cheese is melted. Serve immediately.

Grilled Roast Beef and Sweet Red Pepper Relish

Serves 4

Sweet Red Pepper Relish is the star ingredient in this gooey grilled cheese bursting with flavors.

8	slices sourdough bread (1/2-inch/1 cm thick slices)	8
1/4 cup	butter or margarine, softened	60 mL
1/4 cup	Homemade Mayonnaise (page 321) or store-bought	60 mL
12 oz	thinly sliced roast beef	375 g
1/2 cup	shredded mozzarella cheese	125 mL
1 cup	fresh basil leaves (see Tip, right)	250 mL
1 1/2 cups	Sweet Pepper Relish (page 323) or store-bought relish	375 mL

- **Panini grill or large skillet**
- **Preheat panini grill to medium, if using**

1. Brush one side of each bread slice with butter. Place on a work surface, buttered side down. Spread 4 bread slices equally with mayonnaise. Top equally with roast beef, cheese, basil and Sweet Pepper Relish. Cover with remaining bread slices, buttered side up, and press together gently.

2. Place sandwiches on preheated panini grill or in a large skillet over medium heat and cook, turning once if using a skillet, for 3 to 4 minutes or until golden brown and cheese is melted. Serve immediately

Tip: To store fresh basil, wrap stems in moist paper towels and refrigerate in a tightly sealed plastic bag for up to 2 days. For best flavor, use the basil as soon as you can.

Grilled Roast Beef and Stilton

Serves 4

Stilton is a semisoft, crumbly cheese that is similar to blue cheese. It is terrific paired with roast beef and peppery arugula.

8	slices whole wheat bread	8
1/4 cup	butter or margarine, softened	60 mL
1/4 cup	Homemade Mayonnaise or Fresh Basil Aïoli (pages 321 and 311) or store-bought	60 mL
12 oz	thinly sliced roast beef	375 g
1 cup	fresh arugula leaves	250 mL
2	tomatoes, thinly sliced	2
1 cup	crumbled Stilton cheese or your favorite blue cheese	250 mL

- **Panini grill or large skillet**
- **Preheat panini grill to medium, if using**

1. Brush one side of 4 bread slices with butter. Place on a work surface, buttered side down. Spread 4 bread slices equally with mayonnaise. Top equally with roast beef, arugula, tomatoes and cheese. Cover with remaining bread slices, buttered side up, and press together gently.

2. Place sandwiches on preheated panini grill or in a large skillet over medium heat and cook, turning once if using a skillet, for 3 to 4 minutes or until golden brown and cheese is melted. Serve immediately.

Grilled Ham, Goat Cheese and Figs

Serves 4

This grilled cheese has a terrific mix of sweet and savory flavors.

8	slices Italian bread (1/2-inch/ 1 cm thick slices)	8
1/4 cup	butter or margarine, softened	60 mL
1/4 cup	liquid honey	60 mL
12 oz	thinly sliced ham or turkey	375 g
1 cup	baby spinach leaves	250 mL
1 1/2 cups	chopped figs	375 mL
4 oz	crumbled goat cheese	125 g

Tip: One pound (500 g) fresh figs yields about 2 cups (500 mL) chopped. Figs are usually available June through October. If you can't find fresh figs or they're not in season, substitute dried.

- **Panini grill or large skillet**
- **Preheat panini grill to medium, if using**

1. Brush one side of each bread slice with butter. Place on a work surface, buttered side down. Spread 4 bread slices equally with honey. Top equally with ham, spinach, figs and cheese. Cover with remaining bread slices, buttered side up, and press together gently.

2. Place sandwiches on preheated panini grill or in a large skillet over medium heat and cook, turning once if using a skillet, for 3 to 4 minutes or until golden brown and cheese is melted. Serve immediately.

Grilled Knockwurst and Swiss

Serves 4

Knockwurst, also called "knackwust," is a German-style hot dog that is great served with the Swiss cheese in this sandwich.

8	slices rye bread (½-inch/ 1 cm thick slices)	8
¼ cup	butter or margarine, softened	60 mL
¼ cup	prepared mustard	60 mL
4	knockwurst, grilled and sliced lengthwise (see Tip, below)	4
4	slices Swiss cheese	4

Tip: To grill knockwurst, grill on a lightly greased grill rack over medium-high heat for 5 to 7 minutes.

- **Panini grill or large skillet**
- **Preheat panini grill to medium, if using**

1. Brush one side of each bread slice with butter. Place on a work surface, buttered side down. Spread 4 bread slices equally with mustard. Top equally with knockwurst slices and cheese. Cover with remaining bread slices, buttered side up, and press together gently.

2. Place sandwiches on preheated panini grill or in a large skillet over medium heat and cook, turning once if using a skillet, for 3 to 4 minutes or until golden brown and cheese is melted. Serve immediately.

Chicken, Apple and Smoked Gouda

Serves 4

The roasted chicken pairs nicely with the sweetness of the apple and smokiness of the Gouda cheese.

8	slices Italian or multigrain bread (½-inch/1 cm thick slices)	8
¼ cup	butter or margarine, softened	60 mL
¼ cup	Homemade Mayonnaise (page 321) or store-bought	60 mL
2 cups	thinly sliced roasted or grilled chicken	500 mL
1 cup	baby spinach leaves	250 mL
2	Gala apples, thinly sliced	2
4 oz	smoked Gouda cheese, cut into thin slices	125 g

- **Panini grill or large skillet**
- **Preheat panini grill to medium, if using**

1. Brush one side of each bread slice with butter. Place on a work surface, buttered side down. Spread 4 bread slices equally with mayonnaise. Top equally with chicken, spinach, apples and cheese. Cover with remaining bread slices, buttered side up, and press together gently.

2. Place sandwiches on preheated panini grill or in a large skillet over medium heat and cook, turning once if using a skillet, for 3 to 4 minutes or until golden brown and cheese is melted.

Tip: I use one deli-style rotisserie chicken. It yields the perfect amount.

Grilled Crab, Mango and Avocado

Serves 4

This sandwich is wonderful for summer entertaining at home, the lake or at the beach.

12 oz	fresh crabmeat, drained	375 g
3 tbsp	freshly squeezed lime juice	45 mL
1/8 tsp	freshly ground black pepper	0.5 mL
8	slices French bread (1/2-inch/1 cm thick slices)	8
1/4 cup	butter or margarine, softened	60 mL
2	avocados (see Tips, below)	2
1	mango, thinly sliced	1
4 oz	Muenster cheese, thinly sliced	125 g

Tips: If you're short on time, purchase jarred mango slices and use 1 cup (250 mL), drained.

Avocados turn brown quickly but brushing with lemon juice will help it some. If you end up with half of a cut avocado, store it with the pit still in it and wrap tightly in plastic wrap in the refrigerator.

- **Panini grill or large skillet**
- **Preheat panini grill to medium, if using**

1. In a medium bowl, combine crab, lime juice and pepper.

2. Brush one side of each bread slice with butter. Place on a work surface, buttered side down. Slice avocados. Top 4 bread slices equally with crab mixture, avocados, mango and cheese. Cover with remaining bread slices, buttered side up, and press together gently.

3. Place sandwiches on preheated panini grill or in a large skillet over medium heat and cook, turning once if using a skillet, for 3 to 4 minutes or until golden brown and cheese is melted. Serve immediately.

Variation

Omit mango and use 1 cup (250 mL) Nectarine Relish (page 322) instead.

Mini Grilled Cheese with Marinara

Serves 4

This makes a great appetizer recipe or a fun way to serve grilled cheese for a main dish as well.

8	slices French, white or multigrain bread (1/2-inch/ 1 cm thick slices)	8
1/4 cup	butter or margarine, softened	60 mL
1/4 cup	Homemade Mayonnaise (page 321) or store-bought	60 mL
6 oz	thinly sliced ham	175 g
6 oz	thinly sliced roast beef	175 g
3 oz	sliced pepperoni	90 g
3/4 cup	fresh basil leaves	175 mL
4	slices provolone or mozzarella	4
1 cup	marinara sauce, warmed (see Tip, right)	250 mL

- **Panini grill or large skillet**
- **Preheat panini grill to medium, if using**

1. Brush one side of each bread slice with butter. Place on a work surface, buttered side down. Spread 4 bread slices equally with mayonnaise. Top equally with ham, roast beef, pepperoni, basil and cheese. Cover with remaining bread slices, buttered side up, and press together gently.

2. Place sandwiches on preheated panini grill or in a large skillet over medium heat and cook, turning once if using a skillet, for 3 to 4 minutes or until golden brown and cheese is melted. Cut each sandwich into thirds. Serve immediately with warmed marinara.

Tip: I use jarred marinara sauce in this recipe to save time.

Grilled Gruyère and Caramelized Onions

Serves 4

Caramelizing the onions flavors the Gruyère to perfection in this melt-in-your-mouth sandwich.

1 tbsp	unsalted butter	15 mL
1 tbsp	olive oil	15 mL
4 cups	sliced onions	1 L
1 tbsp	granulated sugar	15 mL
1/8 tsp	salt	0.5 mL
8	slices Italian bread (1/2-inch/1 cm thick slices)	8
1/4 cup	butter or margarine, softened	60 mL
1/4 cup	liquid honey	60 mL
4 oz	Gruyère cheese, thinly sliced	125 g

Tip: Caramelized onions are wonderful on an array of sandwiches and also great on pizza.

- **Large sauté pan**
- **Panini grill or large skillet**
- **Preheat panini grill to medium, if using**

1. In a large sauté pan, melt 1 tbsp (15 mL) of the butter and oil over medium-low heat. Add onions, sugar and salt. Cover and sweat, stirring occasionally, for 20 minutes. Uncover and continue to cook, stirring frequently, for about 15 minutes or until onions are lightly browned.

2. Brush one side of each bread slice with butter. Place on a work surface, buttered side down. Spread 4 bread slices equally with honey. Top equally with cheese and onions. Cover with remaining bread slices, buttered side up, and press together gently.

3. Place sandwiches on preheated panini grill or in a large skillet over medium heat and cook, turning once if using a skillet, for 3 to 4 minutes or until golden brown and cheese is melted. Serve immediately.

Variation

Substitute Swiss cheese for the Gruyère cheese, if you like.

Grilled Roast Beef, Nectarine and Brie

Serves 4

Since I love all of these ingredients, I thought they would pair together beautifully. This is a favorite when I have fresh nectarines.

8	slices multigrain bread (1/2-inch/1 cm thick slices)	8
2 tbsp	butter or margarine, softened	30 mL
1/4 cup	liquid honey	60 mL
12 oz	thinly sliced roast beef	375 g
2	nectarines, thinly sliced	2
4 oz	Brie, thinly sliced	125 g

- **Panini grill or large skillet**
- **Preheat panini grill to medium, if using**

1. Brush one side of 4 bread slices with butter. Place on a work surface, buttered side down. Spread 4 bread slices equally with honey. Top with roast beef, nectarine slices and Brie. Cover with remaining 4 bread slices, buttered side up, and press together gently.

2. Place sandwiches on preheated panini grill or in a large skillet over medium heat and cook, turning once if using a skillet, for 3 to 4 minutes or until golden brown and cheese is melted.

Italian Salami Panini

Serves 4

My 11-year old daughter came up with this panini combination. I was more than impressed when I took a bite.

4	6-inch (15 cm) French bread loaves, cut in half lengthwise	4
1/4 cup	butter or margarine, softened	60 mL
1/4 cup	Homemade Mayonnaise (page 321) or store-bought	60 mL
8 oz	thin slices Italian salami (see Tip, right)	250 g
1 cup	mixed greens	250 mL
4	mozzarella cheese slices	4

- **Panini grill or large skillet**
- **Preheat panini grill to medium, if using**

1. Brush one side of each bread slice with butter. Place on a work surface, buttered side down. Spread mayonnaise equally over 4 of the bread slices. Top equally with salami, mixed greens and cheese. Cover with remaining bread slices, buttered side up, and press together gently.

2. Place sandwiches on preheated panini grill or in a large skillet over medium heat and cook, turning once if using a skillet, for 3 to 4 minutes or until golden brown and cheese is melted.

Tip: I like the smaller circular Italian salami slices. Look for them in the grocery deli.

Grilled Cheese Burgers

Serves 4

I know of a few popular restaurants that serve hamburgers between grilled cheese sandwiches. When I made these, my children's eyes got so big.

1½ lbs	ground sirloin	750 g
1 tbsp	Worcestershire sauce	15 mL
¼ tsp	salt	1 mL
¼ tsp	freshly ground black pepper	1 mL
8	slices sourdough (½-inch/ 1 cm thick slices)	8
¼ cup	butter or margarine, softened	60 mL
4	slices Cheddar cheese	4

Toppings, optional

	Lettuce
	Tomato slices
	Pickles
	Ketchup

Tip: Feel free to cook the burger and grilled cheese in a large skillet over medium-high heat for 4 minutes per side or until an instant-read thermometer registers 160°F (71°C).

- **Preheat greased barbecue grill to medium-high heat (see Tip, left)**
- **Instant-read thermometer**

1. In a large bowl, combine beef, Worcestershire, salt and pepper. Form in to 4 equal patties, about ¾ inch (2 cm) thick.

2. Brush one side of bread slices with butter. Place on a work surface, buttered side down. Top 4 bread slices equally with cheese. Cover with remaining bread slices, buttered side up, and press together gently.

3. Grill hamburgers for 5 minutes per side or until an instant-read thermometer registers 160°F (71°C). Set aside.

4. Reduce barbecue grill to medium heat. Place sandwiches on preheated grill, buttered side down, over medium heat and cook, turning once, for 2 minutes per side or until golden brown and cheese is melted. Place hamburgers between each grilled cheese sandwich, pressing together gently. Top with desired toppings and serve immediately.

Grilled Applewood Smoked Bacon and Almonds

Serves 4

I love the apple flavor from smoked bacon paired with cheese in this sandwich.

8	slices brioche (½-inch/1 cm thick slices)	8
2 tbsp	butter or margarine, softened	30 mL
¼ cup	liquid honey	60 mL
8	slices smoked bacon, preferably Applewood (see Tips, right)	8
8 oz	deli sliced ham	250 g
4 oz	Muenster cheese, cut into 4 slices	125 g
¾ cup	chopped almonds, toasted	175 mL

- **Panini grill or large skillet**
- **Preheat panini grill to medium, if using**

1. Brush one side of each bread slice with butter. Place on a work surface, buttered side down. Spread 4 bread slices equally with honey. Top equally with bacon, ham, cheese and almonds. Cover with remaining bread slices, buttered side up, and press together gently.

2. Place sandwiches on preheated panini grill or in a large skillet over medium heat and cook, turning once if using a skillet, for 3 to 4 minutes or until golden brown and cheese is melted. Serve immediately.

Tips: Look for applewood smoked bacon where bacon is sold in the grocery store.

Feel free to omit the nuts, as desired.

Hawaiian Grilled Cheese

Serves 4

It's fun to make these sandwiches in the wintertime because they always feel like summer.

8	slices Hawaiian bread or 4 rolls (see Tip, right)	8
2 tbsp	olive oil	30 mL
4 tsp	liquid honey	20 mL
8 oz	thinly sliced turkey	250 g
4	slices Monterey Jack cheese	4
1 cup	pineapple slices	250 mL
4	leafy lettuce leaves	4

Tip: I love to grill the pineapple to put on these sandwiches. Grill over medium-high heat for 1 to 2 minutes or until grill marks appear.

- **Panini grill or large skillet**
- **Preheat panini grill to medium, if using**

1. Brush one side of all bread slices with oil. Place on a work surface, oiled side down. Spread bottom halves equally with honey. Top equally with turkey, cheese, pineapple and lettuce. Cover with remaining bread slices, oiled side up, and press together gently.

2. Place sandwiches on preheated panini grill or in a large skillet over medium heat and cook, turning once if using a skillet, for 3 to 4 minutes or until golden brown and cheese is melted. Serve immediately.

Tip: If you can't find Hawaiian bread, use any small rolls.

BLT Grilled Cheese with Avocado

Serves 4

I get a great response whenever I make this sandwich. These are all of my favorite ingredients tied into one great recipe.

8	slices Italian bread (½-inch/ 1 cm thick slices)	8
2 tbsp	butter or margarine, softened	30 mL
¼ cup	Homemade Mayonnaise (page 321) or store-bought	60 mL
8	slices cooked bacon	8
2	tomatoes, thinly sliced	2
2	avocados	2
4 oz	mozzarella, thinly sliced	125 g

- **Panini grill or large skillet**
- **Preheat panini grill to medium, if using**

1. Brush one side of each bread slice with butter. Place on a work surface, buttered side down. Spread 4 bread slices equally with mayonnaise. Thinly slice avocados. Top equally with bacon, tomatoes, avocados and cheese. Cover with remaining bread slices, buttered side up, and press together gently.

2. Place sandwiches on preheated panini grill or in a large skillet over medium heat and cook, turning once if using a skillet, for 3 to 4 minutes or until golden brown and cheese is melted.

Grilled Goat Cheese and Figs

Serves 4

This is one of my favorites in the summertime when figs are in season. The combination of figs and goat cheese makes a delicious sandwich.

8	slices raisin bread (1/2-inch/ 1 cm thick slices)	8
2 tbsp	butter or margarine, softened	30 mL
1/4 cup	fig preserves or jam	60 mL
4 tsp	liquid honey	20 mL
4 oz	crumbled goat cheese	125 g

- **Panini grill or large skillet**
- **Preheat panini grill to medium, if using**

1. Brush one side of each bread slice with butter. Place on a work surface, buttered side down. Spread tops of 4 bread slices equally with fig preserves, 1 tsp (15 mL) of the honey and equally with goat cheese. Cover with remaining bread slices, buttered side up, and press together gently.

2. Place sandwiches on preheated panini grill or in a large skillet over medium heat and cook, turning once if using a skillet, for 3 to 4 minutes or until golden brown and cheese is melted. Serve immediately.

Variation

If you can't find fig preserves, substitute peach, apricot or strawberry preserves or jam.

Grilled Brie with Chutney

Serves 4

This recipe was inspired by a foodie friend of mine, Kelly, in Utah. It makes use of two wonderful combinations: Brie and mango chutney. I made these sandwiches for a shower party and everyone loved them.

8	slices pumpernickel bread (1/2-inch/1 cm thick slices)	8
2 tbsp	butter or margarine, softened	30 mL
1/4 cup	liquid honey	60 mL
4 oz	Brie, thinly sliced	125 g
1 cup	baby spinach leaves	250 mL
1 1/2 cups	Peach-Ginger or Mango Chutney (page 335 or Variation, page 335) or store-bought	375 mL

- **Panini grill or large skillet**
- **Preheat panini grill to medium, if using**

1. Brush one side of each bread slice with butter. Place on a work surface, buttered side down. Spread 4 bread slices equally with honey. Top equally with Brie, spinach leaves and chutney. Cover with remaining bread slices, buttered side up, and press together gently.

2. Place sandwiches on preheated panini grill or in a large skillet over medium heat and cook, turning once if using a skillet, for 3 to 4 minutes or until golden brown and cheese is melted.

Tip: To add protein to this sandwich, add sliced grilled chicken or turkey.

Grilled Spinach, Pepper Jack and Bacon

Serves 4

I love the spice of Pepper Jack cheese with the bacon in this grilled cheese. It's perfect for a weeknight dinner.

8	slices multigrain (1/2-inch/ 1 cm thick slices)	8
2 tbsp	butter or margarine, softened	30 mL
1/2 cup	Basil Pesto (page 329) or store-bought	125 mL
8	slices cooked bacon	8
4	slices pepper Jack cheese	4
1 1/2 cups	baby spinach leaves	375 mL

- **Panini grill or large skillet**
- **Preheat panini grill to medium, if using**

1. Brush one side of each bread slice with butter. Place on a work surface, buttered side down. Spread tops of bread slices equally with pesto. Top 4 slices equally with bacon, cheese and spinach. Cover with remaining bread slices, buttered side up, and press together gently.

2. Place sandwiches on preheated panini grill or in a large skillet over medium heat and cook, turning once if using a skillet, for 3 to 4 minutes or until golden brown and cheese is melted.

Grilled Brie, Apple and Thyme Sandwich

Serves 4

This combination of Brie, apples and fresh thyme can't be beat. It's the perfect fall lunch or appetizer sandwich.

¼ cup	liquid honey	60 mL
1 tbsp	finely chopped fresh thyme	15 mL
8	slices raisin bread (½-inch/1 cm thick slices)	8
2 tbsp	butter or margarine, softened	30 mL
1	apple, such as Fuji, Braeburn or Gala, thinly sliced	1
4 oz	Brie, thinly sliced	125 g

- **Panini grill or large skillet**
- **Preheat panini grill to medium, if using**

1. In a small bowl, combine honey and thyme.

2. Brush one side of each bread slice with butter. Place on a work surface, buttered side down. Spread 4 bread slices equally with honey mixture. Top equally with apple and Brie. Cover with remaining bread slices, buttered side up, and press together gently.

3. Place sandwiches on preheated panini grill or in a large skillet over medium heat and cook, turning once if using a skillet, for 3 to 4 minutes or until golden brown and cheese is melted. Serve immediately.

Variation

I love to substitute fresh sliced plums for the apples in this recipe.

Grilled Smoked Salmon and Brie

Serves 4

The saltiness of smoked salmon and buttery Brie make a wonderful gooey combination.

8	slices sourdough bread (½-inch/1 cm thick slices)	8
2 tbsp	butter or margarine, softened	30 mL
4 oz	cream cheese, softened	125 g
8 oz	sliced smoked salmon	250 g
4 oz	Brie, thinly sliced	125 g
1 cup	sliced red onions	250 mL

Tip: To keep Brie fresher longer, wrap it in parchment or wax paper and refrigerate.

- **Panini grill or large skillet**
- **Preheat panini grill to medium, if using**

1. Brush one side of each bread slice with butter. Place on a work surface, buttered side down. Spread 4 bread slices equally with cream cheese. Top equally with smoked salmon, Brie and red onions. Cover with remaining bread slices, buttered side up, and press together gently.

2. Place sandwiches on preheated panini grill or in a large skillet over medium heat and cook, turning once if using a skillet, for 3 to 4 minutes or until golden brown and cheese is melted. Serve immediately.

Variation

If desired, substitute goat cheese for the Brie in this recipe.

Grilled Apple Cheddar Sandwich

Serves 4

This is a twist on an old-fashioned Cheddar pie recipe, and it makes a fabulous sweet and savory warm sandwich.

8	slices multigrain bread (½-inch/1 cm thick slices)	8
¼ cup	butter or margarine, softened	60 mL
¼ cup	liquid honey	60 mL
2	apples, thinly sliced	2
8	slices sharp (aged) Cheddar cheese	8

- **Panini grill or large skillet**
- **Preheat panini grill to medium, if using**

1. Brush one side of each bread slice with butter. Place on a work surface, buttered side down. Spread 4 bread slices equally with honey. Top equally with apple slices and cheese. Cover with remaining bread slices, buttered side up, and press together gently.

2. Place on panini grill or in skillet over medium heat and cook, turning once if using skillet, 3 to 4 minutes until cheese is melted.

Huevos Rancheros Wraps (page 17)

Overnight Stuffed French Toast (page 20)

Coconut Shrimp Tea Sandwich (page 33)

Pear, Pecan and Gorgonzola Crostini (page 36)

Lunch Box Sushi (page 52)

Garden Tuna Checkerboard Sandwich (page 55)

Italian Sub Sandwich (page 64)

Classic Club Sandwich (page 74)

Smoked Mozzarella, Arugula and Tomato

Serves 4

Using peppery arugula and smoked mozzarella makes this grilled cheese unique. I love to serve this sandwich when I am entertaining.

8	slices Italian bread (½-inch/ 1 cm thick slices)	8
2 tbsp	butter or margarine, softened	30 mL
¼ cup	Basil Pesto (page 329) or store-bought	60 mL
4 oz	smoked mozzarella, thinly sliced	125 g
1 cup	arugula leaves (see Tips, below)	250 mL
2	tomatoes, thinly sliced (see Tips, below)	2

Tips: Make sure you wash arugula well before using because dirt clings to the leaves easily.

Do not store tomatoes in the refrigerator as cool temperatures reduce their flavor. Store at room temperature. Once ripened, use within a few days.

- **Panini grill or large skillet**
- **Preheat panini grill to medium, if using**

1. Brush one side of each bread slice with butter. Place on a work surface, buttered side down. Spread 4 bread slices equally with pesto. Top equally with cheese, arugula and tomatoes. Cover with remaining bread slices, buttered side up, and press together gently.

2. Place sandwiches on preheated panini grill or in a large skillet over medium heat and cook, turning once if using a skillet, for 3 to 4 minutes or until golden brown and cheese is melted. Serve immediately.

Variation

Watercress also works great in this recipe instead of the arugula.

Grilled Roast Beef and Manchego

Serves 4

Take deli roast beef to the next level with the flavors and textures of this fabulous Spanish-style cheese.

8	slices sourdough bread (1/2-inch/1 cm thick slices)	8
2 tbsp	butter or margarine, softened	30 mL
1/2 cup	Dijon mustard (see Tip, below)	125 mL
8 oz	thinly sliced roasted beef	250 g
4 oz	Manchego cheese, thinly sliced	125 g
1 cup	watercress leaves	250 mL
3/4 cup	Spanish olives, sliced	175 mL

Tip: Dijon mustard originated in France and is made from brown mustard seeds and white wine, thus is more flavorful than yellow mustard.

- **Panini grill or large skillet**
- **Preheat panini grill to medium, if using**

1. Brush one side of each bread slice with butter. Place on a work surface, buttered side down. Spread tops of 8 bread slices equally with Dijon mustard. Top equally with roast beef, cheese, watercress and olives. Press bread slices together gently, buttered side up.

2. Place sandwiches on preheated panini grill or in a large skillet over medium heat and cook, turning once if using a skillet, for 3 to 4 minutes or until golden brown and cheese is melted. Serve immediately.

Variations

If you're having trouble finding watercress, use green leafy lettuce or baby spinach.

Substitute 8 oz (250 g) thinly sliced prosciutto or turkey for the roast beef.

Grilled Apricot Blues

Serves 4

Believe it or not, my kids love blue cheese and apricots. I created this sandwich for them one day and it was gone within minutes.

8	slices sourdough bread (1/2-inch/1 cm thick slices)	8
2 tbsp	butter or margarine, softened	30 mL
1/4 cup	apricot preserves or jam	60 mL
1 cup	spinach leaves	250 mL
3/4 cup	dried apricots	175 mL
4 oz	crumbled blue cheese	125 g

Tip: If you have leftover blue cheese, use it in salads, on vegetables, on top of burgers or steak and in salad dressings.

- **Panini grill or large skillet**
- **Preheat panini grill to medium, if using**

1. Brush one side of each bread slice with butter. Place on a work surface, buttered side down. Spread 4 slices equally with apricot preserves. Top equally with spinach leaves, apricots and blue cheese. Cover with remaining bread slices, buttered side up, and press together gently.

2. Place sandwiches on preheated panini grill or in a large skillet over medium heat and cook, turning once if using a skillet, for 3 to 4 minutes or until golden brown and cheese is melted. Serve immediately.

Grilled Pear, Walnut and Goat Cheese

Serves 4

This fall-inspired recipe is so creamy, crunchy and tasty all in one. I like to cut these into small pieces for appetizers as well.

8	slices multigrain bread (1/2-inch/1 cm thick slices)	8
2 tbsp	butter or margarine, softened	30 mL
1/2 cup	pear preserves or jam	125 mL
2	pears, thinly sliced (see Tip, below)	2
1 cup	chopped walnuts, toasted	250 mL
4 oz	crumbled goat cheese	125 g

Tip: Purchase pears when they are firm and not hard. To ripen faster, place in a paper bag or in a covered bowl. Once ripe, pears can be kept in the refrigerator up to 3 days.

- **Panini grill or large skillet**
- **Preheat panini grill to medium, if using**

1. Brush one side of each bread slice with butter. Place on a work surface, buttered side down. Spread 8 bread slices equally with pear preserves. Top equally with pears, walnuts and goat cheese. Press slices together gently, buttered side up, to form 4 sandwiches.

2. Place sandwiches on preheated panini grill or in a large skillet over medium heat and cook, turning once if using a skillet, for 3 to 4 minutes or until golden brown and cheese is melted. Serve immediately.

Grilled Asparagus Swiss Pesto

Serves 4

This four-ingredient sandwich is a winner. Try it, and you will see. I also like to use flour tortillas and make this as a wrap sandwich.

1 lb	asparagus, cut into 2-inch (5 cm) pieces	500 g
¼ tsp	salt	1 mL
¼ tsp	freshly ground black pepper	1 mL
2 tbsp	olive oil	30 mL
8	slices sourdough bread (½-inch/1 cm thick slices)	8
2 tbsp	butter or margarine, softened	30 mL
½ cup	Basil Pesto (page 329) or store-bought	125 mL
4	slices Swiss cheese	4

Tip: This would be great served with fontina instead or in addition to Swiss.

- **Panini grill or large skillet**
- **Preheat oven to 350°F (180°C) or panini grill to medium, if using**

1. Season asparagus with salt and pepper and drizzle with olive oil. Place on a large baking sheet and bake in preheated oven for 10 minutes or until tender. Let cool.

2. Brush one side of each bread slice with butter. Place on a work surface, buttered side down. Spread bread slices equally with pesto. Top 4 slices equally with asparagus and cheese. Cover with remaining slices, buttered side up, and press together gently.

3. Place sandwiches on preheated panini grill or in a large skillet over medium heat and cook, turning once if using a skillet, for 3 to 4 minutes or until golden brown and cheese is melted. Serve immediately.

Variation

Add turkey or grilled chicken for added protein.

Mozzarella en Carozza

Serves 4

This Italian appetizer sandwich translates to "in a carriage," meaning the mozzarella is encased between two layers of firm sandwich bread and dipped in egg and fried. It is so delectable!

2	eggs	2
1/2 cup	milk	125 mL
1/2 tsp	kosher salt (see Tip, right)	2 mL
8	slices white bread (1/2-inch/1 cm thick slices)	8
8	slices mozzarella cheese	8

Tips: If you want a thicker bread for this rich sandwich, try challah bread.

- **Panini grill or large skillet**
- **Preheat greased panini grill to medium, if using**

1. In a small bowl, whisk together eggs, milk and salt. Set aside.

2. Place bread slices on a work surface. Top with 4 slices cheese. Cover with bread slices. Press slices together gently to form 4 sandwiches. Dip sandwiches in egg mixture, one at a time, coating each side.

3. Place sandwiches on preheated panini grill or in a large skillet over medium heat and cook, turning once if using a skillet, for 3 to 4 minutes or until golden brown and cheese is melted. Serve immediately.

Tip: I typically use kosher or sea salt in my recipes, but feel free to use what you have on hand.

Grilled Olive Caponata and Goat Cheese

Serves 4

I love cooking with olives and goat cheese. When these two ingredients are melted together in a sandwich, it tastes even better.

8	slices sourdough bread (1/2-inch/1 cm thick slices)	8
2 tbsp	olive oil	30 mL
1/2 cup	Caponata Spread (page 320) or store-bought	125 mL
1/2 cup	fresh basil leaves	125 mL
4 oz	crumbled goat cheese (see Tip, below)	125 g
	Balsamic vinegar, optional	

Tip: Goat cheese is often labeled as "chèvre" and is sold in a variety of sizes and shapes, such as logs and cones.

- **Panini grill or large skillet**
- **Preheat panini grill to medium, if using**

1. Brush one side of each bread slice with olive oil. Place on a work surface, oiled side down. Spread caponata equally over bread slices. Top 4 slices equally with basil and goat cheese. Cover with remaining bread slices, oiled side up, and press together gently.

2. Place sandwiches on preheated panini grill or in a large skillet over medium heat and cook, turning once if using a skillet, for 3 to 4 minutes or until golden brown and cheese is melted. Drizzle with balsamic vinegar, if desired. Serve immediately.

Grilled Steak, Beets and Parmesan

Serves 4

The sweetness of beets and fresh Parmesan create an upscale grilled cheese. People love when I serve these sandwiches because they are so unique.

8	slices sourdough bread (1/2-inch/1 cm thick slices)	8
2 tbsp	olive oil	30 mL
1 1/2 cups	thinly sliced cooked steak	375 g
1 cup	thinly sliced beets (see Tip, right)	250 mL
1/2 cup	baby spinach leaves	125 mL
1/2 cup	freshly grated Parmesan cheese	125 mL

- **Panini grill or large skillet**
- **Preheat panini grill to medium, if using**

1. Brush one side of each bread slice with olive oil. Place on a work surface, oiled side down. Top 4 bread slices with steak, beets, spinach and Parmesan. Cover with remaining bread slices, oiled side up, and press together gently.

2. Place sandwiches on preheated panini grill or in a large skillet over medium heat and cook, turning once if using a skillet, for 3 to 4 minutes or until golden brown and cheese is melted. Serve immediately.

Tip: Instead of fresh beets, use 1 cup (250 mL) sliced canned beets.

Black Russian

This idea came to me from a New York friend who said she used to eat this often as a cold sandwich. Either way, I love the rustic combination of ingredients.

½ cup	stone-ground mustard	125 mL
1 tbsp	chopped fresh parsley	15 mL
1 tsp	grated lemon zest	2 mL
8	slices pumpernickel bread (½-inch/1 cm thick slices)	8
¼ cup	olive oil	60 mL
8 oz	black forest ham	250 g
1 cup	lettuce leaves	250 mL
4 oz	cracked pepper Brie	125 g

Tip: You can substitute regular Brie for the cracked pepper one.

- **Panini grill or large skillet**
- **Preheat panini grill to medium, if using**

1. In a small bowl, combine mustard, parsley and lemon zest.

2. Brush one side of each bread slice with olive oil. Place on a work surface, oiled side down. Spread bread slices equally with mustard mixture. Top 4 slices equally with ham, lettuce and Brie. Cover with remaining bread slices, oiled side up, and press together gently.

3. Place sandwiches on preheated panini grill or in a large skillet over medium heat and cook, turning once if using a skillet, for 3 to 4 minutes or until golden brown and cheese is melted.

The Pilgrim

This sandwich became popular in the 1950s, but it still is a hit today, especially during Thanksgiving.

8	slices pumpernickel bread (½-inch/1 cm thick slices)	8
2 tbsp	butter or margarine, softened	30 mL
¼ cup	Dijon mustard	60 mL
8 oz	thinly sliced roast beef	250 g
1 cup	baby spinach leaves	250 mL
4 oz	Gouda cheese, thinly sliced	125 g
¾ cup	dried cranberries	175 mL

- **Panini grill or large skillet**
- **Preheat panini grill to medium, if using**

1. Brush one side of each bread slice with butter. Place on a work surface, buttered side down. Spread 4 bread slices equally with Dijon mustard. Top equally with roast beef, spinach, cheese and cranberries. Cover with remaining bread slices, buttered side up, and press together gently.

2. Place sandwiches on preheated panini grill or in a large skillet over medium heat and cook, turning once if using a skillet, for 3 to 4 minutes or until golden brown and cheese is melted. Serve immediately.

Grilled Chicken, Tomatoes and Olives

Serves 4

This sandwich is a take off of a chicken dish I cook in a skillet or a grill pan. It makes a wonderful grilled cheese that's sure to please.

8	slices sourdough bread (1/2-inch/1 cm thick slices)	8
2 tbsp	butter or margarine, softened	30 mL
1/4 cup	Homemade Mayonnaise (page 321) or store-bought or Chipotle Aïoli (page 311)	60 mL
8 oz	thinly sliced cooked chicken (see Tip, right)	250 g
8	slices Swiss cheese	8
2	tomatoes, thinly sliced	2
1 cup	sliced black olives	250 mL

- **Panini grill or large skillet**
- **Preheat panini grill to medium, if using**

1. Brush one side of each bread slice with butter. Place on a work surface, buttered side down. Spread 4 bread slices equally with mayonnaise. Top equally with chicken, cheese, tomatoes and olives. Cover with remaining bread slices, buttered side up, and press together gently.

2. Place sandwiches on preheated panini grill or in a large skillet over medium heat and cook, turning once if using a skillet, for 3 to 4 minutes or until golden brown and cheese is melted. Serve immediately.

Tip: If you're cooking your own chicken for this sandwich, season 1 1/2 lbs (750 g) boneless skinless chicken breasts with 1/2 to 1 tsp (2 to 5 mL) chipotle seasoning, depending on your heat preference.

Chorizo Melts

Serves 4

Chorizo is a ground pork sausage flavored with garlic and chili powder with a Spanish influence. It is so flavorful in this spicy warm sandwich.

12 oz	dry-cured chorizo, removed from casings and thinly sliced	375 g
8	slices sourdough bread (½-inch/1 cm thick slices)	8
¼ cup	butter or margarine, softened	60 mL
¼ cup	Homemade Mayonnaise (page 321) or store-bought	60 mL
4	slices pepper Jack cheese	4
2	tomatoes, thinly sliced	2

- **Panini grill or large skillet**
- **Preheat panini grill to medium, if using**

1. In a large skillet, cook chorizo over medium-high heat for 5 to 7 minutes or until lightly browned. Set aside

2. Brush one side of each bread slice with butter. Place on a work surface, buttered side down. Spread 4 bread slices equally with mayonnaise. Top equally with chorizo, cheese and tomatoes. Cover with remaining bread slices, buttered side up, and press together gently.

3. Place sandwiches on preheated panini grill or in a large skillet over medium heat and cook, turning once if using a skillet, for 3 to 4 minutes or until golden brown and cheese is melted. Serve immediately.

Variations

If you can't find chorizo, you can use your favorite sausage.

Monterey Jack cheese may be used instead of pepper Jack.

Lasagna Grilled Cheese

Serves 4

When I don't have time to make lasagna, I cook these up really quickly. The kids love them!

8	slices Italian bread (½-inch/1 cm thick slices)	8
¼ cup	butter or margarine, softened	60 mL
¼ cup	marinara sauce	60 mL
8	thin slices mozzarella cheese	8
1 cup	freshly grated Parmesan cheese	250 mL

Tip: If you're short on time, purchase already shredded cheese. If you do have time, grate your own for better quality

- **Panini grill or large skillet**
- **Preheat panini grill to medium, if using**

1. Brush one side of each bread slice with butter. Place on a work surface, buttered side down. Spread 4 bread slices equally with marinara sauce. Top equally with mozzarella and Parmesan. Cover with remaining bread slices, buttered side up, and press together gently.

2. Place sandwiches on preheated panini grill or in a large skillet over medium heat and cook, turning once if using a skillet, for 3 to 4 minutes or until golden brown and cheese is melted. Serve immediately.

Variation

Add 1½ cups (375 mL) baby spinach leaves with the cheeses in Step 1 and proceed as directed.

Grilled Flounder and Feta Cheese

Serves 4

I cook a lot of flounder at my house, and this recipe was a result of some leftovers. It came out great with melted feta.

1½ lbs	flounder fillets	750 g
½ tsp	sea salt	2 mL
½ tsp	freshly ground black pepper	2 mL
½ tsp	paprika	2 mL
¼ cup	freshly squeezed lemon juice (see Tips, below)	60 mL
8	slices Italian bread (½-inch/1 cm thick slices)	8
2 tbsp	butter or margarine, softened	30 mL
¼ cup	Tartar Sauce (page 333) or store-bought	60 mL
1 cup	baby spinach leaves	250 mL
4 oz	crumbled feta cheese (see Tips, below)	125 g

Tips: There are concerns about the sustainability of some fish and seafood so we recommend you check reliable sites such as www.seachoice.org for the latest information.

Let lemons come to room temperature before juicing for more juice.

Feta is a white Greek cheese that has a tangy flavor. It's made from goat's milk, sheep's milk or a combination. I use low-fat feta. You can find it crumbled in the cheese section at the grocery store.

- **Preheat lightly greased barbecue grill to medium heat**

1. Season flounder with salt, pepper and paprika. Drizzle with lemon juice. Grill for 6 minutes or until fish flakes easily with a fork. Slice and then set aside. Slice flounder into 4 pieces. Leave barbecue grill on.

2. Brush one side of each bread slice with butter. Place on a work surface, buttered side down. Spread 4 bread slices equally with tartar sauce. Top equally with flounder, spinach and cheese. Cover with remaining bread slices, buttered side up, and press together gently.

3. Place sandwiches, buttered side down, on preheated barbecue grill. Cook, turning once, for 3 to 4 minutes or until golden brown and cheese is melted. Serve immediately.

Variation

Substitute any white fish fillets, such as halibut or tilapia, for the flounder.

Shrimp-Avocado Grilled Cheese

Serves 4

Shrimp, avocado and Havarti are three of my favorite ingredients that work well together in this mouthwatering sandwich.

8	slices Italian bread (½-inch/1 cm thick slices)	8
2 tbsp	olive oil	30 mL
1 lb	cooked shrimp (see Tip, page 109)	500 g
2	tomatoes, thinly sliced	2
2	avocados, thinly sliced	2
4	thin slices Havarti cheese	4

- **Panini grill or large skillet**
- **Preheat panini grill to medium, if using**

1. Brush one side of each bread slice with olive oil. Place on a work surface, oiled side down. Top 4 bread slices equally with shrimp, tomatoes, avocados and cheese. Cover with remaining bread slices, oiled side up, and press together gently.

2. Place sandwiches on preheated panini grill or in a large skillet over medium heat and cook, turning once if using a skillet, for 3 to 4 minutes or until golden brown and cheese is melted. Serve immediately.

Shrimp Gremolata Panini

Serves 4

Gremolata is a mixture of parsley, lemon and garlic. It pairs well with the shrimp and provolone in this flavorful grilled cheese.

1 lb	cooked shrimp (see Tip, page 109)	500 g
2	cloves garlic, minced	2
3 tbsp	chopped fresh flat-leaf Italian parsley	45 mL
1 tsp	grated lemon zest	5 mL
8	slices French bread (½-inch/1 cm thick slices)	8
2 tbsp	olive oil	30 mL
4	slices provolone cheese	4

Tip: Once lemon zest is removed from a lemon, the lemon can be refrigerated up to 1 week.

- **Panini grill or large skillet**
- **Preheat panini grill to medium, if using**

1. In a large bowl, toss together shrimp, garlic, parsley and lemon zest.

2. Brush one side of each bread slice with olive oil. Place on a work surface, oiled side down. Top 4 bread slices equally with shrimp mixture and cheese. Cover with remaining bread slices, oiled side up, and press together gently.

3. Place sandwiches on preheated panini grill or in a large skillet over medium heat and cook, turning once if using a skillet, for 3 to 4 minutes or until golden brown and cheese is melted. Serve immediately.

Grilled Shrimp Parmesan

Serves 4

This Italian-style shrimp sandwich is great to serve for lunch and dinner. It's my family's favorite spring and summertime sandwich.

8	slices Italian bread (1/2-inch/ 1 cm thick slices)	8
1/4 cup	olive oil	60 mL
1 lb	cooked shrimp (see Tip, below)	500 g
3/4 cup	fresh basil leaves	175 mL
1/2 cup	freshly grated Parmesan cheese	125 mL

Tip: Fresh shrimp cook very quickly. In a skillet, heat 1 tbsp (15 mL) olive oil over medium heat. Sauté shrimp for about 2 minutes per side or until pink and opaque. Pour in a colander to drain.

- **Panini grill or large skillet**
- **Preheat panini grill to medium, if using**

1. Brush one side of each bread slice with olive oil. Place on a work surface, oiled side down. Top 4 bread slices equally with shrimp, basil and cheese. Cover with remaining bread slices, oiled side up, and press together gently.

2. Place sandwiches on preheated panini grill or in a large skillet over medium heat and cook, turning once if using a skillet, for 3 to 4 minutes or until golden brown and cheese is melted. Serve immediately.

Variation

Sourdough bread can be substituted for the Italian.

Shrimp, Mushroom and Fontina

Serves 4

I love shrimp, mushrooms and fontina, so this grilled cheese is heaven to me. We serve these a lot for simple entertaining, and guests love them.

8	slices Italian bread (1/2-inch/1 cm thick slices)	8
2 tbsp	butter or margarine, softened	30 mL
1 lb	cooked shrimp (see Tip, above)	500 g
1 1/3 cups	sliced fresh button mushrooms	325 mL
1/2 cup	grated fontina cheese	125 mL

- **Panini grill or large skillet**
- **Preheat panini grill to medium, if using**

1. Brush one side of each bread slice with butter. Place on a work surface, buttered side down. Top 4 bread slices equally with shrimp, mushrooms and cheese. Cover with remaining bread slices, buttered side up, and press together gently.

2. Place sandwiches on preheated panini grill or in a large skillet over medium heat and cook, turning once if using a skillet, for 3 to 4 minutes or until golden brown and cheese is melted. Serve immediately.

Grilled Salmon and Gorgonzola

Serves 4

This is an awesome grilled cheese sandwich that I love to make when I buy fresh salmon. It makes great use of Gorgonzola cheese.

1¼ lbs	salmon fillets, skin on (see Tip, below)	625 g
½ tsp	sea salt	2 mL
½ tsp	paprika	2 mL
¼ tsp	cayenne pepper	1 mL
2 tbsp	freshly squeezed lemon juice	30 mL
3 tbsp	olive oil, divided	45 mL
8	slices sourdough bread (½-inch/1 cm thick slices)	8
1 cup	arugula leaves	250 mL
4 oz	crumbled Gorgonzola cheese	125 g

Tip: Buy wild or Alaskan salmon when possible. I cook mine with the skin on because it holds the fish together and makes it easier to transfer from the grill.

- **11- by 7-inch (28 by 18 cm) glass baking dish, lined with foil**
- **Panini grill or large skillet**
- **Preheat oven to 400°F (200°C)**
- **Preheat panini grill to medium, if using**

1. Place salmon, skin side down, in prepared baking dish. Season with salt, paprika and cayenne. Drizzle with lemon juice and 1 tbsp (15 mL) of the olive oil. Bake in preheated oven for 10 minutes or until salmon flakes easily when tested with a fork. Slice into 4 pieces.

2. Brush one side of each bread slice with remaining olive oil. Place on a work surface, oiled side down. Top 4 bread slices equally with salmon, arugula and cheese. Cover with remaining bread slices, oiled side up, and press together gently.

3. Place sandwiches on preheated panini grill or in a large skillet over medium heat and cook, turning once if using a skillet, for 3 to 4 minutes or until golden brown and cheese is melted. Serve immediately.

Turkey Antipasto Grilled Cheese

This Italian-style sandwich has a delicious mixture of meats, cheese and vegetables. It's not only great tasting but also pretty and colorful.

8	slices Italian bread (½-inch/ 1 cm thick slices	8
2 tbsp	olive oil	30 mL
4 oz	thinly sliced turkey	125 g
4 oz	thinly sliced Italian salami	125 g
2	slices provolone cheese	2
2	slices fontina cheese	2
¾ cup	roasted red peppers	175 mL
½ cup	chopped kalamata olives	125 mL

- **Panini grill or large skillet**
- **Preheat panini grill to medium, if using**

1. Brush one side of each bread slice with olive oil. Place on a work surface, oiled side down. Top 4 bread slices equally with turkey, salami and provolone and fontina cheeses. Arrange red peppers and olives equally on top. Cover with remaining bread slices, oiled side up, and press together gently.

2. Place sandwiches on preheated panini grill or in a large skillet over medium heat and cook, turning once if using a skillet, for 3 to 4 minutes or until golden brown and cheese is melted. Serve immediately.

Variation

Substitute mozzarella cheese for the fontina or just double the amount of provolone.

Grilled Turkey Cobb

Serves 4

I love Cobb salad, and turkey, bacon, spinach, blue cheese and mozzarella make a delicious grilled cheese sandwich.

8	slices white or wheat bread (1/2-inch/1 cm thick slices)	8
1/4 cup	olive oil	60 mL
6 oz	thinly sliced turkey	175 g
1 cup	fresh baby spinach leaves	250 mL
8	slices cooked bacon (see Tip, right)	8
2	tomatoes, thinly sliced	2
4	slices mozzarella cheese	4
1/2 cup	crumbled blue cheese	125 mL

- **Panini grill or large skillet**
- **Preheat panini grill to medium, if using**

1. Brush one side of each bread slice with olive oil. Place on a work surface, oiled side down. Top 4 bread slices equally with turkey, spinach, bacon, tomato slices, mozzarella and blue cheese. Cover with remaining bread slices, oiled side up, and press together gently.

2. Place sandwiches on preheated panini grill or in a large skillet over medium heat and cook, turning once if using a skillet, for 3 to 4 minutes or until golden brown and cheese is melted. Serve immediately.

Tip: To make this sandwich lower in fat, try turkey bacon. It isn't as crisp but tastes great.

Grilled Southern Barbecue Sandwich

Serves 4

I make these all the time, and they are just as good as the ones served in Southern barbecue restaurants.

8	slices sourdough bread (1/2-inch/1 cm thick slices)	8
1/4 cup	butter or margarine, softened	60 mL
1/4 cup	Barbecue Sauce (page 325) or store-bought	60 mL
2 cups	thinly sliced cooked chicken	500 mL
4	slices mozzarella cheese	4
1/2 cup	sliced dill pickles	125 mL

- **Panini grill or large skillet**
- **Preheat panini grill to medium, if using**

1. Brush one side of each bread slice with butter. Place on a work surface, buttered side down. Spread 4 bread slices equally with barbecue sauce. Top equally with chicken, cheese and pickles. Cover with remaining bread slices, buttered side up, and press together gently.

2. Place sandwiches on preheated panini grill or in a large skillet over medium heat and cook, turning once if using a skillet, for 3 to 4 minutes or until golden brown and cheese is melted.

Caprese Panini

This twist on caprese salad makes a simple grilled cheese that everyone will love.

8	slices sourdough bread (½-inch/1 cm thick slices)	8
2 tbsp	olive oil	30 mL
2	tomatoes, thinly sliced	2
4 oz	fresh mozzarella, sliced into 4 slices (see Tip, below)	125 g
½ cup	fresh basil leaves	125 mL
	Balsamic vinegar, optional	

Tip: Purchase fresh mozzarella packed in water for best quality.

- **Panini grill or large skillet**
- **Preheat panini grill to medium, if using**

1. Brush one side of each bread slice with olive oil. Place on a work surface, oiled side down. Top 4 bread slices equally with tomatoes, mozzarella slices and basil. Cover with remaining bread slices, oiled side up, and press together gently.

2. Place sandwiches on preheated panini grill or in a large skillet over medium heat and cook, turning once if using a skillet, for 3 to 4 minutes or until golden brown and cheese is melted. Drizzle with balsamic vinegar, if desired. Serve immediately.

Grilled Pimiento Cheese BLT

These delicious sandwiches are a Southern favorite. You can't go wrong with warmed pimiento cheese slightly melted on sourdough bread.

8	slices sourdough bread (½-inch/1 cm thick slices)	8
4 tbsp	butter or margarine, softened (see Tip, below)	60 mL
2 cups	Pimiento Cheese (page 114) or store-bought	500 mL
8	lettuce leaves	8
8	slices cooked bacon	8
1	large tomato, cut into 8 slices	1

Tip: Be sure to butter the bread, not the skillet, when making grilled sandwiches.

- **Panini grill or large skillet**
- **Preheat panini grill to medium, if using**

1. Brush one side of each bread slice with butter. Place on a work surface, buttered side down. Top 4 bread slices equally with Pimiento Cheese, lettuce, bacon and tomato. Cover with remaining bread slices, buttered side up, and press together gently.

2. Place sandwiches on preheated panini grill or in a large skillet over medium heat and cook, turning once if using a skillet, for 3 to 4 minutes or until golden brown and cheese is melted. Serve immediately.

Grilled Gourmet Pimiento Cheese

Serves 4

When someone asked me how to make a gourmet grilled cheese, I told them to add white Cheddar, fresh watercress and prosciutto.

Pimiento Cheese

¼ cup	Homemade Mayonnaise (page 321) or store-bought	60 mL
2 tbsp	finely chopped red onion	30 mL
4 oz	diced pimientos, drained	125 g
⅛ tsp	cayenne pepper	0.5 mL
4 oz	shredded sharp (aged) Cheddar cheese (see Tip, right)	125 g
4 oz	shredded white Cheddar	125 g
8	slices Italian bread (½-inch/1 cm thick slices)	8
¼ cup	butter or margarine, softened	60 mL
8 oz	thinly sliced prosciutto	250 g
1⅓ cups	watercress	325 mL

- **Panini grill or large skillet**
- **Preheat panini grill to medium, if using**

1. *Pimiento Cheese:* In a medium bowl, combine mayonnaise, red onion, pimientos and cayenne. Gently stir in sharp and white Cheddar cheeses.

2. Brush one side of each bread slice with butter. Place on a work surface, buttered side down. Top 4 bread slices equally with Pimiento Cheese, prosciutto and watercress. Cover with remaining bread slices, buttered side up, and press together gently.

3. Place sandwiches on preheated panini grill or in a large skillet over medium heat and cook, turning once if using a skillet, for 3 to 4 minutes or until golden brown and cheese is melted. Serve immediately.

Tips: Shred Cheddar cheese by hand or by using a food processor. If you're using hard cheese, such as Parmesan, let it get to room temperature before grating.

The pimiento cheese can be stored, covered and refrigerated, for up to 3 days.

Grilled Pimiento Cheese with Bacon and Pickles

Serves 4

This sandwich was crafted by my assistant, Alatia. It's a true family favorite.

8	slices sourdough bread (½-inch/1 cm thick slices)	8
¼ cup	butter or margarine, softened	60 mL
1 cup	Pimiento Cheese (page 114) or store-bought	250 mL
1½ cups	small dill pickles	375 mL
8	slices cooked bacon	8

Tip: This sandwich is also good served with lettuce and tomato after it's cooked.

- **Panini grill or large skillet**
- **Preheat panini grill to medium, if using**

1. Brush one side of each bread slice with butter. Place on a work surface, buttered side down. Top 4 bread slices equally with Pimiento Cheese, pickles and bacon. Cover with remaining bread slices, buttered side up, and press together gently.

2. Place sandwiches on preheated panini grill or in a large skillet over medium heat and cook, turning once if using a skillet, for 3 to 4 minutes or until golden brown and cheese is melted.

Grilled Turkey and Brie with Apricot

Serves 4

This sandwich is wonderfully sweet and savory because the Brie and Granny Smith apple pair so well together.

8	slices sourdough bread (½-inch/1 cm thick slices)	8
2 tbsp	butter or margarine, softened	30 mL
½ cup	apricot preserves or jam	125 mL
8 oz	thinly sliced maple-glazed turkey	250 g
4 oz	Brie, sliced	125 g
2	medium Granny Smith apples, thinly sliced (see Tip, below)	2

Tip: Apples ripen quickly so be sure to store them in the coldest part of the refrigerator if you're not going to eat them for a while.

- **Panini grill or large skillet**
- **Preheat panini grill to medium, if using**

1. Brush one side of each bread slice with butter. Place 4 slices on a work surface, buttered side down. Spread remaining 4 bread slices equally with apricot preserves. Top equally with turkey, Brie and apples. Cover with remaining bread slices, buttered side up, and press together gently.

2. Place sandwiches on preheated panini grill or in a large skillet over medium heat and cook, turning once if using a skillet, for 3 to 4 minutes or until golden brown and cheese is melted. Serve immediately.

Grilled Bacon and Fried Green Tomatoes

Serves 4

It doesn't get more Southern than this. I make these on very special occasions.

¼ cup	self-rising cornmeal	60 mL
2 tbsp	all-purpose flour	30 mL
2 tbsp	panko bread crumbs	30 mL
¼ tsp	salt	1 mL
¼ tsp	freshly ground black pepper	1 mL
2	green tomatoes, thinly sliced (see Tip, right)	2
⅓ cup	olive oil	75 mL
8	slices sourdough bread (½-inch/1 cm thick slices)	8
¼ cup	butter or margarine, softened	60 mL
¼ cup	Homemade Mayonnaise (page 321) or store-bought or Rémoulade Sauce (page 333)	60 mL
8	slices cooked bacon	8
4	slices Cheddar cheese	4

- **Panini grill or large skillet**
- **Preheat panini grill to medium, if using**

1. In a small bowl, combine cornmeal, flour, bread crumbs, salt and pepper. Coat green tomatoes with cornmeal mixture.

2. In a large skillet, heat oil over medium heat. Add tomatoes and cook for 5 minutes per side or until lightly browned.

3. Brush one side of each bread slice with butter. Place on a work surface, buttered side down. Spread 4 bread slices equally with mayonnaise. Top equally with bacon, tomatoes and cheese. Cover with remaining bread slices, buttered side up, and press together gently.

4. Place sandwiches on preheated panini grill or in a large skillet over medium heat and cook, turning once if using a skillet, for 3 to 4 minutes or until golden brown and cheese is melted. Serve immediately.

Tip: If you can't find green tomatoes, feel free to use fresh tomatoes and omit the frying step.

Prosciutto and Fontina Grilled Cheese

Serves 4

I call this a "dressy" grilled cheese. It's definitely for special occasions and also works well for an appetizer.

8	slices Italian bread (1/2-inch/1 cm thick slices)	8
1/4 cup	olive oil	60 mL
1/4 cup	Basil Pesto (page 329) or store-bought	60 mL
8 oz	thinly sliced prosciutto	250 g
1 cup	arugula leaves	125 mL
4	slices fontina cheese	4

- **Panini grill or large skillet**
- **Preheat panini grill to medium, if using**

1. Brush one side of each bread slice with olive oil. Place on a work surface, oiled side down. Spread 4 bread slices equally with pesto. Top equally with prosciutto, arugula leaves and fontina. Cover with remaining bread slices, oiled side up, and press together gently.

2. Place sandwiches on preheated panini grill or in a large skillet over medium heat and cook, turning once if using a skillet, for 3 to 4 minutes or until golden brown and cheese is melted. Serve immediately.

Prosciutto and Melon Grilled Cheese

Serves 4

This is a twist on a one of my favorite appetizers: prosciutto and melon. I turned it into a grilled cheese with a touch of Havarti, and now it's better than ever.

8	slices sourdough bread (1/2-inch/1 cm thick slices)	8
1/4 cup	olive oil	60 mL
4 tsp	liquid honey	20 mL
12 oz	thinly sliced prosciutto	375 mL
1 cup	thinly sliced honeydew melon	250 mL
4	slices Havarti cheese	4
4 tsp	balsamic vinegar	20 mL

- **Panini grill or large skillet**
- **Preheat panini grill to medium, if using**

1. Brush one side of each bread slice with olive oil. Place on a work surface, oiled side down. Spread 4 bread slices equally with honey. Top equally with prosciutto, melon slices and Havarti. Drizzle equally with balsamic vinegar. Cover with remaining bread slices, oiled side up, and press together gently.

2. Place sandwiches on preheated panini grill or in a large skillet over medium heat and cook, turning once if using a skillet, for 3 to 4 minutes or until golden brown and cheese is melted. Serve immediately.

Ham and Gouda Melts

Serves 4

The buttery, nutty flavor of Gouda pairs well with the ham in this hot sandwich. I call this a "comfort food" sandwich.

8	slices country white or sourdough bread (½-inch/ 1 cm thick slices)	8
2 tbsp	butter or margarine, softened	30 mL
¼ cup	Homemade Mayonnaise (page 321) or store-bought	60 mL
12 oz	thinly sliced ham	375 g
1 cup	chopped mixed greens	250 mL
4 oz	Gouda cheese, thinly sliced	125 g

Tip: If you have leftover ham, it works great instead of the deli sliced.

- **Panini grill or large skillet**
- **Preheated panini grill to medium, if using**

1. Brush one side of each bread slice with butter. Place on a work surface, buttered side down. Spread 4 bread slices equally with mayonnaise. Top equally with ham, greens and Gouda. Cover with remaining bread slices, buttered side up, and press together gently.

2. Place sandwiches on preheated panini grill or in a large skillet over medium heat and cook, turning once if using a skillet, for 3 to 4 minutes or until golden brown and cheese is melted. Serve immediately.

Pastrami and White Cheddar Grilled Cheese

Serves 4

This grilled cheese is my oldest son's favorite. He suggested it one day, and now it's a keeper.

8	slices rye bread (½-inch/ 1 cm thick slices)	8
2 tbsp	butter or margarine, softened	30 mL
¼ cup	spicy deli or Dijon mustard	60 mL
12 oz	sliced pastrami	375 g
4	slices white Cheddar cheese	4

Tip: If you can't find white Cheddar, feel free to substitute equal amounts of regular Cheddar.

- **Panini grill or large skillet**
- **Preheat panini grill to medium, if using**

1. Brush one side of each bread slice with butter. Place on a work surface, buttered side down. Spread 4 bread slices equally with mustard. Top equally with pastrami and cheese. Cover with remaining bread slices, buttered side up, and press gently.

2. Place sandwiches on preheated panini grill or in a large skillet over medium heat and cook, turning once if using a skillet, for 3 to 4 minutes or until golden brown and cheese is melted. Serve immediately.

Roast Beef with Asiago and Watercress

Serves 4

The rich, nutty flavor of Asiago makes the perfect flavor profile with the roast beef and watercress. I love to serve these for a simple dinner.

8	slices whole-grain bread (1/2-inch/1 cm thick slices)	8
1/4 cup	butter or margarine, softened	60 mL
1/4 cup	Dijon mustard	60 mL
12 oz	sliced roast beef	375 g
1 cup	watercress leaves	250 mL
4 oz	Asiago cheese, thinly sliced	125 g

- **Panini grill or large skillet**
- **Preheat panini grill to medium, if using**

1. Brush one side of each bread slice with butter. Place on a work surface, buttered side down. Spread 4 bread slices equally with mustard. Top equally with roast beef, watercress and cheese. Cover with remaining bread slices, buttered side up, and press gently.

2. Place sandwiches on preheated panini grill or in a large skillet over medium heat and cook, turning once if using a skillet, for 3 to 4 minutes or until golden brown and cheese is melted.

Variation

Feel free to substitute mixed lettuce for the watercress.

Classic Grilled Two Cheese

Serves 4

This is back to the basics and a classic. I love to serve it with a creamy tomato soup in the wintertime.

8	slices white or whole grain bread (1/2-inch/1 cm thick slices)	8
2 tbsp	butter or margarine, softened	30 mL
4 oz	Muenster cheese, thinly sliced	125 g
4 oz	Cheddar cheese, thinly sliced	125 g

- **Panini grill or large skillet**
- **Preheat panini grill to medium, if using**

1. Brush one side of each bread slice with butter. Place on a work surface, buttered side down. Top 4 bread slices equally with Muenster and Cheddar cheeses. Cover with remaining bread slices, buttered side up, and press gently.

2. Place sandwiches on preheated panini grill or in a large skillet over medium heat and cook, turning once if using a skillet, for 3 to 4 minutes or until golden brown and cheese is melted.

Southwestern Grilled Cheese

Serves 4

I love this grilled cheese recipe. I can never go wrong with Southwestern foods. Serve with an avocado salad for a complete meal.

8	slices white or whole-grain bread (½-inch/1 cm thick slices)	8
2 tbsp	butter or margarine, softened	30 mL
4	slices pepper Jack cheese	4
2	tomatoes, thinly sliced	2
2	avocados, thinly sliced	2

Toppings, optional

Salsa
Sour cream
Chopped jalapeños
Freshly chopped cilantro

Tip: Jalapeños can be found in the produce section at almost any grocery store. Store them in a plastic bag in the refrigerator for up to 1 week.

- **Panini grill or large skillet**
- **Preheat panini grill to medium, if using**

1. Brush one side of each bread slice with butter. Place on a work surface, buttered side down. Top 4 bread slices equally with cheese, tomato slices and avocado slices. Cover with remaining bread slices, buttered side up, and press together gently.

2. Place sandwiches on preheated panini grill or in a large skillet over medium heat and cook, turning once if using a skillet, for 3 to 4 minutes or until golden brown and cheese is melted. Serve immediately with desired toppings.

Variation

Substitute nonfat Greek yogurt for the sour cream. It tastes great, has zero fat and has a lot of protein.

Provençal Panini

I love to serve this sandwich with a Caesar salad for a simple meal.

8	slices white or whole-grain bread (½-inch/1 cm thick slices)	8
2 tbsp	olive oil	30 mL
2	tomatoes, thinly sliced	2
1 cup	sun-dried tomatoes, packed in oil, drained	250 mL
¾ cup	sliced kalamata olives	175 mL
4	slices mozzarella cheese	4
½ cup	freshly grated Parmesan cheese	125 mL
½ tsp	hot pepper flakes	2 mL

Tip: If you want to limit fat intake, use dehydrated sun-dried tomatoes. They even sell them already sliced.

- **Panini grill or large skillet**
- **Preheat panini grill to medium, if using**

1. Brush one side of each bread slice with olive oil. Place on a work surface, oiled side down. Spread 4 bread slices equally with tomatoes, sun-dried tomatoes, olives, and mozzarella and Parmesan cheeses. Sprinkle equally with hot pepper flakes. Cover with remaining bread slices, oiled side up, and press together gently.

2. Place sandwiches on preheated panini grill or in a large skillet over medium heat and cook, turning once if using a skillet, for 3 to 4 minutes or until golden brown and cheese is melted. Serve immediately.

Prosciutto Feta Grilled Cheese

Serves 4

This grilled cheese makes a great lunch, dinner or appetizer. The melted feta is so delicious on the prosciutto.

8	slices whole-grain bread (1/2-inch/1 cm thick slices)	8
2 tbsp	olive oil	30 mL
1/4 cup	Homemade Mayonnaise (page 321) or store-bought	60 mL
8 oz	thinly sliced prosciutto	250 g
1 cup	baby spinach leaves	250 mL
2	tomatoes, thinly sliced	2
4 oz	crumbled feta cheese	125 g

Tip: This sandwich is also great served on sliced Italian bread.

- **Panini grill or large skillet**
- **Preheat panini grill to medium, if using**

1. Brush one side of each bread slice with olive oil. Place on a work surface, oiled side down. Spread 4 bread slices equally with mayonnaise. Top equally with prosciutto, spinach, tomatoes and cheese. Cover with remaining bread slices, oiled side up, and press together gently.

2. Place sandwiches on preheated panini grill or in a large skillet over medium heat and cook, turning once if using a skillet, for 3 to 4 minutes or until golden brown and cheese is melted. Serve immediately.

California Grilled Cheese

Serves 4

I love making California-style sandwiches. They are always fabulous and seem so fresh and healthy.

8	slices whole-grain bread (1/2-inch/1 cm thick slices)	8
2 tbsp	olive oil	30 mL
4	slices Havarti cheese	4
2	avocados, sliced	2
2	tomatoes, thinly sliced	2
1 cup	alfalfa sprouts	250 mL

- **Panini grill or large skillet**
- **Preheat panini grill to medium, if using**

1. Brush one side of each bread slice with olive oil. Place on a work surface, oiled side down. Top 4 bread slices equally with cheese, avocados, tomatoes and sprouts. Cover with remaining bread slices, oiled side up, and press gently.

2. Place sandwiches on preheated panini grill or in a large skillet over medium heat and cook, turning once if using a skillet, for 3 to 4 minutes or until golden brown and cheese is melted.

Variation

Substitute provolone or Muenster cheese for the Havarti.

On-the-Grill Grilled Cheese

Serves 4

For something different, I like to make my grilled cheese on the grill outside. My kids think it's so different, and it's really just as simple.

8	slices whole-grain bread (½-inch/1 cm thick slices)	8
¼ cup	butter or margarine, softened	60 mL
4	slices Colby cheese	4
4	slices Havarti cheese	4
2	tomatoes, thinly sliced	2

Tip: Make sure the grill is lightly greased so the sandwiches don't stick.

- **Preheat lightly greased barbecue grill to medium**

1. Brush one side of each bread slice with butter. Place on a work surface, buttered side down. Top 4 bread slices equally with Colby and Havarti cheeses and tomato slices. Cover with remaining bread slices, buttered side up, and press gently.

2. Place on prepared grill rack, for 3 to 4 minutes, turning once, until golden brown and cheese is melted. Serve immediately.

Grilled Carnegie Sandwich

Serves 4

This sandwich is similar to the "Carnegie Deli" in New York. I love serving these with matzo ball or chicken and rice soup.

8	slices rye bread (½-inch/1 cm thick slices)	8
2 tbsp	butter or margarine, softened	30 mL
¾ cup	deli mustard	175 mL
8 oz	thinly sliced pastrami	250 g
3	kosher dill pickles, thinly sliced	3
4	slices Swiss cheese	4

- **Panini grill or large skillet**
- **Preheat panini grill to medium, if using**

1. Brush one side of each bread slice with butter. Place on a work surface, buttered side down. Spread mustard on tops of bread slices. Top 4 bread slices equally with pastrami, pickles and cheese. Cover with remaining bread slices, buttered side up, and press gently.

2. Place sandwiches on preheated panini grill or in a large skillet over medium-high heat and cook, turning once if using a skillet, for 3 to 4 minutes or until golden brown and cheese is melted. Serve immediately.

Variation

Substitute Thousand Island dressing for the deli mustard.

Grilled Salmon and Gruyère

Serves 4

Gruyère cheese is my all-time favorite. It is great paired with the salmon in this grilled cheese.

8	slices sourdough bread (½-inch/1 cm thick slices)	8
2 tbsp	butter or margarine, softened	30 mL
8 oz	smoked salmon, thinly sliced	250 g
4 oz	Gruyère or Swiss cheese, thinly sliced	125 g
2	tomatoes, thinly sliced	2
½ cup	chopped fresh basil	250 mL

- **Panini grill or large skillet**
- **Preheat panini grill to medium-high, if using**

1. Brush one side of each bread slice with butter. Place on a work surface, buttered side down. Top 4 bread slices equally with smoked salmon, cheese, tomatoes and basil. Cover with remaining bread slices, buttered side up, and press gently.

2. Place sandwiches on preheated panini grill or in a large skillet over medium-high heat and cook, turning once if using a skillet, for 3 to 4 minutes or until golden brown and cheese is melted. Serve immediately.

Grilled Cheese Pizza Sandwich

Serves 4

Using marinara and pesto sauces creates awesome flavors in this sandwich. Serve with a tossed salad for lunch or dinner on busy weeknights.

8	slices Italian bread (½-inch/ 1 cm thick slices)	8
2 tbsp	olive oil	30 mL
¼ cup	Basil Pesto (page 329) or store-bought	60 mL
¼ cup	marinara sauce	60 mL
6 oz	sliced pepperoni	175 mL
4	slices mozzarella cheese	4

- **Panini grill or large skillet**
- **Preheat panini grill to medium, if using**

1. Brush one side of each bread slice with olive oil. Place on a work surface, oiled side down. Spread 4 bread slices equally with pesto and the 4 other bottom halves with 1 tbsp (15 mL) of the marinara. Top marinara with pepperoni and cheese. Cover with remaining bread slices, oiled side up, and press together gently.

2. Place sandwiches on preheated panini grill or in a skillet over medium heat and cook, turning once if using a skillet, for 3 to 4 minutes or until golden brown and cheese is melted.

Lemon Basil Chicken Panini

Serves 4

This chicken is my daughter's favorite. When I made it as a grilled cheese, it was an instant hit.

1/4 cup	olive oil, divided	60 mL
1/3 cup	freshly squeezed lemon juice	75 mL
2	cloves garlic, minced	2
1 tbsp	chopped fresh basil	15 mL
1 tbsp	chopped fresh rosemary	15 mL
1/4 tsp	kosher salt	1 mL
1/4 tsp	freshly ground black pepper	1 mL
4	boneless skinless chicken cutlets (about 1 1/2 lbs/750 g total) (see Tips, below)	4
8	slices Italian bread (1/2-inch/ 1 cm thick slices)	8
1/3 cup	freshly grated Parmesan cheese	175 mL

Tips: You can also broil chicken. Place on a baking sheet, lined with parchment paper. Broil chicken, turning once, for 4 to 6 minutes per side or until chicken is no longer pink inside.

I love using chicken cutlets because they are thinner and cook so much more quickly than chicken breasts.

- **Preheat greased barbecue grill to medium**
- **Panini grill or large skillet**
- **Preheat panini grill to medium-high, if using**

1. In a small bowl, combine 2 tbsp (30 mL) of the olive oil, lemon juice, garlic, basil, rosemary, salt and pepper. Place chicken in a large bowl and pour marinade over chicken and marinate for at least 30 minutes or for up to 8 hours in the refrigerator.

2. Remove chicken from marinade and discard marinade. Grill chicken on prepared grill or panini grill for 4 to 6 minutes per side or until chicken is no longer pink inside. Set aside.

3. Brush one side of each bread slice with remaining olive oil. Place on a work surface, oiled side down. Top 4 bread slices equally with chicken and cheese. Top with remaining bread slices, oiled side up, and press together gently.

4. Place sandwiches on preheated panini grill or in a large skillet over medium heat and cook, turning once if using a skillet, for 3 to 4 minutes or until golden brown and cheese is melted. Serve immediately.

Roast Beef and Fontina Focaccia Panini

Serves 4

Serve this sandwich with a spinach salad and fresh fruit for a complete meal.

4	4-inch (10 cm) focaccia, halved horizontally	4
¼ cup	olive oil, divided	60 mL
¼ cup	Basil Pesto (page 329) or store-bought	60 mL
4 oz	sliced turkey	125 g
2 oz	sliced roast beef	60 g
2 cups	arugula	500 mL
1	tomato, thinly sliced	1
4 oz	thinly sliced fontina	125 g
2 tbsp	balsamic vinegar	30 mL
⅛ tsp	freshly ground black pepper	0.5 mL

- **Panini grill or large skillet**
- **Preheat panini grill to medium, if using**

1. Place focaccia, cut side down, on a work surface and brush crusts with 2 tbsp (30 mL) of the olive oil. Turn over and spread equally with pesto. Top equally with turkey, roast beef, arugula, tomato and cheese. Drizzle with balsamic vinegar and sprinkle with pepper.

2. Place sandwiches on a preheated panini grill or in a skillet over medium heat and cook, turning once if using a skillet, for 3 to 4 minutes or until golden brown and cheese is melted.

Variation

Substitute 8 Italian bread slices or sourdough bread for the focaccia in this recipe.

Grilled Chicken Gremolata Sandwich

Serves 4

Gremolata is a paste made of herbs, garlic and citrus often found in Italy.

1/4 cup	chopped fresh parsley	60 mL
2 tbsp	grated lemon zest	30 mL
2	cloves garlic, minced	2
1 1/2 tsp	dried Italian seasoning	7 mL
1 tsp	sea salt, divided	5 mL
8 tbsp	olive oil, divided	120 mL
1/4 cup	freshly squeezed lemon juice	60 mL
4	boneless skinless chicken cutlets, about 1 1/2 lbs (750 g)	4
1/4 tsp	freshly ground black pepper	1 mL
8	ciabatta or Italian bread (1/2-inch/1 cm thick slices), toasted	8
4	slices mozzarella cheese	4

Tips: You can also broil chicken. Place on a baking sheet, lined with foil. Broil chicken, turning once, for 4 to 6 minutes per side or until chicken is no longer pink inside.

If you have leftover grilled chicken on hand, feel free to use that in this sandwich.

- **Preheat lightly greased barbecue grill to medium-high**
- **Panini grill or large skillet**
- **Preheat panini grill to medium, if using**

1. In a small bowl, combine parsley, lemon zest, garlic, Italian seasoning and 1/2 tsp (2 mL) of the salt. Stir in 6 tbsp (90 mL) of the olive oil. Set aside.

2. Drizzle lemon juice over chicken and season with remaining salt and pepper. Cook chicken on prepared grill or panini grill for 4 to 6 minutes per side or until chicken is no longer pink inside. Set aside.

3. Brush one side of each bread slice with remaining olive oil. Place on a work surface, oiled side down. Spread 4 bread slices with parsley mixture. Top 4 bread slices equally with chicken and cheese. Press together gently, oiled side up.

4. Place sandwiches on preheated grill, panini grill or in a skillet and cook, turning once if using a skillet, for 3 to 4 minutes or until golden brown and cheese is melted. Serve immediately.

Grilled Turkey Tenderloin Sandwich

Serves 4

The balsamic and brown sugar sauce goes great on this turkey sandwich topped with provolone cheese.

5 tbsp	olive oil, divided	75 mL
1/2 cup	chopped onion	125 mL
1 cup	balsamic vinegar	250 mL
1 tbsp	tomato paste	15 mL
1/4 cup	packed brown sugar	60 mL
1 tbsp	Worcestershire sauce	15 mL
1 tbsp	Dijon mustard	15 mL
4	turkey tenderloins (about 1 1/2 lbs/750 g total)	4
1/4 tsp	salt	1 mL
1/4 tsp	freshly ground black pepper	1 mL
8	slices Italian bread (1/2-inch/1 cm thick slices)	8
4	slices provolone cheese	4

- **Preheat greased barbecue grill to medium**
- **Panini grill or large skillet**
- **Preheat panini grill to medium, if using**

1. In a medium skillet, heat 2 tbsp (30 mL) of the olive oil over medium heat. Saute onion for about 5 minutes or until softened. Add vinegar, tomato paste, brown sugar, Worcestershire sauce and Dijon mustard. Increase to medium-high. Bring to a boil. Reduce heat and simmer for about 10 minutes or until reduced by half. Set aside.

2. Sprinkle tenderloins with salt and pepper and drizzle with 1 tbsp (15 mL) of olive oil. Separate 3 tbsp (45 mL) of the vinegar mixture and brush on turkey. Grill turkey on preheated grill for 4 minutes per side or until no longer pink inside.

3. Brush one side of each bread slice with remaining 2 tbsp (30 mL) of olive oil. Place bread on a work surface, oiled side down. Spread 4 bread slices equally with remaining vinegar mixture. Top equally with turkey and cheese. Cover with remaining bread slices, oiled side up, and press together gently.

4. Place sandwiches on preheated grill, panini grill or in a skillet and cook, turning once if using a skillet, for 3 to 4 minutes or until golden brown and cheese is melted. Serve immediately.

Variation

Substitute chicken cutlets or thinly sliced pork tenderloin for the turkey tenderloins.

Seasonal Vegetable Panini

Serves 4

These are one of my favorite panini sandwiches. I love to serve them with minestrone soup for a soup and sandwich night.

1	medium eggplant, peeled and sliced into $\frac{1}{4}$-inch (0.5 cm) slices (see Tip, below)	1
7 tbsp	olive oil, divided	105 mL
$\frac{1}{2}$ tsp	sea salt, divided	2 mL
$\frac{1}{2}$ tsp	freshly ground black pepper, divided	2 mL
6	Roma (plum) tomatoes, thinly sliced	6
2	cloves garlic, minced	2
4 oz	crumbled goat cheese	125 g
8	slices ciabatta bread or Italian bread ($\frac{1}{2}$-inch/1 cm thick slices)	8
4	slices mozzarella cheese	4
$\frac{1}{2}$ cup	chopped fresh basil	125 mL

Tip: Since eggplant can often taste bitter depending on the variety, I like to sprinkle it with salt and let stand for about 30 minutes. Then wash off and cook.

- **Large baking sheet, lined with parchment paper**
- **Preheat oven to 400°F (200°C)**
- **Panini grill or large skillet**
- **Preheat panini grill to medium, if using**

1. On prepared baking sheet, place eggplant in a single layer. Drizzle with 3 tbsp (45 mL) of the olive oil. Sprinkle with $\frac{1}{4}$ tsp (1 mL) of the salt and $\frac{1}{4}$ tsp (1 mL) of the pepper. Bake in preheated oven for 20 minutes or until eggplant is tender.

2. Place tomatoes on prepared baking sheet and drizzle with 2 tbsp (30 mL) of olive oil, garlic and remaining salt and pepper. Bake in preheated oven for 15 minutes. Set aside.

3. Brush one side of each bread slice with remaining 2 tbsp (30 mL) of oil. Place on work surface, oiled side down. Spread goat cheese on one side of each bread slice. Top 4 slices equally with mozzarella, eggplant, tomatoes and basil. Sandwich with remaining bread, oiled side up.

4. Place sandwiches on preheated panini grill or in a large skillet over medium heat and cook, turning once if using a skillet, for 5 minutes or until golden brown and cheese is melted. Serve immediately.

Grilled Tequila Citrus Panini

This sandwich was inspired by a tequila chicken recipe I like. Serve it with chips, salsa and guacamole.

¼ cup	tequila	60 mL
¼ cup	freshly squeezed orange juice	60 mL
¼ cup	freshly squeezed lime juice	60 mL
2 tsp	chili powder	10 mL
1	clove garlic, minced	1
1 tsp	salt	5 mL
1 tsp	freshly ground black pepper	5 mL
4	boneless skinless chicken cutlets, about 1½ lbs (750 g) total (see Tip, below)	4
8	slices sourdough bread (½-inch/1 cm thick slices)	8
2 tbsp	olive oil	30 mL
4	slices Monterey Jack cheese	4

Tip: You can also broil chicken. Place on a baking sheet, lined with parchment paper. Broil chicken, turning once, for 4 to 6 minutes per side or until chicken is no longer pink inside.

- **Preheat greased barbecue grill to medium-high**
- **Panini grill or large skillet**
- **Preheat panini grill to medium, if using**

1. In a shallow dish, combine tequila, orange juice, lime juice, chili powder, garlic, salt and pepper. Add chicken, turning to coat. Cover and marinate in the refrigerator for at least 2 hours.

2. Remove chicken from marinade. Discard marinade. Grill chicken on preheated grill for 4 minutes per side or until chicken is no longer pink inside.

3. Brush one side of each bread slice with olive oil. Place on a work surface, oiled side down. Top 4 bread slices equally with chicken cutlets and cheese. Cover with remaining bread slices, oiled side up, and press together gently.

4. Place sandwiches on preheated panini grill or in a large skilled over medium heat and cook, turning once if using a skillet, for 3 to 4 minutes or until golden brown and cheese is melted. Serve immediately.

Variation

You can omit the tequila if you want. Use the same amounts for orange juice and lime juice.

Grilled Apple Blue Cheese Sandwich

Serves 4

This sandwich says fall with the mixture of apples, walnuts and blue cheese. If you can't find apple preserves, apricot is a nice substitute.

4 oz	cream cheese, softened	125 g
3 tbsp	crumbled blue cheese	45 mL
2 tbsp	apple preserves or apple jelly	30 mL
4 tsp	liquid honey	20 mL
8	slices whole wheat bread or oat bread ($\frac{1}{2}$-inch/1 cm thick slices)	8
$\frac{1}{4}$ cup	butter or margarine, softened	60 mL
2	Gala apples, thinly sliced	2
1 cup	mesclun lettuce or mixed spring greens	250 mL
$\frac{1}{2}$ cup	chopped toasted walnuts (see Tip, below)	125 mL

Tip: Toasting nuts intensifies their flavors. I like to toast mine in a skillet over medium heat, tossing gently, for 3 to 5 minutes or in 350°F (180°C) oven for 5 to 10 minutes or until fragrant and golden brown.

- **Panini grill or large skillet**
- **Preheat panini grill to medium, if using**

1. In a small bowl, combine cream cheese and blue cheese. Set aside.

2. In a separate bowl, combine apple preserves and honey. Brush one side of each bread slice equally with butter. Place bread on work surface, buttered side down. Spread preserve mixture equally on half of bread slices and cream cheese mixture on the other halves. Top 4 halves with apples, lettuce and walnuts. Cover with remaining bread slices, buttered side up, and press gently.

3. Place sandwiches on preheated panini grill or in a large skillet over medium heat and cook, turning once if using a skillet, for 3 to 4 minutes or until golden brown and cheese is melted. Serve immediately.

Tip: If you like a less potent blue cheese flavor, reduce the blue cheese to 2 tbsp (30 mL).

Spicy Paprika Salmon–Goat Cheese Sandwich

Serves 4

Chipotle seasoning can be found in the spice aisle of the grocery store. If you prefer less spicy food, use only 1 to 2 tsp (5 to 10 mL) chipotle seasoning.

2 tbsp	paprika	30 mL
1 tbsp	chipotle seasoning	15 mL
2	clove garlic, minced	2
½ tsp	kosher salt	2 mL
1½ lbs	salmon fillets (see Tip, below)	750 g
⅓ cup	freshly squeezed lemon juice	75 mL
4 tbsp	olive oil, divided	60 mL
8	slices Italian bread (½-inch/ 1 cm thick slices)	8
½ cup	Homemade Mayonnaise (page 321) or store-bought	125 mL
½ cup	arugula	125 mL
1 cup	crumbled goat cheese	250 mL

Tip: For best results, try to cook salmon within 24 hours of its purchase for optimal freshness.

- **Preheat greased barbecue grill to medium-high**
- **Panini grill or large skillet**
- **Preheat panini grill to medium, if using**

1. In a small bowl, combine paprika, chipotle seasoning, garlic and salt. Rub over salmon. Drizzle salmon with lemon juice and 2 tbsp (30 mL) of the olive oil.

2. Place salmon on a lightly greased grill rack or grill pan coated with cooking spray. Grill over medium-high heat for 5 minutes or until fish flakes easily when pierced with a fork.

3. Brush one side of each bread slice with remaining 2 tbsp (30 mL) of olive oil. Place on a work surface, oiled side down. Spread mayonnaise equally over bottom halves. Top equally with salmon, arugula and cheese. Cover with top halves, oiled side up, and press together gently.

4. Place sandwiches on preheated panini grill or in a large skillet over medium heat and cook, turning once if using a skillet, for 3 to 4 minutes or until golden brown and cheese is melted. Serve immediately.

Grilled Cowboy-Spiced Pork

Serves 4

This western-spiced pork is wonderful with pepper Jack cheese and avocado. I serve this with chips and salsa to start, and that's all you need.

3	cloves garlic, minced	3
2 tbsp	ground cumin	30 mL
1 tbsp	chili powder	15 mL
1/2 tsp	kosher salt	2 mL
1/4 tsp	hot pepper flakes	1 mL
4	boneless pork chops (about 1 1/2 lbs/750 g total)	4
1/4 cup	olive oil, divided	60 mL
2 tbsp	freshly squeezed lime juice	30 mL
8	slices crusty French bread (1/2-inch/1 cm thick slices)	8
1	avocado, thinly sliced	1
4	slices pepper Jack cheese	4

Toppings, optional

	Salsa
	Sour cream

- **Preheat greased barbecue grill to medium-high**
- **Instant-read thermometer**
- **Panini grill or large skillet**
- **Preheat panini grill to medium, if using**

1. In a small bowl, stir together garlic, cumin, chili powder, salt and hot pepper flakes. Rub over both sides of pork. Drizzle pork with 2 tbsp (30 mL) of the olive oil and lime juice.

2. Grill pork, turning once, for 10 to 12 minutes or until a meat thermometer inserted in thickest portion registers 155°F (68°C).

3. Brush one side of each bread slice with remaining olive oil. Place on a work surface, oiled side down. Top 4 bread slices equally with pork, avocado, cheese and desired toppings. Cover with remaining bread slices, oiled side up, and press together gently.

4. Place sandwiches on preheated panini grill or a large skillet over medium heat and cook, turning once if using a skillet, for 3 to 4 minutes or until golden brown and cheese is melted. Serve immediately.

Variation

Monterey Jack cheese or a shredded Mexican cheese blend also works great in this sandwich instead of the pepper Jack.

Muffuletta Grilled Cheese

Serves 4

I love taking this New Orleans sandwich to a new level by cooking it as a grilled cheese. It doesn't get much better than this.

1/3 cup	chopped green olives	75 mL
1 cup	black olives, chopped	250 mL
1	clove garlic, minced	1
2 tbsp	chopped fresh parsley	30 mL
1 tbsp	olive oil	15 mL
1/2 cup	olive juice	125 mL
1 tbsp	red wine vinegar	15 mL
8	slices French bread (1/2-inch/1 cm thick slices)	8
8 oz	thinly sliced deli ham	250 g
8 oz	thinly sliced salami	250 g
6	slices provolone cheese	6

- **Panini grill or large nonstick skillet**
- **Preheat panini grill to medium, sprayed with cooking spray, if using**

1. In a medium bowl, combine green olives, black olives, garlic, parsley, olive oil, olive juice and vinegar.

2. Place bread slices on a work surface. Spread olive mixture equally over 4 bread slices. Top with ham and salami. Place 1 cheese slice on top and cover with remaining bread slice. Press together gently.

3. Place sandwiches in preheated panini grill or large nonstick skillet, turning once if using a skillet, for 3 to 5 minutes per side or until lightly browned and cheese is melted. Serve immediately.

Turkey-Havarti Grinder

Serves 4

Other names of this sandwich are Po'Boy, Cuban, Torpedo and Zep. Whatever the name, this version is good.

1/3 cup	Dijon mustard	75 mL
2 tbsp	Homemade Mayonnaise (page 321) or store-bought	30 mL
1/8 tsp	hot pepper flakes	0.5 mL
8	slices French bread (1/2-inch/1 cm thick slices)	8
2 tbsp	butter or margarine, softened	30 mL
1 lb	thinly sliced turkey	500 g
2 cups	fresh spinach leaves	500 mL
2	small tomatoes, thinly sliced	2
4	sweet pickle slices	4
2 oz	Havarti cheese, thinly sliced	60 g

- **Panini grill or large skillet**
- **Preheat panini grill to medium, if using**

1. In a small bowl, combine mustard, mayonnaise and hot pepper flakes.

2. Brush one side of each bread slice with butter. Place on a work surface, buttered side down. Spread 4 bread slices equally with mayonnaise mixture. Top equally with turkey, spinach, tomatoes, pickles and cheese. Cover with remaining bread slices, buttered side up, and press together gently.

3. Place sandwiches on preheated panini grill or in a large skillet over medium-high heat and cook, turning once if using a skillet, for 3 to 4 minutes or until golden brown and cheese is melted. Serve immediately.

Variation

You can omit the sweet pickles or use fresh dill.

Grilled Roasted Pepper and Feta

Serves 4 to 6

I believe roasted red peppers are great with any cheese, but I am very fond of this version with feta.

4	large red or yellow bell peppers (see Tip, below)	4
3 tbsp	olive oil, divided	45 mL
1 tbsp	balsamic vinegar	15 mL
2	cloves garlic, minced	2
1/2 tsp	sea salt	2 mL
1/2 tsp	freshly ground black pepper	2 mL
1	large ciabatta or French bread, cut into 1/2-inch/1 cm thick slices	1
1 cup	fresh baby spinach leaves	250 mL
1/2 cup	fresh basil leaves	125 mL
1 cup	crumbled feta cheese	250 mL

Tip: You can also roast bell peppers in the microwave. Place peppers in a microwave-safe dish and cover with an airtight lid to allow for the steam to build up inside. Microwave on High for 3 to 4 minutes. Turn peppers with tongs, cover and microwave for 6 minutes more or until peppers look blistered. Let stand for 10 to 20 minutes or until cool.

- **Preheat broiler**
- **Panini grill or large skillet**
- **Preheat panini grill to medium, if using**

1. Place peppers on a large baking sheet. Broil for 7 to 12 minutes or until entire pepper skin has turned black and blistery. Immediately place peppers in an airtight container such as a bowl with a lid or plastic bag and seal for 15 to 20 minutes. Peel off the blackened skin. Cut peppers in half, core and remove seeds. Slice peppers into strips and place in a bowl.

2. In a small bowl, combine 1 tbsp (15 mL) of the olive oil, vinegar, garlic, salt and pepper. Pour over peppers. Cover and refrigerate for at least 1 hour.

3. To assemble, brush one side of each bread slice with remaining olive oil. Place on a work surface, oiled side down. Top 4 bread slices equally with spinach, basil, roasted pepper mixture and feta. Cover with remaining bread slices, oiled side up, and press together gently.

4. Place sandwiches on preheated panini grill or in a large skillet over medium heat and cook, turning once if using a skillet, for 3 to 4 minutes or until golden brown and cheese is melted. Serve immediately.

Chicken-Provolone Sandwich

Serves 4

The secret ingredient in this sandwich is the red wine vinaigrette.

1/2 cup	red wine vinaigrette, divided	125 mL
4	boneless skinless chicken cutlets (about 1 1/2 lbs/ 750 g total)	4
3/4 cup	sliced baby bella mushrooms (see Tips, below)	175 mL
1/2 cup	diced red onion	125 g
4	slices French bread (1/2-inch/ 1 cm thick slices), cut in half diagonally	4
2 tbsp	olive oil	30 mL
1 cup	romaine lettuce leaves	250 mL
1	avocado, sliced	1
4	provolone cheese slices	4

Tips: The best way to clean fresh mushrooms is with a mushroom brush or damp paper towel right before using.

Baby bella mushrooms look like button mushrooms but are mini immature portobello mushrooms that have more flavor than button mushrooms. They are often found in the produce section of the grocery store where the other mushrooms are sold.

You can also broil chicken. Place on a baking sheet, lined with parchment paper. Broil chicken, turning once, for 4 to 6 minutes per side or until chicken is no longer pink inside.

- **Panini grill or large skillet**
- **Preheat panini grill to medium, if using**

1. In a shallow dish or resealable plastic bag, combine 1/4 cup (60 mL) of the vinaigrette and chicken, coating evenly. Cover and refrigerate for 15 minutes. Drain and discard marinade.

2. Brush mushrooms and red onion with remaining vinaigrette. Set aside.

3. In a large skillet, cook chicken for 6 minutes per side or until no longer pink inside.

4. In skillet over medium heat, sauté mushrooms and red onions for 4 minutes or until onions are softened.

5. Brush one side of each bread slice with olive oil. Place on a work surface, oiled side down. Top 4 bread slices equally with chicken, lettuce, mushroom mixture, avocado and cheese. Cover with remaining bread slices, oiled side up, and press together gently.

6. Place sandwiches on preheated panini grill or in a large skillet over medium-high heat and cook, turning once if using a skillet, for 3 to 4 minutes or until golden brown and cheese is melted. Serve immediately.

Grilled Swiss, Artichokes, Tomato and Olives

Serves 4

This makes great use of artichokes and a delicious vegetarian grilled cheese. It's perfect for lunch or a weeknight dinner served with a tossed salad.

8	slices multigrain, country whole wheat or oat bread (1/2-inch/1 cm thick slices)	8
2 tbsp	butter or margarine, softened	30 mL
2 tbsp	coarse-grain mustard	30 mL
1 cup	drained canned chopped artichokes	250 mL
3/4 cup	baby spinach leaves	175 mL
4	Swiss cheese slices	4
1 cup	thinly sliced black olives	250 mL

- **Panini grill or large skillet**
- **Preheat panini grill to medium, if using**

1. Brush one side of each bread slice with butter. Place on a work surface, buttered side down. Spread mustard equally over 4 slices. Top equally with artichokes, spinach, cheese and olives. Cover with remaining bread slices, buttered side up, and press together gently.

2. Place sandwiches on preheated panini grill or in a large skillet over medium heat and cook, turning once if using a skillet, for 3 to 4 minutes or until golden brown and cheese is melted. Serve immediately.

Grilled Peach and Brie Sandwich

Serve 4

I make these very often in the summertime. It's a top request at my house.

8	slices multigrain, country whole wheat or oat bread (1/2-inch/1 cm thick slices)	8
2 tbsp	butter or margarine, softened	30 mL
2 tbsp	liquid honey	30 mL
3/4 cup	baby spinach leaves	175 mL
2	large peaches, thinly sliced	2
5 oz	Brie, thinly sliced	150 g
2 tbsp	chopped fresh chives	30 mL

Tip: Use leftover chives in salads, chicken dishes and any recipe in which you might want to replace the onions.

- **Panini grill or large skillet**
- **Preheat panini grill to medium, if using**

1. Brush one side of each bread slice with butter. Place on a work surface, buttered side down. Spread honey equally over 4 slices. Top equally with spinach, peaches, Brie and chives. Cover with remaining bread slices, buttered side up, and press together gently.

2. Place sandwiches on preheated panini grill or in a large skillet over medium heat and cook, turning once if using a skillet, for 3 to 4 minutes or until golden brown and cheese is melted. Serve immediately.

Grilled Pear and Swiss Cheese

Serves 4

Celebrate fresh pears in fall with this super easy, warm and comforting sandwich.

8	slices multigrain bread (1/2-inch/1 cm thick slices)	8
1/4 cup	butter or margarine, softened	60 mL
1/4 cup	honey mustard	60 mL
2	pears, thinly sliced (see Tip, below)	2
1 cup	arugula or spinach leaves	250 mL
4	Swiss cheese slices	4

Tip: Feel free to use any of your favorite pear varieties.

- **Panini grill or large skillet**
- **Preheat panini grill to medium, if using**

1. Brush one side of each bread slice with butter. Place on a work surface, buttered side down. Spread 4 bread slices equally with honey mustard. Top 4 slices with pears, arugula and cheese. Cover with remaining bread slices, buttered side up, and press together gently.

2. Place sandwiches on preheated panini grill or in a large skillet over medium heat and cook, turning once if using a skillet, for 3 to 4 minutes or until golden brown and cheese is melted. Serve immediately.

Grilled Prosciutto, Cantaloupe and Fontina

Serves 4

My friend and fellow foodie, Kelly, from Park City, Utah, gave me this idea. She told me it's her favorite summertime grilled cheese.

8	slices multigrain bread ($\frac{1}{2}$-inch/1 cm thick slices)	8
$\frac{1}{4}$ cup	butter or margarine, softened	60 mL
$\frac{1}{4}$ cup	honey mustard	60 mL
8 oz	thinly sliced prosciutto	250 g
1 cup	arugula or spinach leaves	250 mL
$\frac{1}{2}$	small cantaloupe, thinly sliced (see Tip, right)	$\frac{1}{2}$
4	slices fontina cheese	4

- **Panini grill or large skillet**
- **Preheat panini grill to medium, if using**

1. Brush one side of each bread slice with butter. Place on a work surface, buttered side down. Spread 4 bread slices equally with honey mustard. Top equally with prosciutto, arugula, cantaloupe and cheese. Cover with remaining bread slices, buttered side up, and press together gently.

2. Place sandwiches on preheated panini grill or in a large skillet over medium heat and cook, turning once if using a skillet, for 3 to 4 minutes or until golden brown and cheese is melted. Serve immediately.

Tip: To pick a cantaloupe, look for one with a fresh melon odor, that is heavy for its size and yields slightly to pressure.

Eggplant and Pesto Grilled Cheese

Serves 4

Serve this sandwich with a glass of Chianti and a tossed salad for a winning sandwich night meal.

1	medium eggplant, sliced into 1/4-inch (0.5 cm) slices	1
1/4 cup + 2 tbsp	olive oil, divided	90 mL
2 tbsp	balsamic vinegar	30 mL
1/8 tsp	salt	0.5 mL
1/8 tsp	freshly ground black pepper	0.5 mL
2	large tomatoes, sliced	2
8	slices Italian or sourdough bread (1/2-inch/1 cm thick slices)	8
1/2 cup	Basil Pesto (page 329) or store-bought	125 mL
4	slices mozzarella cheese	4

- **Preheat greased barbecue grill to medium**

1. Coat eggplant with 1/4 cup (60 mL) of the olive oil and vinegar. Season with salt and pepper. Grill on preheated grill for 5 minutes or until tender. Add tomatoes and grill for 1 minute per side.

2. Brush one side of each bread slice with remaining olive oil. Place on a work surface, oiled side down. Spread all slices equally with pesto. Top 4 slices with eggplant, tomatoes and cheese. Cover with remaining bread slices, oiled side up, and press together gently.

3. Place sandwiches on preheated grill or grill pan over medium heat and cook, turning once if using a skillet, for 3 to 4 minutes or until golden brown and cheese is melted. Serve immediately.

Tip: If you decide to use fresh sliced mozzarella instead of regular mozzarella, it adds a creamier texture.

Feta, Tomato and Basil Grilled Cheese

This sandwich is filled with the most popular ingredients at my house. This is so easy and a crowd (and family) pleaser.

8	slices Italian bread (½-inch/ 1 cm thick slices)	8
½ cup	olive oil	125 mL
12	large fresh tomatoes, thinly sliced	12
½ cup	chopped fresh basil (see Tip, right)	125 g
4	slices provolone cheese	4
½ cup	crumbled feta cheese	125 mL

Great Late-Season Produce for Sandwiches

Basil and other fresh herbs add color and fresh vibrant flavors.

Tomatoes add juicy texture, flavor, color and tang.

Bell peppers, available in green, red, yellow and purple, add color and crunch and are sweeter in the summer.

Corn, peaches and nectarines also add flavor, crunch and color.

Figs make sandwiches fresh, sweet and elegant.

- **Panini grill or large skillet**
- **Preheat panini grill to medium, if using**

1. Brush one side of each bread slice with olive oil. Place on a work surface, oiled side down. Top 4 bread slices equally with tomatoes, basil, provolone and feta. Cover with remaining bread slices, oiled side up, and press together gently.

2. Place sandwiches on preheated panini grill or in a large skillet over medium-high heat and cook, turning once if using a skillet, for 3 to 4 minutes or until golden brown and cheese is melted. Serve immediately.

Tip: To slice basil more quickly, roll up a small bunch of leaves and cut into shreds with a knife or kitchen shears. This is called chiffonade.

Grilled Steak and Blue Cheese

Serves 4

This sandwich is awesome served with an iceberg lettuce wedges topped with diced tomatoes, red onion and crumbled blue cheese.

1/4 cup	olive oil	60 mL
1 tbsp	chopped fresh parsley	15 mL
1 tbsp	chopped fresh thyme	15 mL
1	clove garlic, minced	1
1/2 tsp	salt	2 mL
1/2 tsp	freshly ground black pepper	2 mL
8	slices French bread (1/2-inch/1 cm slices)	8
2 tbsp	butter or margarine, softened	30 mL
1 lb	grilled steak, very thinly sliced (see Tip, right)	500 g
1/2 cup	baby spinach leaves	125 mL
1/2 cup	crumbled blue cheese	125 mL

- **Panini grill or large skillet**
- **Preheat panini grill to medium, if using**

1. In a small bowl, combine olive oil, parsley, thyme, garlic, salt and pepper.

2. Brush one side of each bread slice with butter. Place on a work surface, buttered side down. Spread 4 bottom halves equally with oil mixture. Top other 4 bread slices equally with steak, spinach and blue cheese. Press slices together gently.

3. Place sandwiches on preheated panini grill or in a large skillet over medium heat and cook, turning once if using a skillet, for 3 to 4 minutes or until golden brown and cheese is melted. Serve immediately.

Tip: Broil steak 5 1/2 inches (14 cm) from heat. (If using an electric oven, leave door partially opened.) Or grill over medium-high heat for 6 to 8 minutes per side for well done. Cut steak across the grain into thin slices.

Crab Mushroom Melts

Serves 4

These sandwiches are delightful served with a side of slaw or a spinach salad.

¼ cup + 2 tbsp	butter or margarine, softened, divided	90 mL
1½ cups	sliced fresh mushrooms	375 mL
2 tbsp	Homemade Mayonnaise (page 321) or store-bought	30 mL
1 tbsp	Dijon mustard	15 mL
1 tbsp	white wine vinegar	15 mL
½ tsp	dried oregano	2 mL
⅛ tsp	freshly ground black pepper	0.5 mL
2 cups	crabmeat, shell pieces removed (about 12 oz/375 g) (see Tip, below)	500 mL
8	slices sourdough bread (½-inch/1 cm slices)	8
4 oz	Muenster cheese, cut into 4 slices	125 g

Tip: When purchasing crab, I figure 3 to 4 oz (90 to 125 g) per person.

- **Preheat broiler**
- **Panini grill or large skillet**
- **Preheat panini grill to medium, if using**

1. In a large nonstick skillet, melt 2 tbsp (30 mL) of the butter over medium heat. Saute mushrooms for 4 minutes or until tender. Drain and set aside.

2. In a medium bowl, combine mayonnaise, mustard, vinegar, oregano and pepper. Add crabmeat and mushrooms and toss gently to coat.

3. Brush one side of each bread slice with remaining butter. Place on a work surface, buttered side down. Spoon crabmeat mixture on 4 bread slices. Top with cheese and press bread slices together, buttered side up.

4. Place sandwiches on preheated panini grill or in a large skillet over medium heat and cook, turning once if using a skillet, for 3 to 4 minutes or until golden brown and cheese is melted. Serve immediately.

Burgers

Burgers with Grilled Onion and Smoked Cheddar

Serves 4

These burgers were created with the help of my assistant, Alatia. The combination of chipotle and smoked Cheddar pairs well with the grilled onions and tomatoes.

1 lb	lean ground beef	500 g
1 tsp	garlic powder, divided	5 mL
1/2 tsp	salt, divided	2 mL
1/2 tsp	freshly ground black pepper, divided	2 mL
2	tomatoes, cut in half crosswise	2
1	onion, sliced into 4 thick round slices	1
1 tbsp	olive oil	15 mL
4 oz	smoked Cheddar cheese, cut into 4 slices	125 g
4	hamburger buns, split and toasted	4
1/4 cup	Chipotle Aïoli or Homemade Mayonnaise (pages 311 and 321) or store-bought	60 mL
1	avocado, thinly sliced	1

Tip: Make sure you lightly grease your grill so the burgers, tomatoes and onions don't stick when turning.

- **Preheat lightly greased barbecue grill to medium-high**
- **Instant-read thermometer**

1. In a large bowl, combine beef, 1/2 tsp (2 mL) of the garlic powder, 1/4 tsp (1 mL) of the salt and 1/4 tsp (1 mL) of the pepper. Shape into 4 equal patties, about 3/4 inch (2 cm) thick.

2. In a shallow plate, place tomatoes and onion and drizzle both sides with olive oil and remaining garlic powder, salt and pepper.

3. Place burgers on grill, close lid and grill, turning once, for 5 minutes per side until an instant-read thermometer inserted in the center registers 160°F (71°C). Place cheese on burgers and tomatoes and onions onto rack, close lid and grill for 5 minutes or until cheese is melted and vegetables are tender.

4. Place hamburger buns on a work surface. Spread Chipotle Aïoli equally over cut sides of buns. Arrange burgers, tomatoes, onions and avocado on buns. Top with remaining bun.

Variation

Omit the Chipotle Aïoli and use ketchup and mayonnaise instead.

Tip: Using a vegetable grill rack on the grill makes cooking tomatoes and onions easier so they don't fall through the cracks.

Ham and Cheese Topped Burgers

Serves 4

This recipe was requested by a friend whose kids love ham and cheese sandwiches. I told her, "Why not top a burger with it?" Here's the recipe.

1 lb	extra-lean ground beef, preferably ground round	500 g
1½ tsp	garlic powder	7 mL
½ tsp	salt	2 mL
½ tsp	freshly ground black pepper	2 mL
4 oz	thinly sliced ham	125 g
4	slices Swiss cheese	4
4	hamburger buns, split and toasted	4

Toppings, optional

	Dijon mustard
	Pickles
	Lettuce
	Tomato

- **Preheat lightly greased barbecue grill to medium-high**
- **Instant-read thermometer**

1. In a large bowl, combine beef, garlic powder, salt and pepper. Shape into 4 equal patties, about ¾ inch (2 cm) thick.

2. Place burgers on preheated grill, close lid and grill, turning once, for 5 minutes per side or until an instant-read thermometer registers 160°F (71°C). Arrange ham and cheese slices on top of burgers. Cook for 2 minutes more or until cheese is melted. Serve on buns with desired toppings.

Variations

If you don't want to grill outdoors, these burgers are also great cooked in the skillet. Place burgers on a lightly greased large skillet over medium-high heat for 5 minutes per side or until an instant-read thermometer registers 160°F (71°C).

Substitute 1 lb (500 g) ground turkey for the beef in this recipe.

Aussie Burgers

Serves 4

For a classic Australian combination, try this really simple burger. I love the combination of sliced beets and pineapple rings piled on top.

1½ lbs	lean ground beef, preferably ground chuck	750 g
½ tsp	salt	2 mL
½ tsp	freshly ground black pepper	2 mL
1 cup	thinly sliced onion	250 mL
4	Kaiser rolls or sesame buns, split and toasted	4
4	large eggs, cooked over easy	4

Toppings, optional

Tomatoes
Lettuce
Ketchup
Sliced beets
Pineapple slices

- **Preheat greased barbecue grill to medium**
- **Instant-read thermometer**

1. In a small bowl, combine ground beef, salt and pepper. Shape into 4 equal patties, about ¾ inch (2 cm) thick.

2. Place burgers and onion on preheated grill, close lid and grill, turning once, for 4 to 6 minutes per side or until an instant-read thermometer registers 160°F (71°C). Serve on buns with eggs, and top with tomatoes, lettuce, ketchup, beets and pineapple slices, if desired.

Tip: To grill pineapple rings, grill over medium heat for 1 to 2 minutes per side or until grill marks appear.

Brick Burger Bites

Serves 12

I developed this recipe for Wisconsin Milk and Marketing Board using Brick cheese for a kid's brochure. Kids love these little burger bites.

1 lb	lean ground beef	500 g
	Salt and freshly ground black pepper	
6 oz	Wisconsin Brick or your favorite cheese, cut into 12 slices	175 g
12	mini burger buns, split	12
$\frac{1}{2}$ cup	lettuce, shredded	125 mL
$\frac{1}{2}$ cup	diced tomatoes	125 mL
$\frac{1}{4}$ cup	diced onion	60 mL

Tip: Brick cheese, native to Wisconsin, got its name from the method used to process the cheese, which was pressing it using bricks. This cheese is usually pale and mild, but it can also be found as medium or sharp. If you can't find Brick cheese, you can use Havarti or Cheddar.

- **Preheat oven to 375°F (190°C)**
- **Broiler pan, lightly coated with cooking spray**
- **Instant-read thermometer**

1. Divide beef into 12 equal portions. Shape into 12 equal patties about $\frac{1}{4}$ inch (0.5 cm) thick.

2. Place patties on prepared broiler pan. Lightly sprinkle with salt and pepper. Bake in preheated oven for 10 to 12 minutes per side or until an instant-read thermometer registers 160°F (71°C). Arrange cheese equally over top and bake for 1 to 2 minutes more or until cheese is melted.

3. Place buns on a work surface. Arrange patties on buns and top with lettuce, tomatoes and onions.

Tip: You can make the patties ahead of time and store, tightly covered, in the refrigerator for up to 1 day.

Pizza Sliders with a Twist

Serves 12

These mini pizza burgers are a hit with kids and adults alike. I love to serve these during football season or for big sports parties.

1 lb	lean ground beef	500 g
1/2 tsp	Italian seasoning	2 mL
1 1/2 cups	sliced fresh mushrooms	375 mL
1/2 cup	pizza sauce	125 mL
24	slices turkey pepperoni (see Tip, below)	24
2 cups	coarsely shredded mozzarella cheese	500 mL
2 tbsp	sliced black olives	30 mL
12	mini burger buns, split	12

Tip: Sometimes pepperoni is difficult to find because it can be either in the refrigerated or non-refrigerated section. (I have seen it in both places.) You can find turkey pepperoni where the prebaked pizza shells are located.

- **Preheat oven to 375°F (190°C)**
- **13- by 9-inch (33 by 23 cm) baking dish, sprayed with cooking spray**
- **Instant-read thermometer**

1. Spread ground beef firmly into baking dish, covering bottom in a thin layer. Sprinkle beef with Italian seasoning and top with mushrooms. Bake in preheated oven for 10 minutes.

2. Spread pizza sauce over top and cover with pepperoni. Sprinkle with mozzarella and olives. Return to oven and bake for 5 minutes or until cheese is melted and an instant-read thermometer registers 160°F (71°C). When pizza patty is done, cut into 12 portions.

3. Place buns on a work surface. Place one pizza burger on each bun bottom and replace top.

Brie-Mushroom Burgers

Serves 4

I love Brie on just about anything, but Brie, mushrooms and burgers? You just can't go wrong with this combination. When I made these for friends, they begged me to invite them again.

1½ lbs	lean ground beef	750 g
¼ cup	finely chopped onion	60 mL
1 tbsp	Worcestershire sauce	15 mL
¼ tsp	freshly ground black pepper	1 mL
2 tbsp	butter	30 mL
1 cup	sliced fresh mushrooms	250 mL
1 cup	thinly sliced onion (about 1 small)	250 mL
4 oz	Brie, thinly sliced	60 g
4	hamburger buns, split and toasted	4
	Lettuce leaves, optional	

Tip: When purchasing Brie, look for rounds that are about 1 inch (2.5 cm) thick. When they are too thick, they get overripe more quickly.

- **Instant-read thermometer**

1. In a medium bowl, combine beef, chopped onion, Worcestershire sauce and pepper. Shape into 4 equal patties, about ¾ inch (2 cm) thick.

2. In a nonstick skillet, melt butter over medium heat. Sauté mushrooms and sliced onion for 5 minutes or until tender. Set aside.

3. Fry patties in same skillet over medium heat for 4 minutes per side or until an instant-read thermometer registers 160°F (71°C). Top with Brie slices and cook for 2 minutes or until slightly melted.

4. Place buns on a work surface. Place Brie-coated burgers in buns. Top with mushrooms and onions and lettuce, if using.

Variation

If you want to make this more kid-friendly, substitute Cheddar for the Brie in this recipe.

Fried Green Tomato Cheeseburgers

Serves 8

We get fabulous green tomatoes, and they are such a delight. Enjoy them on these wonderful cheeseburgers for a true taste of the South.

1½ lbs	lean ground beef	750 g
8 oz	ground pork sausage	250 g
½ cup	panko bread crumbs	125 mL
2	large eggs, lightly beaten	2
2 tbsp	Worcestershire sauce	30 mL
½ tsp	freshly ground black pepper	2 mL
3	green tomatoes, cut into ¼-inch (0.5 cm) slices	3
½ tsp	salt	2 mL
¼ tsp	freshly ground black pepper	1 mL
1 cup	yellow cornmeal	250 mL
2 tbsp	vegetable oil	30 mL
4	slices Cheddar cheese, preferably Wisconsin	4
4	Kaiser rolls, split and toasted	4

Toppings, optional

	Lettuce
	Sliced tomatoes
	Onion slices

- **Preheat lightly greased barbecue grill to medium-high**
- **Instant-read thermometer**

1. In a large bowl, combine beef, sausage, bread crumbs, eggs, Worcestershire and pepper. Shape into 8 equal patties, about ¾ inch (2 cm) thick.

2. Sprinkle tomato slices with salt and pepper and dredge in cornmeal.

3. In a large skillet, heat oil over medium heat. Fry tomato slices until golden on each side. Drain on paper towels and keep warm.

4. Place burgers on grill, close lid and grill, turning once, for 5 minutes per side or until an instant-read thermometer inserted in the center registers 160°F (71°C). Place cheese on burgers, close lid and grill for 2 minutes or until cheese is melted. If desired, place rolls on grill to toast. Serve burgers on rolls and top with desired toppings.

Tip: Green tomatoes have a mild flavor and are terrific in salsas and relishes.

Classic Patty Melts

Serves 4

I never really had patty melts growing up. I had a friend that used to tell me her mom served them with cut-up fresh fruit on the side for a wonderful summertime meal.

1½ lbs	ground sirloin	750 g
2 tbsp	Worcestershire sauce	30 mL
¼ tsp	kosher salt	1 mL
¼ tsp	freshly ground black pepper	1 mL
1 tbsp	butter or margarine	15 mL
1 tsp	olive oil	5 mL
8 oz	sliced fresh mushrooms	250 g
½ cup	sliced onion	125 mL
4	slices Swiss cheese	4
8	slices rye bread, toasted	4
2 tbsp	melted butter	30 mL

Tip: I like to purchase ground sirloin because it's leaner, has less fat than ground beef, and tastes great!

- **Preheat greased barbecue grill to medium-high, if using**
- **Instant-read thermometer**

1. In a large bowl, combine sirloin, Worcestershire sauce, salt and pepper. Shape into 4 equal patties, about ¾ inch (2 cm) thick.

2. In a large skillet, melt butter over medium-high heat. Place burgers on skillet or grill, if using, and fry over medium-high heat for 6 to 8 minutes per side or until an instant-read thermometer registers 160°F (71°C).

3. In another large skillet, heat oil over medium heat. Sauté mushrooms and onion for 5 minutes or until golden. Top each burger with one cheese slice and melt.

4. Place bread slices on a work surface. Brush melted butter over half. Place 4 slices in skillet, buttered side down. Top with burger, mushrooms, onion and top with remaining bread. Fry until bread is lightly browned on each side and cheese is melted.

Variation

Light Patty Melt: Add 4 slices turkey bacon, omit the cheese and serve open-faced in lettuce wraps.

Mushroom and Blue Cheese Burgers

Serves 4

With only five ingredients, these burgers have great flavor and a wonderful, simple combination.

1 tbsp	olive oil	15 mL
8 oz	sliced mushrooms	250 g
1¾ lbs	ground sirloin	875 g
¼ tsp	salt	1 mL
¼ tsp	freshly ground black pepper	1 mL
½ cup	crumbled blue cheese	125 mL
4	hamburger buns, split	4

Toppings, optional

	Lettuce leaves
	Tomato slices
	Onion slices
	Pickles

- **Preheat greased barbecue grill to medium-high heat, if using**
- **Instant-read thermometer**

1. In a large skillet, heat oil over medium heat. Sauté mushrooms for 5 to 7 minutes or until softened. Set aside.

2. Shape sirloin into 4 equal patties, about ¾ inch (2 cm) thick. Season with salt and pepper.

3. Place burgers on grill, close lid and grill, turning once, for 6 to 8 minutes per side or until an instant-read thermometer inserted in the center registers 160°F (71°C). Top with mushrooms and blue cheese. Serve on buns with desired toppings.

Tip: Do not press down burgers with a spatula while cooking. This will release some of the juices, which will cause the burgers to be dryer and cause flames on the grill.

Sun-Dried Tomato Sliders

Serves 8

My sister, Julie, gave me a variation of this recipe a few years ago. The first time I ever cooked on television, I made these for a Super Bowl television cooking segment.

1 lb	lean ground beef	500 g
¾ cup	panko bread crumbs	175 mL
½ cup	chopped fresh basil	125 mL
½ cup	marinara sauce	125 mL
½ cup	chopped sun-dried tomatoes	125 mL
2	large egg whites	2
2	cloves garlic, minced	2
¼ tsp	freshly ground black pepper	1 mL
8	mini hamburger buns, split	8

Toppings, optional

	Ketchup
	Lettuce leaves
	Sliced tomatoes

- **Preheat greased barbecue grill to medium-high, if using**
- **Instant-read thermometer**

1. In a large bowl, combine beef, bread crumbs, basil, marinara, sun-dried tomatoes, egg whites, garlic and pepper. Shape into 8 equal patties, about ¼ inch (0.5 cm) thick.

2. Place patties on preheated grill, close lid and grill, turning once, for 5 minutes per side or until an instant-read thermometer registers 160°F (71°C). Serve in buns with desired toppings.

Variation

Sun-Dried Tomato Meat Loaf: These same proportions of ingredients make a meat loaf as well. Use a 9- by 5-inch (23 by 12.5 cm) lightly greased loaf pan and bake at 350°F (180°C) for 1 hour.

Tip: Use your favorite jarred marinara sauce to save time or if you make homemade marinara, make double to freeze.

Stuffed Southwestern Burgers

Serves 4

I love stuffed burgers, and my kids love putting their favorite cheese inside burgers. This Southwestern version is perfect with an ice cold margarita.

2 lbs	lean ground beef	1 kg
1½ tsp	fajita seasoning	7 mL
½ tsp	freshly ground black pepper	2 mL
4	slices Monterey Jack cheese with jalapeño	4
4	whole-grain buns, split and toasted	4

Toppings, optional

	Lettuce
	Tomato slices
	Red onion slices
	Avocado slices
	Salsa

Tip: Leave a separate area on your grill to toast buns. Buns usually toast in about 1 minute on the grill.

- **Preheat greased barbecue grill to medium, if using**
- **Instant-read thermometer**

1. In a large bowl, combine beef, fajita seasoning and pepper. Shape into 8 equal patties, about ¾ inch (2 cm) thick.

2. Top 4 patties with cheese, tearing cheese slices as needed to fit patties. Cover with remaining patties, pressing edges to seal.

3. Place hamburgers on grill, close lid and grill, turning once, for 8 to 10 minutes per side until an instant-read thermometer inserted in the center registers 160°F (71°C). Serve in buns with desired toppings.

Variation

Lower-Fat Version: These may also be served without buns or in 6 large lettuce wraps.

Easy Mushroom Angus Burgers

These classic burgers are my favorite and very simple with garlic, mushrooms, Worcestershire and freshly cracked pepper. Serve with sweet potatoes or sweet potato chips and a tossed salad, and dinner is done.

1 lb	extra-lean ground beef, preferably ground round	500 g
2	cloves garlic, minced	2
½ cup	finely chopped mushrooms	125 mL
2 tsp	Worcestershire sauce	10 mL
¼ tsp	freshly ground black pepper	1 mL
4	whole wheat buns, split	4

Toppings, optional

Lettuce or spinach leaves
Tomato slices
Onion slices
Pickles
Mustard
Ketchup

- **Preheat greased barbecue grill to medium-high heat**
- **Instant-read thermometer**

1. In a large bowl, combine beef, garlic, mushrooms, Worcestershire sauce and pepper. Shape into 4 equal patties, about ¾ inch (2 cm) thick.

2. Place burgers on preheated grill, close lid and grill, turning once, for 4 to 6 minutes per side or until an instant-read thermometer registers 160°F (71°C). Serve in buns with desired toppings.

Tip: To save time, chop the mushrooms in a food processor. You can also combine the beef and seasonings ahead of time, refrigerate overnight and grill the burgers the next day.

Stuffed Pizza Burgers

Serves 6

These are a favorite as I had a similar burger often when I was a child. My kids beg me to make these when they have company coming over.

2 lbs	lean ground beef	1 kg
½ cup	finely chopped onion	125 mL
1	clove garlic, minced	1
1 tsp	ground Italian seasoning	5 mL
½ tsp	kosher salt	2 mL
½ tsp	hot pepper flakes	2 mL
6	slices mozzarella cheese	6
6	sesame seed hamburger buns, split and toasted	6
½ cup	marinara sauce, warmed	125 mL

Toppings, optional

	Lettuce leaves
	Tomato slices
	Hot pepper flakes

- **Preheat broiler**
- **Instant-read thermometer**

1. In a large bowl, combine beef, onion, garlic, Italian seasoning, salt and hot pepper flakes. Shape into 12 equal patties, about ½ inch (1 cm) thick. Top 6 patties with cheese. Cover with remaining patties, pressing to seal.

2. Place burgers on a rack of a broiler pan. Broil 5½ inches (13.5 cm) from heat (with electric oven door partially open) for 8 to 10 minutes per side or until an instant-read thermometer registers 160°F (71°C). Serve in buns with marinara sauce and toppings, if desired.

Tip: I use sea salt and kosher salt. Sea salt has more nutrients and tastes the best to me.

BLT and Pimiento Cheese Sliders

Makes 8

This is a true classic Southern burger. These make great pickup appetizer burgers, and they go very fast.

1 lb	extra-lean ground beef, preferably ground round	500 g
½ tsp	garlic powder	2 mL
½ tsp	freshly ground black pepper	2 mL
8	mini hamburger buns, split and toasted	8
8	slices bacon, cooked and crumbled	8
1 cup	chopped green leaf lettuce	250 mL
2	tomatoes, thinly sliced	2
1 cup	Pimiento Cheese (page 114)	250 mL

- **Preheat greased grill to medium-high**
- **Instant-read thermometer**

1. In a large bowl, combine beef, garlic powder and pepper. Shape into 8 equal patties, about ½ inch (1 cm) thick.

2. Place burgers on preheated grill, close lid and grill, turning once, for 5 minutes per side or until an instant-read thermometer registers 160°F (71°C).

3. Place burger on buns and top with bacon, lettuce, tomato and Pimiento Cheese.

Tip: When making pimiento cheese, start with the freshest and best Cheddar you can find and grate your own for optimal results.

Bacon and Cheese–Stuffed Burgers

Serves 4

This burger was a request by my family. If I serve cheese and bacon on a burger, I can't go wrong.

1 tbsp	olive oil	15 mL
1 lb	sliced fresh mushrooms	500 g
1½ lbs	ground sirloin	750 g
½ tsp	garlic powder	2 mL
½ tsp	freshly ground black pepper	2 mL
¼ tsp	salt	1 mL
4	slices bacon, cooked and finely chopped	4
4	slices Cheddar cheese	4
4	hamburger buns, split and toasted	4

Toppings, optional

	Lettuce
	Tomato slices
	Onion slices
	Ketchup
	Mayonnaise

- **Preheat broiler or greased barbecue grill to medium**
- **Instant-read thermometer**

1. In a large nonstick skillet, heat oil over medium heat. Sauté mushrooms for 4 minutes or until tender. Set aside.

2. In a large bowl, combine beef, garlic powder, pepper and salt. Shape beef into 8 equal patties, about ¾ inch (2 cm) thick. Top each of 4 patties with bacon and Swiss cheese. Top with remaining 4 patties, pinching to seal.

3. Place patties on a grill rack or broiler pan coated with cooking spray. Grill for 8 to 10 minutes per side or until an instant-read thermometer registers 160°F (71°C). Place burgers on buns. Top with mushrooms and desired toppings and remaining bun.

Tip: Feel free to substitute the type of garlic in this recipe. The ratio for garlic is 1 medium clove garlic equals ½ tsp (2 mL) minced or ⅛ tsp (0.5 mL) garlic powder.

Taco Burgers

Just about all of my friends have Mexican or taco night at their house once a week. This is a good twist on usual Mexican fare, and everyone loves this combination of burgers and Mexican all in one.

1 lb	ground sirloin	500 g
2 tsp	taco seasoning mix (see Tips, right)	10 mL
1 cup	refried beans with chiles, divided	250 mL
¾ cup	salsa or Pico de Gallo (page 328) or store-bought, divided	175 mL
2 tbsp	chopped fresh cilantro	30 mL
4	hamburger buns, split and toasted	4
1 cup	shredded iceberg lettuce	250 mL
4	Pepper Jack cheese slices	4

Toppings, optional

	Avocado slices	
	Tomato slices	
	Red onion slices	

- **Instant-read thermometer**

1. In a large bowl, combine sirloin and seasoning mix. Shape into 4 patties, about ¾ inch (2 cm) thick. In a large nonstick skillet coated with cooking spray, fry burgers over medium heat for 4 to 5 minutes per side or until an instant-read thermometer registers 160°F (71°C).

2. In a small bowl, combine ¼ cup (60 mL) of the refried beans, salsa, and cilantro.

3. Serve patties on buns with salsa mixture, lettuce, cheese and remaining refried beans. Top with desired toppings.

Tips: When buying taco seasoning mix, look for the reduced-sodium version.

If you want to prepare these ahead, assemble burgers, refrigerate overnight and cook the next day.

Chicken Burgers with Basil Lemon Aïoli

This recipe is for chicken lovers. These cook well and have very little fat drippings. This is a great weight-watching alternative served without a bun.

1¼ lbs	ground chicken	625 g
½ cup	dill pickle relish	125 mL
1	clove garlic, minced	1
2 tsp	Worcestershire sauce	10 mL
½ tsp	salt	2 mL
½ tsp	freshly ground black pepper	2 mL
4	slices Havarti cheese	4
4	hamburger buns, split	4
	Basil-Lemon Aïoli (page 312)	

Tip: Make sure the ground chicken you purchase says "ground breast of chicken" so you know you're getting the white meat.

- **Preheat greased barbecue grill to medium-high**

1. In a large bowl, combine chicken, relish, garlic, Worcestershire sauce, salt and pepper. Shape into 4 equal patties, about ¾ inch (2 cm) thick.

2. Place burgers on preheated grill, close lid and grill, turning once, for 8 minutes per side or until chicken is no longer pink. Top with cheese and place buns on grill. Grill for 2 minutes more or until cheese is melted and bread is toasted. Place in buns. Top with Basil Lemon Aïoli.

Variation

Turkey Havarti Burgers: Substitute 1¼ lbs (625 g) ground turkey for the ground chicken in this recipe.

Chicken Cutlet Burgers

I love using chicken cutlets because they are so thin and don't take long to cook. I love the bell peppers and onions on this burger.

1½ lbs	chicken breast cutlets (see Tip, right)	750 g
½ tsp	sea salt	2 mL
¼ tsp	freshly ground black pepper	1 mL
2 tbsp	freshly squeezed lemon juice	30 mL
2 tbsp	olive oil	30 mL
1	small red onion, sliced	1
½ cup	thinly sliced red bell peppers	125 mL
4	hamburger buns, split and toasted	4

Toppings, optional

	Baby arugula
	Tomato slices
	Dijon mustard
	Mayonnaise

- **Preheat greased barbecue grill to medium-high**

1. Place chicken in a large shallow dish and season with salt and pepper. Drizzle with lemon juice and olive oil.

2. Place chicken, red onion and bell peppers on preheated grill, close lid and grill, turning once, for 3 minutes per side or until chicken is no longer pink inside and vegetables are tender. Serve on buns with desired toppings.

Variation

To cook burgers indoors, use a grill pan or cast-iron skillet and fry over medium-high heat for 3 minutes per side or until chicken is no longer pink inside.

Tip: If you can't find chicken cutlets, cut a boneless skinless chicken breast in half lengthwise.

Asian-Style Turkey Burgers

Serves 4

These Asian burgers are wonderful served with a side of slaw with red and green cabbage and shredded carrots topped with sesame seeds.

1 lb	lean ground turkey	500 g
2	cloves garlic, minced	2
2 tbsp	finely chopped onion	30 mL
2 tbsp	finely chopped green bell pepper	30 mL
1 tsp	reduced-sodium soy sauce	5 mL
2 tsp	grated fresh gingerroot (see Tip, right)	10 mL
1/2 tsp	salt	2 mL
1/4 tsp	freshly ground black pepper	1 mL
4	whole-grain hamburger buns, split and toasted	4

Toppings, optional

	Lettuce	
	Tomato slices	

- **Preheat greased barbecue grill to medium-high, if using**
- **Instant-read thermometer**

1. In a large bowl, combine turkey, garlic, onion, bell pepper, soy sauce, ginger, salt and pepper. Shape into 4 equal patties, about 3/4 inch (2 cm) thick.

2. Place patties on preheated grill, close lid and grill, turning once, for 6 to 8 minutes per side or until an instant-read thermometer registers 160°F (71°C).

3. Place buns on a work surface. Top with burgers, desired toppings and remaining buns.

Tip: When you're trying to determine how much fresh ginger you will need, usually a 2-inch (5 cm) piece of ginger yields 2 tbsp (30 mL) minced.

Turkey Feta Sliders

Makes 12

I have been making turkey burgers for years, and sometimes just making them smaller with a twist of feta makes them just a little more special.

1 lb	lean ground turkey	500 g
1 tsp	dried oregano	5 mL
1/2 tsp	kosher salt (see Tips, right)	2 mL
1/2 tsp	freshly ground black pepper	2 mL
12	mini burger buns, split	12
1/2 cup	Hummus (page 313) or store-bought	125 mL
1/2 cup	baby spinach leaves	125 mL
1/2 cup	thinly sliced cucumbers	125 mL
1/4 cup	sliced black olives	60 mL
1/4 cup	chopped roasted red pepper (see Tip, below)	60 mL
1 cup	crumbled feta cheese	250 mL

Tip: Look for roasted red peppers in a jar where pickles and olives are sold.

- **Preheat oven to 375°F (190°C)**
- **Broiler pan, lightly coated with cooking spray**
- **Instant-read thermometer**

1. Shape turkey into 6 equal patties, about 1/4 inch (0.5 cm) thick.

2. Place patties on prepared broiler pan. Lightly sprinkle patties with oregano, salt and pepper. Bake in preheated oven for 5 minutes per side or until an instant-read thermometer registers 160°F (71°C).

3. Place buns on a work surface. Spread hummus on both cut sides of buns. Arrange spinach leaves and cucumber slices over top. Sprinkle with black olives and red peppers. Place hot turkey burgers on top. Cover patties with feta and replace bun tops.

Variation

You can substitute 1 lb (500 g) lean ground beef for the turkey.

Tips: Spinach will keep for up to 4 days in a sealed bag in the refrigerator.

I like to use sea salt or kosher salt in most of my recipes because it adds more distinctive flavor.

Goat Cheese Turkey Burgers

Serves 4

The combination of goat cheese and turkey is fabulous on these burgers. Using flavored goat cheese also works great for company.

¼ cup	Homemade Mayonnaise (page 321) or store-bought	60 mL
¼ cup	reduced-fat sour cream	60 mL
2 tbsp	diced drained roasted red peppers	30 mL
1 lb	lean ground turkey	500 g
4 oz	crumbled goat cheese (see Tips, right)	125 g
2 tbsp	finely chopped fresh basil	30 mL
¼ cup	freshly grated Asiago or Parmesan cheese	60 mL
½ tsp	freshly ground black pepper	2 mL
¼ tsp	sea salt	1 mL
4	hamburger buns, split and toasted	4
½ cup	baby spinach leaves	125 mL

- **Preheat greased barbecue grill to medium-high heat**
- **Instant-read thermometer**

1. In a small bowl, stir together mayonnaise, sour cream and red peppers. Cover and refrigerate until chilled.

2. In a large bowl, combine turkey, goat cheese, basil, Asiago, pepper and salt. Shape into 4 equal patties, about ½ inch (1 cm) thick.

3. Place patties on preheated grill, close lid and grill, turning once, for 5 minutes per side or until an instant-read thermometer registers 160°F (71°C).

4. Place buns on a work surface. Spread mayonnaise mixture equally over cut sides of each bun. Serve burgers on buns with spinach leaves.

Tips: You can broil burgers 5½ inches (13.5 cm) from heat (with door to electric oven partially opened) for 5 minutes per side or until an instant-read thermometer registers 160°F (71°C).

When purchasing goat cheese, make sure it is made purely from goat's milk. You will usually see "Pur Chèvre" on the label.

Turkey Guacamole Burgers

Guacamole spread, whole-grain mustard and bacon make these simple burgers truly decadent.

1¼ lbs	lean ground turkey	625 g
½ tsp	kosher salt	2 mL
½ tsp	freshly ground black pepper	2 mL
4	sourdough English muffins, split and toasted	4
⅓ cup	Guacamole (page 336) or store-bought (see Tip, right)	75 mL
4 tbsp	whole-grain mustard	60 mL
4	slices bacon, crisply cooked	4

Toppings, optional

	Lettuce
	Tomato slices
	Red onion slices

- **Preheat greased barbecue grill to medium-high**

1. In a medium bowl, combine turkey, salt and pepper. Shape into 4 equal patties, about ¾ inch (2 cm) thick.

2. Place patties on preheated grill, close lid and grill, turning once, for 5 to 7 minutes per side or until an instant-read thermometer registers 160°F (71°C).

3. Place toasted English muffins on a work surface. Top with burgers. Serve with guacamole, mustard, bacon and desired toppings.

Tip: To keep guacamole from turning brown, add lime juice and cover with plastic directly on the surface.

Mediterranean Burgers

Serves 4

I eat a lot of Greek influenced foods, and these burgers, with fresh parsley, oregano and feta cheese, are a nice change of pace from ordinary burgers. Serve with an appetizer of hummus and fresh sliced cucumber.

1 lb	lean ground turkey	500 g
1 tbsp	chopped flat-leaf Italian parley	15 mL
1 tbsp	chopped fresh oregano	15 mL
1 tbsp	reduced-fat crumbled feta cheese	15 mL
1	clove garlic, minced	1
¼ tsp	sea salt	1 mL
¼ tsp	freshly ground black pepper	1 mL
4	pita pockets, split	4
½ cup	baby spinach leaves	125 mL
2	Roma (plum) tomatoes, sliced	2
½ cup	red onion slices	125 mL
	Greek Cucumber Sauce (page 316), optional (see Tips, right)	

- **Preheat greased barbecue grill to medium-high, if using**

1. In a large bowl, combine turkey, parsley, oregano, feta, garlic, salt and pepper. Shape into 4 equal patties, about ¾ inch (2 cm) thick.

2. Place patties on a large nonstick skillet or preheated grill, close lid and grill, turning once, for 5 to 7 minutes per side or until an instant-read thermometer registers 160°F (71°C).

3. Place pita pockets on a work surface. Arrange spinach inside pockets. Add burgers, tomato and red onion slices. Serve with Greek Cucumber Sauce, if using.

Variation

These burgers are also delicious with ground chicken or pork.

Tips: If you don't have time to purchase fresh herbs or have none on hand, use 1 tsp (5 mL) Greek seasoning in the beef mixture.

Roma, or plum, tomatoes have a juicy, sweet flavor. They work great in recipes in which you want tomatoes to retain their shape.

For a quick sauce, combine 1 cup (250 mL) plain yogurt, 2 tbsp (30 mL) finely chopped cucumber, 1 tbsp (15 mL) finely chopped red onion and salt and pepper to taste.

Stuffed Feta Veal Burgers

Serves 4

These Mediterranean-style burgers can be prepared ahead of time. This recipe also works well with ground lamb and turkey.

1¼ lbs	lean ground veal	625 g
⅓ cup	crumbled feta cheese	75 mL
2	cloves garlic, minced	2
3 tbsp	chopped fresh parsley	45 mL
3 tbsp	chopped fresh mint	45 mL
¼ tsp	kosher salt	1 mL
¼ tsp	freshly ground black pepper	1 mL
4	6-inch (15 cm) pitas or hamburger buns, split and toasted	4

Toppings, optional

	Bibb lettuce
	Red onion slices
	Tomato slices

- **Preheat greased barbecue grill to medium-high, if using**

1. In a large bowl, combine veal, feta, garlic, parsley, mint, salt and pepper. Form into 4 equal patties, about ½ inch (1 cm) thick. Refrigerate for at least 30 minutes.

2. Place patties on a large nonstick skillet or preheated grill, close lid and grill, turning once, for 5 to 7 minutes per side or until an instant-read thermometer registers 160°F (71°C). Serve in pita bread with desired toppings.

Grilled Pork Tenderloin Sliders

Serve 12

These are so easy to make. I make them for large parties all the time, and everyone loves them.

2	pork tenderloins (each about 1 lb/500 g) (see Tip, right)	2
	Teriyaki sauce	
12	mini hamburger buns, split and toasted	12
	Light Horseradish Sauce (page 318)	

Toppings, optional

	Lettuce
	Tomato slices
	Chopped chives

- **Preheat greased barbecue grill to medium-high, if using**

1. In a large bowl, cover pork with teriyaki sauce. Marinate for at least 1 hour or for up to 8 hours covered in the refrigerator.

2. Remove pork from marinade, discarding marinade. Cook pork on a lightly greased grill or large skillet over medium-high heat for 10 minutes for per side or until just a hint of pink remains in pork. Slice and serve on buns with Light Horseradish Sauce and toppings, if desired.

Tip: I like to purchase pre-marinated pork tenderloin, especially the "peppercorn" or "teriyaki" flavor. If you can't find pre-marinated, purchase store-bought teriyaki sauce or your favorite meat or chicken marinade.

Banh Mi Burger

Serves 4

I love these Vietnamese-style burgers. For a low carbohydrate option, serve burgers without a bun with the cucumber, carrot and mixture over the top.

1 cup	thinly sliced cucumber	250 mL
1 cup	shredded carrots	250 mL
½ cup	chopped fresh cilantro, divided	125 mL
¼ cup	rice wine vinegar	60 mL
1 tbsp + 1 tsp	chili garlic sauce, divided	20 mL
¼ tsp	sea salt	1 mL
1½ lbs	ground pork	750 g
3 tbsp	finely chopped green onions (about 2)	45 mL
2 tbsp	minced fresh gingerroot	30 mL
1 tbsp	chopped fresh basil	15 mL
2 tbsp	soy sauce	30 mL
4	hamburger rolls, split and toasted	4
	Homemade Mayonnaise (page 321) or chili sauce, optional	

- **Preheat greased barbecue grill to medium-high**
- **Instant-read thermometer**

1. In a large bowl, combine cucumbers, carrots, 6 tbsp (90 mL) of the cilantro, vinegar, 1 tsp (5 mL) of the chili sauce and salt. Cover, refrigerate and set aside.

2. In a large bowl, combine pork, green onions, ginger, remaining cilantro, basil, soy sauce and remaining chili sauce. Shape into 4 patties, about ¾ inch (2 cm) thick.

3. Place burgers on preheated grill, close lid and grill, turning once, for 4 to 6 minutes per side or until an instant-read thermometer registers 160°F (71°C). Place buns on grill, cut side down, and heat through. To assemble, spread mayonnaise or chili sauce, if using, on buns. Top equally with cucumber and carrot mixture.

Variation

This can also be made with ground beef, turkey or chicken.

Tip: Chili garlic sauce is a blend of chiles and garlic that has a full-bodied flavor. It can be found in the Asian section of your grocery store.

Chipotle Pork Burgers

Serves 4

I love ground chipotle seasoning on pork, and this combination works great with the touch of sweet honey.

4	thin boneless pork chops (see Tip, right)	4
2	cloves garlic, minced	2
1½ tsp	ground chipotle seasoning	7 mL
½ tsp	salt	2 mL
2 tbsp	olive oil	30 mL
1 tbsp	liquid honey	15 mL
4	hamburger buns, split and toasted	4

Toppings, optional

	Lettuce leaves
	Avocado slices
	Nectarine Relish (page 322)
	Cilantro sprigs

- **Grill pan or skillet, coated with cooking spray**
- **Instant-read thermometer**

1. Place pork in a large shallow dish and season with garlic, chipotle seasoning and salt. Drizzle with olive oil and honey.

2. Heat a large prepared grill pan or skillet over medium-high heat. Fry pork chops, turning once, for 3 minutes per side or until just a hint of pink remains in pork. Serve on buns with desired toppings.

Tip: I love to buy the thinly sliced pork loin chops. They are low in fat and cook so quickly.

Lamb Burgers

Lamb burgers are great when you want a "different" burger. It is wonderful topped with the Cucumber-Mango Raita.

1½ lbs	lean ground lamb	750 g
1	clove garlic, minced	1
2 tbsp	finely chopped onion	30 mL
½ tsp	ground cumin	2 mL
½ tsp	paprika	2 mL
½ tsp	salt	2 mL
¼ tsp	freshly ground black pepper	1 mL
4	hamburger buns, split and toasted	4
4	Bibb lettuce leaves	4
	Cucumber-Mango Raita (page 317)	

- **Preheat greased barbecue grill to medium-high**
- **Instant-read thermometer**

1. In a large bowl, combine lamb, garlic, onion, cumin, paprika, salt and pepper. Shape into 4 equal patties, about ¾ inch (2 cm) thick.

2. Place burgers on preheated grill, close lid and grill, turning once, for 4 to 6 minutes per side or until an instant-read thermometer registers 160°F (71°C). Serve on buns with lettuce and Cucumber-Mango Raita.

Variation

This burger also works great with ground beef, pork, turkey or chicken.

Seared Tuna Burgers

Serves 4

Grilled tuna is so delicious and such a treat. It is so simple to make, and these burgers are an example of how easy.

¼ cup	Homemade Mayonnaise (page 321) or store-bought	60 mL
2 tbsp	grated gingerroot, divided	30 mL
2 tsp	soy sauce	10 mL
4	pieces tuna steaks, each about 6 oz (175 g)	4
1	clove garlic, minced	1
¼ tsp	sea salt	1 mL
¼ tsp	freshly ground black pepper	1 mL
2 tbsp	olive oil	30 mL
4	hamburger buns, split and toasted (see Tip, right)	4

Toppings, optional

	Arugula or lettuce leaves
	Tomato slices
	Red onion slices
	Soy sauce

- **Preheat greased barbecue grill to medium-high**

1. In a small bowl, combine mayonnaise, 1 tbsp (15 mL) of the ginger and soy sauce. Set aside.

2. Place tuna steaks in a shallow dish and rub with remaining ginger, garlic, salt and pepper. Drizzle with olive oil. Place tuna on preheated grill, close lid and grill, turning once, for 4 minutes per side for medium-rare or until desired degree of doneness.

3. Serve tuna on buns and top with mayonnaise mixture and desired toppings.

Variations

You can also cook the tuna in a large skillet in 2 tbsp (30 mL) hot oil over medium-high heat for 4 minutes or until desired degree of doneness.

You can substitute reduced-fat mayonnaise for the regular mayonnaise.

Tip: Use a sturdy bun for these burgers.

Tuna Sliders

Serves 6

I love to serve these as appetizers, but sometimes we fill up on these and just eat them with a salad.

2	cans (6 oz/170 g) water-packed tuna, drained (see Tips, right)	2
1 tbsp	Dijon mustard	15 mL
1	clove garlic, chopped	1
½ cup	panko bread crumbs	125 mL
1	large egg, lightly beaten	1
1 tbsp	drained capers, rinsed	15 mL
¼ tsp	freshly ground black pepper	1 mL
2 tbsp	butter or olive oil	30 mL
6	mini hamburger buns, split	6

Toppings, optional

Lemon slices
Hot sauce
Homemade Mayonnaise (page 321) or store-bought

1. In a large bowl, combine tuna, Dijon, garlic, bread crumbs, egg, capers and pepper. Shape into 8 patties, each about ½ inch (1 cm) thick.

2. In a large nonstick skillet, melt butter over medium-high heat. Fry patties, turning once, for 2 to 3 minutes per side or until golden brown (be careful not to overcook to prevent drying out). Serve on buns with desired toppings.

Variation

You can substitute an equal amount of salmon for the tuna.

Tips: If you want to make these ahead, prepare the tuna mixture and cover and refrigerate overnight. Then, cook the next day.

I prefer to purchase tuna packed in water as it is lower in fat and has a great taste.

Salmon Burgers

Serves 4

When I gave my good friend, Kelly, this recipe she said she starting making them once a week as a staple main course that even her kids would eat.

1/3 cup	plain nonfat or Greek yogurt	75 mL
1 tbsp	whole-grain Dijon mustard	15 mL
2	large egg whites	2
1/2 cup	chopped onion	125 mL
1/2 cup	chopped celery	125 mL
1 cup	panko bread crumbs, divided	250 mL
1/4 tsp	dried basil	1 mL
1/8 tsp	freshly ground black pepper	0.5 mL
2	cans (each 7 oz/213 g) wild Alaskan red salmon, skin removed and drained (see Tip, right)	2
4 tsp	olive oil	20 mL
4	hamburger buns, split	4
	Fresh basil sprigs, optional	

1. In a large bowl, combine yogurt, mustard, and egg whites. Set aside.

2. In a nonstick skillet coated with cooking spray, sauté onion and celery over medium-high heat for 4 minutes or until tender. Let cool slightly.

3. In a large bowl, combine onion mixture, yogurt mixture, 1/2 cup (125 mL) of the bread crumbs, dried basil and pepper. Add salmon and toss gently. Cover and refrigerate and let chill for 10 minutes.

4. Divide salmon mixture into 4 equal patties, about 1/2 inch (1 cm) thick. Coat patties equally with remaining bread crumbs.

5. In a large nonstick skillet, heat oil over medium-high heat. Fry patties, turning once, for 4 minutes per side or until lightly browned and hot in the center. Serve salmon burgers on buns and top with fresh basil, if using.

Tip: Look for canned salmon in the grocery store where canned tuna is sold. I prefer the canned wild Alaskan sockeye salmon.

Fish Burgers

Serves 4

Tartar sauce, lime juice and lime zest flavor these fish burgers to perfection. I like to serve these with a side salad and a cold beer.

1 cup	Tartar Sauce (page 333) or store-bought	250 mL
1 tsp	grated lime zest	5 mL
2 tbsp	freshly squeezed lime juice	30 mL
1/4 cup	butter or margarine, divided	60 mL
1 lb	skinless tilapia fillets (see Tip, below)	500 g
1/4 cup	dry bread crumbs	60 mL
1	large egg, lightly beaten	1
1	clove garlic, minced	1
2 tsp	lemon pepper	10 mL
4	lettuce leaves	4
4	buns, split and toasted	4

Tip: If you can't find tilapia, use any mild white fish.

1. In a small bowl, stir together tartar sauce, lime zest and lime juice.

2. In a large nonstick skillet, melt 2 tbsp (30 mL) of the butter over medium heat. Fry fish fillets, turning once, for about 5 minutes per side or until fish flakes when tested with a fork. Transfer to a large bowl and use a fork to flake fish into small pieces. Add 1/3 cup (75 mL) of the tartar sauce mixture, bread crumbs, egg, garlic and lemon pepper, stirring gently to combine. Shape into 4 equal patties, about 3/4 inch (2 cm) thick.

3. In same skillet, melt remaining butter over medium-high heat. In batches, fry patties, turning once, for 5 minutes per side or until golden brown and hot in the center. Serve immediately on buns with lettuce and remaining tartar sauce.

Variation

Substitute panko bread crumbs for the regular bread crumbs in this recipe to create light burgers with a wonderful texture.

Creole Shrimp Sliders

Serves 8

I like to serve these over mixed greens or spinach leaves for a light, healthy supper.

5 tbsp	olive oil, divided	75 mL
1/2 cup	chopped onion (about 1 small)	125 mL
4 cups	chopped cooked shrimp	1 L
1 cup	cracker crumbs, such as crushed saltine crackers, bread crumbs or panko bread crumbs	250 mL
1/2 cup	skim milk	125 mL
1 tbsp	Creole seasoning (see Tip, right)	15 mL
1/4 tsp	hot pepper flakes	1 mL
1	egg white, lightly beaten	1
	Cocktail Sauce (page 326) or store-bought or Tarragon Cocktail Sauce (Variation, page 326)	
	Fresh tarragon sprigs, optional	

1. In a large skillet, heat 2 tbsp (30 mL) of the oil over medium-high. Sauté onion for 5 minutes or until tender. Let cool.

2. In a large bowl, combine shrimp, cracker crumbs, milk, cooled onion, Creole seasoning, hot pepper flakes and egg white. Shape into 8 equal patties, about 3/4 inch (2 cm) thick. Cover and chill for 2 hours.

3. In skillet, heat remaining oil over medium-high heat. Sauté shrimp cakes, in batches, for 4 to 5 minutes per side or until golden. Drain on paper towels. Serve with Cocktail Sauce and garnish with tarragon, if desired.

Tip: If you can't find Creole seasoning, use 1/2 tsp (2 mL) each paprika, garlic powder and cayenne pepper.

Lobster Cakes with Rémoulade Sauce

Serves 4

I created these lobster cakes as a takeoff of shrimp and crab cakes that we make often in the South. This doesn't have to be just a special occasion recipe. See my tip below for finding economical lobster.

Rémoulade Sauce

1 cup	Homemade Mayonnaise (page 321) or store-bought	250 mL
1½ tbsp	Dijon mustard	22 mL
1 tbsp	grated lemon zest	15 mL
1 tbsp	sweet pickle relish	15 mL
1 tbsp	drained capers, rinsed	15 mL
¼ tsp	paprika	1 mL
3 tbsp	freshly squeezed lemon juice, divided	45 mL
¼ cup	chopped parsley, divided	60 mL
½ tsp	hot pepper flakes, divided	2 mL

¾ cup	Italian-seasoned bread crumbs	175 mL
1	large egg, lightly beaten	1
3 tbsp	light mayonnaise	45 mL
1 tsp	Dijon mustard	5 mL
1 lb	shelled frozen lobster chunks, preferably squat lobster, thawed and chopped (see Tip, right)	500 g
2 tbsp	butter or margarine	30 mL
4	kaiser buns, split	4

- **Food processor**

1. *Rémoulade Sauce:* In a food processor, combine mayonnaise, mustard, lemon zest, relish, capers, paprika, 2 tbsp (30 mL) of the lemon juice, 2 tbsp (30 mL) of the parsley and ¼ tsp (1 mL) of the hot pepper flakes. Cover and refrigerate until ready to serve.

2. In a separate bowl, combine bread crumbs, egg, mayonnaise, mustard, remaining lemon juice, parsley and hot pepper flakes. Gently fold in lobster. Shape into 4 equal patties, ¾ inch (2 cm) thick. Cover and chill for 1 hour.

3. In a large nonstick skillet, melt butter over medium-high heat. In batches, fry lobster cakes, turning once, for 3 minutes per side or until golden brown and hot in the center. Drain on paper towels. Place lobster cakes on buns and top with Rémoulade Sauce.

Tip: Squat lobster is the smallest lobster in the world found mainly in the Pacific coastal waters of El Salvador. If you can't find squat lobster, just use chopped, cooked lobster meat. Usually 2 (1½ lbs/750 g) live Maine lobsters equals 2½ cups (625 mL) chopped, cooked meat.

Crab Cake Burgers

Serves 4

I love crab cakes from Baltimore or New Orleans, but making them at home can be just as wonderful. Crab cake night is always a special night, for sure.

1 lb	cooked lump crabmeat	500 g
½ cup	Italian bread crumbs	125 mL
1 tbsp	Cajun seasoning	15 mL
1 tsp	grated lemon zest	5 mL
¼ cup	freshly squeezed lemon juice	60 mL
1	large egg, lightly beaten	1
1 cup	shredded cabbage	250 mL
4	hamburger buns, split and toasted	4

Topping, optional

	Tartar Sauce (page 333) or store-bought

- **Preheat greased grill pan to medium**

1. In a large bowl, combine crabmeat, bread crumbs, Cajun seasoning, lemon zest, lemon juice and egg. Shape into 4 patties, about ¾ inch (2 cm) thick. Cover and refrigerate for at least 30 minutes.

2. Place burgers on preheated grill pan, and grill, turning once, for 4 to 6 minutes per side or until golden brown and hot in the center. Serve on buns with shredded cabbage, and tartar sauce, if desired.

Tip: Crab cakes always work better when I refrigerate them after shaping and let them stand for a while. I like to make them ahead or the night before.

Veggie Bulgur Burgers

Serves 4

Bulgur, a staple in the Middle East, is made from wheat kernels that have been steamed, dried and crushed. It can be simmered in broth or water and used in salads and homemade veggie burgers.

½ cup	bulgur	125 mL
1	can (14 to 19 oz/398 to 540 mL) pinto beans, drained and rinsed	1
½ cup	old-fashioned rolled oats	125 mL
2	cloves garlic, minced	2
½ cup	freshly grated Parmesan cheese	125 mL
½ cup	finely grated carrots	125 mL
2 tbsp	chopped onion	30 mL
1 tsp	soy sauce	5 mL
½ tsp	ground cumin	2 mL
½ tsp	kosher salt	2 mL
1	large egg, lightly beaten	1
3 tbsp	yellow cornmeal	45 mL

Toppings, optional

	Sliced tomatoes
	Avocado slices
	Alfalfa sprouts
	Fresh cilantro sprigs
	Ketchup
	Mayonnaise

- **Food processor**
- **Instant-read thermometer**

1. In a saucepan over high heat, bring 1 cup (250 mL) water to a boil. Add bulgur. Reduce heat to low and cook for 15 minutes or until water is absorbed.

2. In a food processor, pulse bulgur, beans, oats, garlic, cheese, carrots, onion, soy sauce, cumin, salt and egg until combined. Shape into 4 equal patties, about ½ inch (1 cm) thick. Lightly coat both sides with cornmeal.

3. In a large skillet, heat oil over medium-high heat. Fry burgers, turning once, for 5 minutes per side or until an instant-read thermometer registers 160°F (71°C) or until hot in center. Serve on buns with desired toppings.

Tip: You can make these ahead by completing Steps 1 and 2 and chilling in the refrigerator for up to 1 day.

Black Bean Burgers

Serves 4

This is a really popular recipe that is simple to prepare. Serve on a bun or in a lettuce wrap and top with your favorite toppings.

1	can (14 to 19 oz/398 to 540 mL) black beans, drained and rinsed	1
3/4 cup	panko bread crumbs	175 mL
2 tbsp	finely chopped red onion	30 mL
1/2 tsp	ground cumin	2 mL
1/2 tsp	sea salt	2 mL
1/8 tsp	hot pepper flakes	0.5 mL
1	large egg, lightly beaten	1
3 tbsp	yellow cornmeal	45 mL
3 tbsp	olive oil	45 mL
4	hamburger buns, split and toasted	4

Toppings, optional

	Lettuce leaves
	Salsa
	Avocado
	Shredded Monterey Jack cheese or slices

- **Instant-read thermometer**

1. In a large bowl, mash beans with a fork. Stir in bread crumbs, red onion, cumin, salt, hot pepper flakes and egg. Shape into 4 equal patties, about 1/2 inch (1 cm) thick. Lightly coat both sides with cornmeal.

2. In a large nonstick skillet, heat olive oil over medium heat. Fry patties for 5 minutes per side or until an instant-read thermometer registers 160°F (71°C) or until hot in center and lightly browned. Place burgers on buns and serve with desired toppings.

Tip: To make these ahead of time, prep burgers and refrigerate for up to 8 hours.

Portobello-Onion Burger

Serves 4

This burger is for all of my vegetarian friends. The flavors of this burger are wonderful, and you won't miss the meat.

1 cup	fresh bread crumbs	250 mL
1 cup	freshly grated Parmesan cheese	250 mL
4 tbsp	olive oil, divided	60 mL
2 tbsp	chopped fresh chives	30 mL
2 tbsp	chopped fresh parsley	30 mL
$\frac{1}{2}$ tsp	salt	2 mL
$\frac{1}{4}$ tsp	freshly ground black pepper	1 mL
4	portobello mushrooms, stemmed	4
2 cups	baby spinach leaves	500 mL
1 cup	sliced onion (about 1 small)	250 mL
1 cup	yellow bell pepper (about 1 small)	250 mL
1	clove garlic, minced	1
	Salt and freshly ground black pepper	
3	Roma (plum) tomatoes, thinly sliced	3

- **Preheat greased barbecue grill to medium-high or broiler**

1. In a small bowl, combine bread crumbs, Parmesan, 2 tbsp (30 mL) of the oil, chives, parsley, salt and pepper. Set aside.

2. In a large skillet, heat remaining oil over medium heat. Sauté mushrooms for 5 minutes or until lightly browned. Set aside.

3. Add spinach, onion, bell pepper and garlic to skillet, adding more oil if necessary, and sauté over medium heat for 5 minutes or until tender. Add salt and pepper to taste.

4. Place mushroom caps on a work surface. Fill each cap with $\frac{1}{2}$ cup (125 mL) of the vegetable mixture. Top with tomato slices and sprinkle with bread crumb mixture. Place on a baking sheet and grill or broil for 5 minutes or until cheese is melted.

Tip: If you can't find Roma tomatoes (also known as plum), any ripe thinly sliced tomatoes work great.

Lentil Burgers with Yogurt Sauce

Serves 4

I love cooking with lentils because they are high in fiber, protein and B vitamins and low in fat. Best of all, they taste great in this recipe.

⅓ cup	dry bread crumbs	75 mL
2	cloves garlic, chopped	2
2 tsp	ground cumin	10 mL
½ tsp	hot pepper flakes	2 mL
¼ tsp	kosher salt	1 mL
¼ tsp	freshly ground black pepper	1 mL
¾ cup	canned or cooked lentils, rinsed, drained and cooled (see Tips, right)	175 mL
¼ cup	cooked white rice	60 mL
3 tbsp	olive oil, divided	45 mL
2	large egg whites	2
	Cilantro-Yogurt Sauce (page 317), optional	

- **Food processor**

1. In a food processor, pulse bread crumbs, garlic, cumin, hot pepper flakes, salt and pepper. Add lentils, rice, 1 tbsp (15 mL) of the oil and egg whites until coarsely chopped.

2. Divide mixture into 4 equal burgers, about ¾ inch (2 cm) thick.

3. In a large nonstick skillet, heat remaining oil over medium-low heat. Add burgers and fry for 8 to 10 minutes per side or until crisp and browned. Transfer to a paper-towel lined plate to drain. Serve with Cilantro-Yogurt Sauce, if desired.

Tips: Lentils can be found where dried beans are sold in most grocery stores.

To cook lentils, place in a small saucepan and cover with water by 1 inch (2.5 cm). Bring to a boil. Reduce heat and simmer, covered, for 15 to 20 minutes or until lentils are tender but still holding their shape. Drain well.

Wraps

Vegetable Enchiladas

Serves 4

The zucchini, squash and corn pair wonderfully together in these enchiladas. This is a great vegetarian recipe.

8	6-inch (15 cm) corn tortillas	8
1 cup	thinly sliced zucchini	250 mL
1 cup	thinly sliced yellow summer squash (zucchini)	250 mL
1½ cups	shredded Monterey Jack cheese, divided	375 mL
1 cup	cooked corn kernels, drained (see Tip, right)	250 mL
1 cup	cooked brown rice	250 mL
⅓ cup	sour cream	75 mL
¼ cup	chopped green onions	60 mL
¼ tsp	salt	1 mL
¼ tsp	freshly ground pepper	1 mL
2	cans (each 10 oz/284 mL) diced tomatoes with green chiles	2

- **Preheat oven to 350°F (180°C)**
- **11- by 7-inch (28 by 18 cm) glass baking dish, coated with cooking spray**

1. Wrap tortillas in foil and bake in preheated oven for 7 minutes. Keep warm.

2. In a pot of boiling water, blanch zucchini and summer squash for 2 minutes. Drain. Combine zucchini, squash, ½ cup (125 mL) of the cheese, corn, rice, sour cream, green onions, salt and pepper.

3. Place tortillas on a work surface. Spoon zucchini mixture equally down center of tortillas. Fold both edges over and place, seam side down, in prepared baking dish. Top with tomatoes.

4. Bake in preheated oven for 15 minutes. Sprinkle with remaining cheese and bake for 4 minutes or until cheese is melted.

Tip: I used canned corn, but fresh grilled or roasted corn would be great, too.

Veggie and Goat Cheese Wraps

I love a great veggie wrap. Fresh veggies, nuts and hummus tucked inside a flavored tomato-basil tortilla create a wrap that is a home run.

4	8-inch (20 cm) tomato basil-flavored flour tortillas, warmed (see Tips, right and page 197)	4
½ cup	Hummus (page 313) or store-bought	125 mL
1 cup	spring mix greens (see Tip, page 55)	250 mL
1 cup	cucumber slices	250 mL
2	tomatoes, thinly sliced	2
1	red bell pepper, cut into thin slices	1
1 cup	alfalfa sprouts	250 mL
½ cup	whole almonds	125 mL
½ cup	green pumpkin seeds (pepitas), toasted (see Tips, right)	125 mL
4 oz	crumbled goat cheese	125 g

1. Place tortillas on a work surface. Spread 2 tbsp (30 mL) of the hummus down center of tortillas. Arrange greens, cucumber, tomatoes, bell pepper and sprouts over hummus. Top with almonds, pepitas and goat cheese. Fold both edges over filling. Roll up and serve immediately.

Variation

Use feta cheese instead of the goat cheese and whole wheat tortillas instead of tomato basil.

Tips: Flavored wraps are widely available, including plain, wheat, pesto, spinach, tomato basil, multigrain and low carb. Feel free to substitute any of your favorites in these recipes.

Pepitas, or pumpkin seeds, are wonderful roasted or toasted. To toast, place on a lightly greased baking sheet in 300°F (150°C) oven, tossing occasionally, for 45 minutes or until golden brown. You can find them at health food or gourmet grocery stores. They are a great source of protein, iron and zinc.

Classic Spinach Salad Wraps

Serves 4

This twist on spinach salad is really easy to prepare. If you don't have time to make the dressing, use your favorite store-bought dressing instead.

Mustard Dressing

⅓ cup	olive oil	75 mL
3 tbsp	white wine vinegar	45 mL
1 tbsp	coarse-grain mustard	15 mL
1 tbsp	liquid honey	15 mL
⅛ tsp	freshly ground black pepper	0.5 mL

4	8-inch (20 cm) flour tortillas	4
1	package (10 oz/300 g) baby spinach leaves	1
8	slices bacon, cooked	8
1 cup	sliced fresh mushrooms (see Tip, right)	250 mL
2	hard-boiled eggs, thinly sliced	2
4 oz	crumbled goat cheese	125 g

1. *Mustard Dressing:* In a small bowl, whisk together oil, vinegar, mustard, honey and pepper. Set aside.

2. Place tortillas on a work surface. Arrange spinach, bacon, mushrooms and egg slices equally in center of each tortilla. Drizzle each with 1 tbsp (15 mL) of dressing and goat cheese. Fold both edges over filling. Roll up and serve immediately.

Variation

Feel free to omit the goat cheese in this recipe. I like it for added flavor and texture.

Tip: Refrigerate mushrooms for up to 4 days. Make sure you clean them well with moist paper towels.

Nacho Wraps

Serves 4

Instead of making classic nachos, I love to serve them this way. Kids really enjoy these!

¾ cup	refried beans	175 mL
2 tbsp	green chiles (see Tips, right)	30 mL
½ tsp	taco seasoning mix	2 mL
4	8-inch (20 cm) flour tortillas, warmed (see Tip, page 197)	4
¼ cup	Guacamole (page 336) or store-bought	60 mL
2 cups	shredded lettuce	500 mL
1 cup	crushed tortilla chips	250 mL
1 cup	diced tomatoes	250 mL
1 cup	shredded Cheddar cheese	250 mL
2 tbsp	chopped fresh cilantro	30 mL
½ cup	Pico de Gallo (page 328) or store-bought salsa	125 mL
½ cup	sour cream	125 mL

Toppings, optional

	Nacho cheese dip
	Chopped jalapeños

1. In a medium bowl, combine beans, green chiles and taco seasoning.

2. Place tortillas on a work surface. Spread bean mixture equally in center of each tortilla. Spread guacamole over beans. Arrange lettuce, tortilla chips, tomatoes, cheese, cilantro, salsa, sour cream and desired toppings over top. Fold both edges over filling. Roll up and serve immediately.

Variations

Add 1½ cups (375 mL) chopped cooked chicken and arrange over bean mixture. Add remaining ingredients and proceed with recipe.

You could also use 1½ cups (375 mL) black beans instead of refried beans.

Tips: I like to prep all of my ingredients ahead of time for this, then all I have to do is assemble.

I use green chiles from the can. Just drain and use.

Trail Mix Wraps

Serves 4

Since I eat yogurt, cereal and fruit often for breakfast, I made this into a wrap. This makes a great after school snack.

2 cups	Greek yogurt	500 mL
1/2 cup	dried apricots	250 mL
1/2 cup	dried cranberries	250 mL
1/4 cup	chopped almonds, toasted	60 mL
1/4 cup	chopped walnuts, toasted	60 mL
1 tbsp	liquid honey	15 mL
1 1/4 cups	granola	300 mL
4	8-inch (20 cm) flour tortillas, warmed (see Tip, page 197)	4
1/4 cup	apricot preserves or jam	60 mL

1. In a small bowl, combine yogurt, apricots, cranberries, almonds, walnuts and honey. Fold in granola.

2. Place tortillas on a work surface. Spread apricot preserves equally in center of each tortilla. Add yogurt mixture. Fold both edges over filling. Roll up and refrigerate or serve immediately.

Variation

Substitute 1 cup (250 mL) chopped bananas or peaches for the dried fruit and regular low-fat yogurt for the Greek yogurt.

Crunchy Vegetable Wraps

Serves 4

Chilled vegetable wraps are perfect for no-cook dinners, especially during the summertime.

1 1/2 cups	shredded red cabbage	375 mL
1	medium tomato, chopped	1
1 cup	shredded carrots	250 mL
1/2 cup	diced red onion	125 mL
1	clove garlic, minced	1
4 oz	crumbled feta or blue cheese	125 g
1/2 cup	Italian dressing	125 mL
4	8-inch (20 cm) flour tortillas	4
4	leaf lettuce leaves	4
1 cup	alfalfa sprouts	250 mL

1. In a large bowl, toss together cabbage, tomato, carrots, red onion, garlic, cheese and dressing. Refrigerate for 1 hour to drain.

2. Place tortillas on a work surface. Top tortillas equally with lettuce leaves, alfalfa sprouts and cabbage mixture. Fold both edges over filling. Roll up and refrigerate or serve immediately.

Tip: Feel free to add or delete any of your favorite vegetables and substitute spinach or sun-dried tomato-flavored tortillas.

Warm Italian Wraps

If you're in the mood for something Italian, this recipe is great. The roasted vegetables are also fabulous on top of a pizza.

2	eggplants, cut into 1-inch (2.5 cm) pieces	2
3	Roma (plum) tomatoes, thinly sliced	3
1 cup	sliced onion	250 mL
1 cup	sliced red bell pepper	250 mL
1 cup	sliced yellow bell red peppers	250 mL
2	cloves garlic, minced	2
1 tbsp	Italian seasoning	15 mL
1/4 tsp	hot pepper flakes	1 mL
2 tbsp	balsamic vinegar	30 mL
2 tbsp	olive oil	30 mL
4	8-inch (20 cm) white or whole wheat tortillas	4
4	slices mozzarella cheese	4
2 oz	freshly grated Parmesan cheese	60 g

- **Preheat oven to 450°F (230°C)**
- **Large baking sheet, lightly greased**

1. On a prepared baking sheet, arrange eggplant, tomatoes, onion and red and yellow bell peppers. Sprinkle with garlic, Italian seasoning and hot pepper flakes. Drizzle with balsamic vinegar and olive oil. Bake vegetables in preheated oven for 30 minutes or until tender.

2. Place tortillas on a work surface. Arrange vegetables equally in center of each tortilla. Top with mozzarella and Parmesan cheeses. Fold both edges over filling and wrap each filled tortilla in foil. Reduce oven temperature to 325°F (160°C) and bake for 5 minutes or until cheese is melted.

Tip: I used shredded mozzarella cheese rather than fresh mozzarella packed in brine, because it melts better.

Greek Salad Wraps

Serves 4

This wrap is a twist on a classic Greek salad. I love to add shrimp and chicken to this (see Variation, right).

4 cups	torn romaine lettuce	1 L
1 cup	thinly sliced cucumber	250 mL
½ cup	sliced grape tomatoes	125 mL
½ cup	pitted kalamata olives	125 mL
¼ cup	chopped red onion	60 mL
¼ cup	crumbled feta cheese	60 mL
2 tbsp	chopped flat-leaf Italian parsley	30 mL
¼ cup	red wine vinegar	60 mL
¼ cup	olive oil	60 mL
4	10-inch (25 cm) whole wheat flour tortillas	4
	Salt and freshly ground black pepper	

1. In a large bowl, gently combine lettuce, cucumber, tomatoes, olives, red onion, feta and parsley. Drizzle with vinegar and oil and toss to coat.

2. Place tortillas on a work surface. Spoon lettuce mixture equally in center of each tortilla. Sprinkle with salt and pepper to taste. Fold both edges over filling. Roll up and serve immediately.

Variation

Add 1 cup (250 mL) chopped cooked chicken breast or 8 oz (250 g) cooked shrimp if you want some extra protein in this recipe.

Tip: Substitute store-bought Greek dressing for the vinegar and olive oil in this recipe.

Almond Butter, Honey and Banana Chips Wraps

Serves 4

My running partner, Caroline, gave me the idea to add banana chips to this sandwich for some extra crunch.

4	(8-inch/20 cm) white or whole wheat tortillas	4
¼ cup	almond butter	60 mL
2 tbsp	liquid honey	30 mL
1 cup	sliced banana	250 mL
½ cup	banana chips	125 mL
1 cup	granola	250 mL

1. Place tortillas on a work surface. Spread almond butter and honey equally in center of tortillas. Top with banana, banana chips and granola. Fold both edges over filling. Roll up and serve immediately.

Variation

Almond Butter-Apricot Wrap: Omit honey, bananas and banana chips. Substitute apricot preserves or jam and dried apricots.

Grilled Ham, Goat Cheese
and Figs (page 84)

Grilled Crab, Mango and Avocado (page 86)

Lamb Burgers (page 173)

Veggie Bulgur Burgers (page 181)

Quinoa Tabbouleh Wraps (page 193)

Vietnamese Pork Wraps (page 216)

Croque Monsieur (page 247)

Banh Mi (page 254)

Quinoa Tabbouleh Wraps

Serves 4

This recipe was shared by a friend of mine, Kiel, who is a great runner and clever cook. Quinoa (KEEN-wah) is a tiny grain, often called "supergrain" because it's rich in so many nutrients, particularly protein.

1 cup	quinoa, rinsed and drained	250 mL
1/2 tsp	salt	2 mL
3 cups	chopped tomatoes (about 3 medium)	750 mL
1 1/4 cups	finely chopped cucumber	300 mL
3/4 cup	chopped red bell peppers	175 mL
3/4 cup	chopped green bell peppers	175 mL
2 tbsp	chopped green onions	30 mL
2 tbsp	chopped flat-leaf Italian parsley	30 mL
1/3 cup	freshly squeezed lemon juice	75 mL
1/4 cup	olive oil	60 mL
	Salt and freshly ground black pepper, optional	
4	8-inch (20 cm) flour tortillas	4
4	lettuce leaves	4

1. In a large saucepan over high heat, bring 2 cups (500 mL) water, quinoa and salt to a boil. Reduce heat and simmer for 15 minutes. Drain well and let cool.

2. In a large bowl, combine tomatoes, cucumber, red and green bell peppers, green onions and parsley. Drizzle with lemon juice, olive oil, and salt and pepper, if using.

3. Place tortillas on a work surface. Line each tortilla with a lettuce leaf. Spread quinoa mixture equally in center of tortillas over lettuce leaves. Fold both edges over filling. Roll up and serve immediately.

Tip: This recipe can be halved or if you have leftovers, this is a great, healthy salad to have on hand.

Roasted Vegetable Wraps

Serves 4

This great vegetarian wrap is filled with some of my favorite roasted vegetables. Feel free to add or delete some of your own favorite vegetables.

1	large red bell pepper, sliced	1
1	yellow bell pepper, sliced	1
1	red onion, chopped	1
1	yellow squash (zucchini), sliced into ¼-inch (0.5 cm) pieces	1
1	zucchini, thinly sliced	1
¼ cup	olive oil, divided	60 mL
¼ cup	balsamic vinegar, divided	60 mL
½ tsp	kosher salt	2 mL
½ tsp	freshly ground black pepper	2 mL
4	8-inch (20 cm) flour tortilla wraps, warmed (see Tip, page 197)	4
½ cup	crumbled goat cheese	125 mL
¼ cup	chopped fresh basil	60 mL

- **Preheat oven to 500°F (260°C)**
- **Large baking sheet, lightly greased**

1 On a prepared baking sheet, place red and yellow bell peppers, red onion, squash and zucchini. Drizzle with 2 tbsp (30 mL) of the olive oil and 2 tbsp (30 mL) of the vinegar. Sprinkle with salt and pepper. Roast in preheated oven for 30 minutes or until tender. Toss with remaining olive oil and vinegar.

2. Place tortillas on a work surface. Divide vegetables and cheese equally among tortillas. Top with basil. Fold both edges over filling. Roll up and serve immediately.

Tip: You can roast the vegetables on parchment paper for less cleanup and still great roasted texture. It also removes the need for oil.

Southwestern Wraps

This vegetarian wrap is super easy to make. It's one of my favorite weeknight wraps.

1	can (14 to 19 oz/398 to 540 mL) black beans, rinsed and drained	1
1 cup	Pico de Gallo (page 328) or store-bought salsa	250 mL
1	package (8 oz/250 g) cream cheese, softened	1
2 tbsp	freshly squeezed lime juice	30 mL
2	cloves garlic, coarsely chopped	2
4	10-inch (25 cm) flour tortillas, warmed (see Tip, page 197)	4
1 cup	shredded iceberg lettuce	250 mL
1	can (11 oz/330 mL) Mexican-style corn, drained well	1
2	green onions, chopped	2
2 cups	shredded Monterey Jack cheese	500 mL
	Toppings	
	Pico de Gallo (page 328) or store-bought salsa	
	Sour cream	
	Guacamole (page 336) or store-bought	
	Chopped jalapeño pepper	

- **Food processor**

1. In a food processor, purée black beans, salsa, cream cheese, lime juice and garlic until smooth, stopping to scrape down sides of bowl.

2. Place tortillas on a work surface. Spread bean mixture equally in center of each tortilla. Arrange lettuce, corn, green onions and cheese over bean mixture. Fold both edges over filling. Roll up and serve with desired toppings.

Chicken Fajita Wraps

Serves 4

These classic fajitas are very easy to prepare and always a crowd pleaser.

1 lb	boneless skinless chicken breasts or cutlets, cut into thin slices	500 g
1/2 cup + 1 tbsp	freshly squeezed lime juice, divided	140 mL
2	cloves garlic, minced	2
1 tbsp	chili powder	15 mL
1 tsp	ground cumin	5 mL
1 tsp	salt	5 mL
1/2 tsp	freshly ground black pepper	2 mL
1 tbsp	olive oil	15 mL
1 cup	sliced onion	250 mL
1 cup	sliced green and red bell peppers	250 mL
4	10-inch (25 cm) flour tortillas, warmed (see Tip, page 197)	4
1 cup	diced tomatoes	250 mL
1/4 cup	chopped fresh cilantro	60 mL

Toppings, optional

	Sour cream
	Salsa
	Chopped green onions

1. In a shallow dish, combine chicken, 1/2 cup (125 mL) of the lime juice, garlic, chili powder, cumin, salt and pepper. Cover and refrigerate for at least 2 hours.

2. Remove chicken from marinade, discarding marinade. In a large skillet, heat oil over medium-high heat. Sauté chicken for 5 to 7 minutes or until chicken is no longer pink inside. Add onion, bell peppers and remaining 1 tbsp (15 mL) of lime juice and sauté for 2 minutes or until vegetables are tender.

3. Place tortillas on a work surface. Arrange chicken and vegetables equally in center of each tortilla. Top with tomatoes, cilantro and desired toppings. Fold both edges over filling. Roll up and serve immediately.

Variations

Steak Fajita Wraps: You can substitute 1 lb (500 g) thinly sliced beef flank steak for the chicken. Sauté over medium-high heat until a hint of pink remains in beef or until desired doneness.

If you're in a hurry, use 2 tbsp (30 mL) fajita seasoning to marinate the chicken and omit garlic, chili powder, cumin, salt and pepper.

Chicken and Asparagus Wraps

Serves 4

I love serving chicken with asparagus, and this combination works great in a wrap sandwich. Spread with a Classic Aïoli and sprinkle with Parmesan cheese.

½ cup	freshly squeezed lemon juice (about 3 lemons)	125 mL
6 tbsp	olive oil, divided	90 mL
2	cloves garlic, minced	2
1 tsp	sea salt, divided	5 mL
½ tsp	freshly ground black pepper, divided	2 mL
1½ lbs	boneless skinless chicken cutlets or chicken tenders, cut into thin strips	750 g
1 lb	asparagus, trimmed and cut into 1-inch (2.5 cm) pieces	500 g
4	8-inch (20 cm) flour tortillas, warmed (see Tip, right)	4
	Classic Aïoli (page 310)	
½ cup	freshly grated Parmesan cheese	125 mL

Toppings, optional

	Diced tomatoes
	Arugula Leaves

- **Large rimmed baking sheet, greased**
- **Preheat oven to 450°F (230°C)**

1. In a shallow dish, combine lemon juice, 2 tbsp (30 mL) of the olive oil, garlic, ¼ tsp (1 mL) each of the salt and pepper. Add chicken and coat well. Let stand at room temperature for 15 minutes or cover and refrigerate for up to 8 hours.

2. In a saucepan of boiling water, blanch asparagus for 2 minutes. Drain well. Arrange in a single layer on prepared baking sheet and sprinkle with remaining salt and pepper. Drizzle with 2 tbsp (30 mL) of olive oil. Bake in preheated oven for 6 to 8 minutes or until asparagus is tender. Set aside.

3. Meanwhile, in a large skillet, heat remaining oil over medium-high heat. Sauté chicken for 5 minutes or until no longer pink inside. Spread 1 tbsp (15 mL) Classic Aïoli equally along center of each tortilla. Arrange chicken, asparagus, Parmesan and desired toppings on top. Fold both edges over filling. Roll up and serve immediately.

Variation

Feel free to substitute thinly sliced turkey for the chicken in this sandwich.

Tip: To warm tortillas, place on a plate, layered with paper towels, alternating paper towels and tortillas, covering top layer with a towel. Microwave on High for 10 to 20 seconds or until warm.

Indian-Spiced Chicken Wraps

Serves 4

The flavors of a cardamom-spiced mixture combined with the Cucumber-Mango Raita make this chicken wrap very delicious.

1 tsp	ground cumin	5 mL
½ tsp	ground coriander	2 mL
½ tsp	ground cardamom	2 mL
½ tsp	salt	2 mL
¼ tsp	freshly ground black pepper	1 mL
¼ tsp	ground cinnamon	1 mL
1½ lbs	boneless skinless chicken cutlets	750 g
¼ cup	freshly squeezed lime juice	60 mL
2 tbsp	olive oil	30 mL
4	naan bread wraps, warmed	4
1 cup	Cucumber-Mango Raita (page 317)	250 mL
4	lettuce leaves	4

1. In a small bowl, combine cumin, coriander, cardamom, salt, pepper and cinnamon. Rub over chicken and drizzle with lime juice. Toss gently. Cover and refrigerate for at least 1 hour.

2. In a large skillet, heat olive oil over medium heat. In batches as necessary, fry cutlets, turning once, for about 4 minutes per side or until chicken is longer pink inside.

3. Place naan on a work surface. Place chicken equally in wraps with Cucumber-Mango Raita and lettuce leaves. Fold both edges over filling. Roll up and serve immediately.

Variation

Substitute four 6-inch (15 cm) flour tortillas for the naan wraps.

Tip: To grill chicken, preheat greased barbecue grill to medium-high. Place cutlets on preheated grill, cover and grill, turning once, for about 4 minutes per side or until no longer pink inside.

Buffalo Chicken Wraps

Serves 4

My kids love Buffalo chicken wings, and when I made this sandwich they were so excited. This is really fun to serve during or after my kids sporting events.

1 lb	boneless skinless chicken tenders	500 g
½ cup	hot wing sauce (approx.) (see Tips, right)	125 mL
¼ cup	plain yogurt	60 mL
¼ cup	crumbled blue cheese	60 mL
¼ tsp	hot pepper sauce (approx.)	1 mL
2 tbsp	olive oil	30 mL
4	8-inch (20 cm) flour tortillas, warmed (see Tip, page 197)	4
1 cup	shredded lettuce	250 mL
1	large tomato, diced	1

1. In shallow dish or resealable plastic bag, combine chicken and hot wing sauce. Cover or seal and marinate in refrigerator for at least 2 hours or for up to 8 hours.

2. In a bowl, combine yogurt, blue cheese and hot sauce. Set aside.

3. In a large nonstick skillet, heat oil over medium-high heat. Fry chicken tenders, turning once, for 4 minutes per side or until chicken is no longer pink inside.

4. Place tortillas on a work surface. Spread each with 1 tbsp (15 mL) of the blue cheese sauce. Arrange chicken, lettuce and tomato equally in center of tortillas. Top with additional hot wing or hot sauce, if using. Fold edges over filling. Roll up and serve immediately.

Tips: To grill chicken, preheat greased barbecue grill to medium-high. Place cutlets on preheated grill, cover and grill, turning once, for about 4 minutes per side or until no longer pink inside.

If you can't find hot wing sauce, also known as Buffalo wing sauce, combine 2 tbsp (30 mL) hot sauce, 2 tbsp (30 mL) white wine vinegar, 2 tsp (10 mL) extra virgin olive oil and ¼ tsp (1 mL) cayenne pepper.

Easy Spicy Chicken Quesadillas

Serves 4

These simple quesadillas can also be made with chicken, steak or shrimp. They are great for a family-friendly weeknight dinner.

4	boneless skinless chicken breasts, cut into 1-inch (2.5 cm) pieces	4
¼ cup	freshly squeezed lime juice, divided	60 mL
2 tbsp	fajita seasoning mix	30 mL
2 tbsp	olive oil	30 mL
½ cup	chopped red bell pepper	125 mL
½ cup	chopped green bell pepper	125 mL
4	10-inch (25 cm) flour tortillas	4
¼ cup	melted butter	60 mL
⅔ cup	Pico de Gallo (page 328) or store-bought salsa	150 mL
2 cups	shredded Monterey Jack or Cheddar cheese	500 mL

Toppings, optional

	Salsa or Pico de Gallo (page 328) or store-bought
	Sour cream or Greek yogurt

• **Large baking sheet, lightly greased**

1 Place chicken in a heavy-duty resealable plastic bag or on a shallow plate. Drizzle with 2 tbsp (30 mL) of the lime juice. Add fajita seasoning. Seal and shake or mix to coat. Refrigerate for at least 1 hour.

2. In a large nonstick skillet, heat oil over medium-high heat. Sauté chicken for 5 minutes. Add red and green bell peppers and remaining lime juice and sauté for 3 minutes or until chicken is no longer pink inside. Remove from skillet and wipe skillet clean.

3. Place tortillas on a work surface. Spread 1 tbsp (15 mL) of the butter on one side of each tortilla. Place tortillas in skillet, buttered side down. Arrange chicken, pepper mixture, Pico de Gallo and cheese equally on one half of each tortilla. Cook for 3 minutes and fold tortilla in half. Cook for 2 minutes per side or until lightly browned and cheese is melted. Serve immediately with desired toppings.

Tip: Feel free to omit the chicken and substitute additional vegetables for a vegetarian wrap. Or substitute steak, turkey or shrimp for the chicken.

Thai Chicken Curry Wraps

Serves 4

Curry, pineapple and almonds make this chicken recipe fabulous. The curry gives it an extra hint of flavor.

1½ cups	chopped cooked chicken	375 mL
⅓ cup	fresh diced pineapple	75 mL
¼ cup	finely chopped red onion	60 mL
¼ cup	chopped almonds, toasted	60 mL
2 tbsp	chopped fresh cilantro	30 mL
2 tbsp	freshly grated gingerroot	30 mL
¼ cup	Homemade Mayonnaise (page 321) or store-bought	60 mL
2 tbsp	plain nonfat yogurt	30 mL
1 tbsp	liquid honey	15 mL
1 tbsp	freshly squeezed lime juice	15 mL
1 tsp	Thai red curry paste (see Tip, right)	5 mL
4	8-inch (20 cm) flour tortillas	4
2 cups	fresh baby spinach, wilted	500 mL
	Vegetable cooking spray	

1. In a large bowl, combine chicken, pineapple, red onion, almonds, cilantro and ginger.

2. In a small bowl, combine mayonnaise, yogurt, honey, lime juice and curry paste. Toss lime-mayonnaise mixture with chicken mixture.

3. Place tortillas on a work surface. Place ½ cup (125 mL) of the chicken mixture on each tortilla. Add spinach. Fold both edges over filling. Heat a nonstick skillet over medium-high heat. Coat tortillas with cooking spray and cook until golden on each side. Roll up and serve warm.

Tip: Thai red curry paste can be found in a jar in the international section of the grocery store. It's a blend of herbs such as lemongrass, Thai ginger and fresh chiles. Serve as a seasoning or a soup base or mixed with your favorite marinades to add spice.

Chicken Thai Wraps

Serves 4

This simple chicken wrap has great Thai flavor using basil, lime juice and chili garlic paste.

2 cups	chopped cooked chicken	500 mL
¼ cup	Homemade Mayonnaise (page 321) or store-bought	60 mL
3 tbsp	chopped fresh basil	45 mL
2 tbsp	freshly squeezed lime juice	30 mL
1 tsp	chili garlic paste (see Tip, right)	5 mL
4	8-inch (20 cm) flour tortillas	4
2	avocados, chopped	2
1 cup	chopped lettuce	250 mL
⅓ cup	chopped cashews, toasted	75 mL

1. In a large bowl, combine chicken, mayonnaise, basil, lime juice and chili paste.

2. Place tortillas on a work surface. Divide chicken mixture equally among tortillas. Top with chopped avocados, lettuce and cashews. Fold both edges over filling. Roll up and serve immediately or chill, if desired.

Tip: You can find chili garlic paste in the international section of your local grocery store.

Caribbean Chicken Wraps

Serves 4

This was a recipe I developed for a kids' class, and it is a hit with the adults as well as the children.

2 cups	cooked chopped chicken (see Tips, right)	500 mL
⅓ cup	fresh diced pineapple	75 mL
⅓ cup	finely chopped red onion	75 mL
¼ cup	slivered almonds, toasted	60 mL
2 tbsp	chopped fresh cilantro	30 mL
2 tbsp	grated fresh gingerroot	30 mL
4	8-inch (20 cm) whole wheat flour tortillas, warmed (see Tips, 197)	4
¼ cup	Homemade Mayonnaise (page 321) or store-bought	60 mL
1½ cups	baby spinach leaves	375 mL
4	slices pepper Jack cheese	4

1. In a large bowl, combine chicken, pineapple, red onion, almonds, cilantro and ginger. Cover and refrigerate for at least 1 hour.

2. Place tortillas on a work surface. Spread 1 tbsp (15 mL) of the mayonnaise over each tortilla. Top equally with spinach leaves, chicken mixture and cheese. Fold both edges over filling. Roll up and serve immediately.

Variation

Substitute 1 lb (500 g) peeled cooked shrimp for the chicken in this recipe.

Tips: Use rotisserie chicken for the cooked chicken in this recipe.

Warm tortillas on a griddle or in the microwave on paper towels or a microwave-safe plate for 15 seconds to soften.

Curried Chicken Wraps

The combination of chutney, curry, cranberries and raisins make this chicken sandwich a "wow."

½ cup	Homemade Mayonnaise (page 321) or store-bought	125 mL
¼ cup	dry white wine	60 mL
¼ cup	chutney	60 mL
3 tbsp	curry powder	45 mL
2 cups	chopped cooked chicken	500 mL
2	large stalks celery, cut into ¾-inch (2 cm) pieces (about ¾ cup/175 mL)	2
¾ cup	chopped pecans, toasted	175 mL
¼ cup	chopped red onion	60 mL
2 tbsp	golden raisins	30 mL
2 tbsp	dried cranberries	30 mL
4	8-inch (20 cm) flour tortillas	4
1½ cups	watercress leaves (see Tips, left)	375 mL

1. In a medium bowl, combine mayonnaise, wine, chutney and curry powder. Add chicken, celery, pecans, red onion, raisins and cranberries. Cover and refrigerate for at least 1 hour.

2. Place tortillas on a work surface. Arrange chicken and watercress equally in center of each tortilla. Fold both edges over filling. Roll up and serve immediately.

Tips: Watercress can be purchased at most grocery stores and should be refrigerated in a plastic bag for up to 5 days. Wash and shake dry before using. Use leftover watercress in salads, soups and sandwiches and with meats, seafood or pork.

Feel free to use reduced-fat mayonnaise in this recipe.

Smoked Turkey Wraps

Serves 4

These simple turkey wraps are great with turkey bacon and the flavorful stone-ground mustard mixture.

¼ cup	stone-ground mustard	60 mL
1 tbsp	liquid honey	15 mL
½ tsp	apple cider vinegar	2 mL
4	10-inch (25 cm) flour tortillas	4
12 oz	thinly sliced smoked turkey	375 g
8	turkey bacon slices, cooked and crumbled	8
2 cups	loosely packed baby spinach or arugula leaves	500 mL

1. In a small bowl, whisk together mustard, honey and vinegar.

2. Place tortillas on a work surface. Spread honey mustard mixture equally in center of each tortilla. Top with turkey, bacon and spinach. Fold both edges over filling. Roll up and serve immediately or wrap in parchment paper and refrigerate for 30 minutes. Cut in half and serve immediately.

Tip: Substitute Dijon mustard for the stone-ground.

Turkey Hummus Wraps

Serves 4

Turkey and hummus paired with bacon and arugula make a wonderful lunchtime wrap for a picnic or a ladies lunch.

4	10-inch (25 cm) whole wheat flour tortillas	4
1 cup	Hummus (page 313) or store-bought	250 mL
12 oz	thinly sliced smoked turkey	375 g
8	turkey bacon slices, cooked and crumbled	8
2 cups	loosely packed arugula or baby spinach leaves	500 mL
2	Roma (plum) tomatoes, thinly sliced	2
1	small cucumber, thinly sliced	1

1. Place tortillas on a work surface. Spread Hummus equally over wraps. Top with turkey, bacon, arugula, tomatoes and cucumber. Fold both edges over filling. Roll up and serve immediately or chill, if desired.

Tip: To make ahead, wrap sandwiches in parchment paper to keep them fresh for up to 4 hours.

Turkey Spinach Cobb Wraps

Serves 4

This twist on Cobb salad was a hit with my friend Carrie and her family. They loved these with and without the addition of salsa.

4	10-inch (25 cm) flour tortillas	4
2 cups	baby spinach leaves	500 mL
8 oz	thinly sliced deli turkey	250 g
8	bacon slices, cooked	8
2	tomatoes, thinly sliced	2
2	avocados, thinly sliced	2
1 cup	shredded Cheddar cheese	250 mL
2	hard-boiled eggs, thinly sliced	2
1 cup	ranch dressing	250 mL
1/8 tsp	salt	0.5 mL
1/8 tsp	freshly ground black pepper	0.5 mL

1. Place tortillas on a work surface. Arrange spinach, turkey, bacon, tomatoes, avocados, Cheddar cheese and eggs equally in center of each tortilla. Top each with ranch dressing and sprinkle with salt and pepper. Fold both edges over filling. Roll up and serve immediately.

Tips: Feel free to add 1/4 cup (60 mL) salsa with the ranch dressing to give this an added kick.

Serve with Chipotle Aïoli (page 311), Creole Honey Mustard (page 324) or White Barbecue Sauce (page 325).

Thanksgiving Turkey Wraps

Serves 4

This is one of my family's fall favorites, which I make often for football get-togethers.

4	10-inch (25 cm) flour tortillas, warmed (see Tip, page 197)	4
¼ cup	spicy brown mustard, divided	60 mL
¼ cup	cranberry sauce, preferably whole berry, divided	60 mL
4	slices sharp (aged) Cheddar cheese	4
2 cups	chopped cooked turkey (see Tip, right)	500 mL
⅓ cup	pecan halves, toasted	75 mL
2 cups	mixed salad greens or arugula	500 mL

1. Place tortillas on a work surface. Spread 1 tbsp (15 mL) of the mustard and 1 tbsp (15 mL) of the cranberry sauce in center of each tortilla. Top each with one slice Cheddar cheese.

2. In a bowl, combine turkey and pecans. Spoon equally over cranberry mixture and top with lettuce. Fold both edges over filling. Roll up and serve immediately.

Variation

Leftover Thanksgiving Turkey Wrap: Omit mustard, cheese and pecans. For each wrap, spread tortillas with turkey, 1 tbsp (15 mL) mayonnaise, ½ cup (125 mL) leftover stuffing, 2 tbsp (30 mL) cranberries and 1 tbsp (15 mL) leftover gravy. Top with mixed greens and roll up.

Tip: If you don't have leftover turkey, purchase thinly sliced deli turkey.

Turkey Panzanella Wraps

Serves 4

When tomatoes are at their peak, this wrap is a great way to serve a version of the classic Italian panzanella salad.

2 cups	cooked turkey or chicken, chopped	500 mL
2	medium red tomatoes, seeded and chopped	2
2	medium yellow tomatoes, seeded and chopped	2
1	English cucumber, chopped	1
3 tbsp	chopped fresh basil	45 mL
2 tbsp	diced red onion	30 mL
2 cups	chopped French or Italian bread, cut into 1-inch (2.5 cm) cubes and toasted	500 mL
1/4 cup	olive oil	60 mL
1/4 cup	red wine vinegar	60 mL
2 tbsp	drained capers, rinsed	30 mL
4	10-inch (25 cm) flour tortillas, warmed (see Tip, page 197)	4
1 cup	mixed baby lettuce or spinach leaves	250 mL

1. In a large bowl, combine turkey, red and yellow tomatoes, cucumber, basil and red onion. Add bread cubes, olive oil, vinegar and capers. Toss gently to combine.

2. Place tortillas on a work surface. Spread tomato mixture and lettuce leaves equally in center of each tortilla. Fold both edges over filling. Roll up and serve immediately.

Variation

These wraps also work great in pita bread pockets.

Tip: The panzanella mixture makes wonderful leftovers. Serve these immediately because they can get soggy.

Barbecued Brisket Wraps

The best way to cook brisket is braised in liquid. Use either of my barbecue sauce recipes from the Condiment chapter: Barbecue Sauce (page 325) or Orange-Soy Barbecue Sauce (page 326).

2 lbs	beef brisket, trimmed of any visible fat (see Tips, right)	1 kg
2	cloves garlic, minced	2
1 tsp	salt	5 mL
1 tsp	freshly ground black pepper	5 mL
1	medium onion, thinly sliced	1
1½ cups	barbecue sauce, store-bought or homemade (pages 325 or 326)	375 mL
4	8-inch (20 cm) flour tortillas	4

- **Preheat oven to 350°F (180°C)**
- **Dutch oven**

1. Sprinkle brisket with garlic, salt and pepper. Place brisket in a large Dutch oven. Arrange onion on top and pour in barbecue sauce. Cover and bake in preheated oven for 3½ to 4 hours or until meat is tender.

2. Transfer beef to a bowl, reserving sauce in pot. Shred beef, using 2 forks, return meat to Dutch oven, mixing well.

3. Warm tortillas (see Tip, page 197). Spoon beef mixture equally over tortillas. Fold both edges over filling and roll up and serve immediately.

Variation

Serve on 8 crusty toasted bread slices, such as sourdough, for a Knife and Fork Brisket Sandwich.

Tips: To make in advance, prepare the meat 1 day ahead and shred. Refrigerate for up to 2 days and reheat before serving on sandwiches.

If you can't find a smaller brisket, ask the meat department to cut you one smaller.

Beef Tenderloin and Watercress Wraps

Serves 4

When I have leftover steak, I love to make this wrap sandwich. Watercress and avocados make it even better.

¼ cup	soy sauce	60 mL
1	clove garlic, minced	1
2 tbsp	butter, melted	30 mL
2 tbsp	chopped fresh rosemary	30 mL
2 tbsp	freshly ground black pepper	30 mL
1 lb	beef tenderloin	500 g
⅓ cup	Homemade Mayonnaise (page 321) or store-bought	75 mL
1 tbsp	Dijon mustard	15 mL
1 tbsp	freshly squeezed lemon juice	15 mL
2 tbsp	chopped fresh basil	30 mL
4	8-inch (20 cm) flour tortillas, warmed (see Tip, page 197)	4
1 cup	watercress leaves	250 mL
2	tomatoes, thinly sliced	2
2	avocados, thinly sliced	2

- **Preheat oven to 400°F (200°C)**
- **Large roasting pan**

1. In a large bowl, combine soy sauce, garlic, butter, rosemary and pepper. Rub over beef and refrigerate for at least 1 hour or for up to 8 hours.

2. Place beef in a large roasting pan and bake tenderloin in preheated oven for 40 minutes or until an instant-read thermometer registers 140°F (60°C) for rare. Let stand for 10 minutes before carving into thin slices.

3. In a small bowl, combine mayonnaise, Dijon, lemon juice and basil.

4. Place tortillas on a work surface. Spread 1 tbsp (15 mL) of the mayonnaise mixture equally in center of each tortilla. Top with tenderloin slices, watercress, tomatoes and avocados. Fold both edges over filling. Roll up and serve immediately.

Thai Beef Salad Wraps

This sandwich is a twist of a favorite local Thai restaurant's Thai beef salad. It is even better served in a tortilla.

1/2 cup	freshly squeezed lime juice	125 mL
1/4 cup	chopped fresh cilantro	60 mL
2	cloves garlic, minced	2
2 tbsp	brown sugar	30 mL
2 tbsp	chili paste with garlic	30 mL
1 tbsp	Thai fish sauce	15 mL
1 1/2 lbs	beef flank steak	750 g
1 tbsp	olive oil	15 mL
1 1/4 cups	sliced red onion	300 mL
3	Roma (plum) tomatoes, sliced	3
4 cups	romaine lettuce	1 L
1 cup	thinly sliced seedless cucumber	250 mL
3 tbsp	chopped fresh mint	45 mL
4	8-inch (20 cm) flour tortillas	4

- **Preheat broiler or lightly greased barbecue grill to medium-high**

1. In a small bowl, combine lime juice, cilantro, garlic, brown sugar, chili paste and fish sauce. Set half of dressing aside for later use.

2. Place steak in a shallow dish or resealable bag and pour remaining half of marinade over top. Mix well. Cover or seal and refrigerate for at least 1 hour or for up to 8 hours.

3. Remove steaks from marinade, discarding marinade. Place on preheated grill or broiler pan and grill or broil, turning once, for 6 minutes per side for medium or until desired degree of doneness. Transfer to a cutting board and let stand for 5 minutes. Cut diagonally across the grain into 1/2-inch (1 cm) slices.

4. In a large nonstick skillet, heat oil over medium-high heat. Sauté red onion for 3 minutes. Add tomatoes and sauté for 2 minutes. Remove from pan and toss with lettuce, cucumber and mint.

5. Place tortillas on a work surface. Divide tomato mixture equally in center of each tortilla. Add steak and drizzle with remaining dressing. Fold both edges over filling. Roll up and serve immediately.

Variation

This recipe is also great on its own as a salad or served in pita pockets.

Beef-Vegetable Quesadillas

We make these easy quesadillas on "Mexican night" at my house. They are very popular with the kids.

1 lb	extra-lean ground beef, preferably ground round	500 g
½ cup	diced red onion	125 mL
8 oz	sliced fresh mushrooms	250 g
2 cups	baby spinach	500 mL
2 tbsp	taco seasoning	30 mL
¼ tsp	freshly ground black pepper	1 mL
⅛ tsp	salt	0.5 mL
4	8-inch (20 cm) flour tortillas	4
4	slices pepper Jack cheese	4

Toppings, optional

	Pico de Gallo (page 328) or store-bought salsa
	Low-fat sour cream
	Chopped fresh cilantro

1. In a large nonstick skillet over medium-high heat, sauté beef and red onion, breaking up beef with a spoon, for 5 minutes or until beef is browned. Drain off any fat. Add mushrooms, spinach, taco seasoning, pepper and salt. Sauté for 5 minutes or until mushrooms are tender and beef is no longer pink inside. Drain off any excess liquid.

2. Place tortillas on a work surface. Sprinkle beef mixture equally over one-half of each tortilla. Top each with one cheese slice. Carefully fold each tortilla in half.

3. Heat a nonstick skillet over medium heat. Add 2 quesadillas to pan and cook for 2 minutes per side or until lightly browned and cheese is melted. Repeat with remaining quesadillas. Serve immediately with desired toppings.

Tip: Be sure to use the largest skillet you own. The spinach will seem like a lot at first, but it will cook down.

Steak, Tomato and Basil Wraps

Serves 4

This easy wrap is a great combination of fresh basil, tomatoes and mozzarella. It's the perfect summer sandwich.

2 tbsp + 4 tsp	balsamic vinegar, divided	50 mL
1 tbsp	Worcestershire sauce	15 mL
1 lb	boneless beef rib-eye steak	500 g
¼ tsp	kosher salt	1 mL
¼ tsp	freshly ground black pepper	1 mL
4	8-inch (20 cm) flour tortillas, warmed (see Tip, page 197)	4
2	medium tomatoes, thinly sliced	2
⅓ cup	chopped fresh basil	75 mL
3 oz	fresh mozzarella, thinly sliced	90 g

- **Preheat greased barbecue grill to medium-high**

1. In a small bowl, combine 2 tbsp (30 mL) of the balsamic vinegar and Worcestershire. Brush on steaks and season with salt and pepper.

2. Place steaks on preheated grill, cover and grill, turning once, for 6 to 8 minutes per side for medium or to desired degree of doneness. Transfer to a cutting board and let stand for 5 minutes. Cut across the grain into thin slices.

3. Place tortillas on a work surface. Layer steak, tomatoes, basil and mozzarella equally in center of each tortilla. Drizzle each with 1 tsp (5 mL) of the balsamic vinegar. Fold both edges over filling. Roll up and serve immediately.

Variation

Feel free to substitute New York strip steak for the rib-eye steaks in this recipe.

Classic Steak Fajitas

This classic recipe uses flank steak, but hanger steak also works great. These are really fun to make for "girl's night" dinners.

2 tsp	ground cumin	10 mL
2 tsp	chili powder	10 mL
1/2 tsp	salt	2 mL
1/4 tsp	garlic powder	1 mL
1/4 tsp	cayenne pepper	1 mL
1 lb	beef flank steak, cut across the grain into 1 1/2-inch (4 cm) strips	500 g
5 tbsp	freshly squeezed lime juice, divided	75 mL
1 tbsp	vegetable oil	15 mL
1/2 cup	thinly sliced green bell pepper	125 mL
1/2 cup	thinly sliced red bell pepper	125 mL
1/2 cup	thinly sliced yellow bell pepper	125 mL
1	onion, sliced	1
4	8-inch (20 cm) flour tortillas, warmed (see Tip, page 197)	4

Toppings, optional

	Pico de Gallo (page 328) or store-bought salsa
	Chopped fresh cilantro
	Chopped green onions
	Sour cream

1 In a small bowl, combine cumin, chili powder, salt, garlic powder and cayenne pepper. Rub over steak. Place steak in a shallow dish or in a resealable plastic bag. Add 3 tbsp (45 mL) of the lime juice and seal and shake to coat. Cover and refrigerate for at least 2 hours or for up to 8 hours.

2. In a large skillet, heat oil over medium-high heat. Sauté steak, green, red and yellow bell peppers, onion and remaining lime juice for 6 minutes or until a hint of pink remains in steak.

3. Place tortillas on a work surface. Spoon steak mixture equally in center of each tortilla with desired toppings. Fold both edges over filling. Roll up and serve immediately.

Variation

Feel free to substitute shrimp or chicken for the steak in this recipe.

Hoisin-Marinated Pork Loin Wraps

Serves 4

This wrap combines Asian and Southwestern flavors. It makes a wonderful weeknight dinner option.

1/3 cup	hoisin sauce	75 mL
2 tbsp	rice wine vinegar	30 mL
1 tbsp	liquid honey	15 mL
2 tbsp	chopped green onions	30 mL
1 tsp	freshly grated gingerroot	5 mL
1 1/2 lbs	pork tenderloins, thinly sliced	750 g
	Vegetable cooking spray	
4	8-inch (20 cm) flour tortillas, warmed (see Tip, page 197)	4

Toppings, optional

	Pico de Gallo salsa (page 328) or store-bought	
	Chopped fresh cilantro	

1 In a small bowl, combine hoisin, vinegar, honey, green onions and ginger. Place pork in a shallow dish or resealable plastic bag. Add marinade, cover or seal and marinate in refrigerator for at least 1 hour or for up to 8 hours.

2. Remove pork from marinade, discarding marinade. In a large skillet coated with cooking spray over medium heat, sauté pork, in batches as necessary to prevent crowding, for 4 to 6 minutes or until a hint of pink remains in pork. Slice into thin strips and serve in warmed tortillas. Fold both edges over filling and top with desired toppings. Roll up and serve immediately.

Jambalaya Wraps

This is a really fun way to serve jambalaya. It's true comfort food with a New Orleans flair.

12 oz	andouille sausage, cut into ¼-inch (0.5 cm) slices	375 g
1 cup	diced onion	250 mL
1 cup	diced celery	250 mL
2 tsp	dried oregano	10 mL
2 tsp	paprika	10 mL
½ tsp	cayenne pepper	2 mL
¼ tsp	salt	1 mL
2 cups	reduced-sodium chicken broth	500 mL
1	can (14 oz/398 mL) fire-roasted tomatoes with garlic	1
1 cup	cooked long-grain rice	250 mL
4	8-inch (20 cm) flour tortillas, warmed (see Tip, page 197)	4
2 tbsp	chopped green onions	30 mL

- **Dutch oven or large pot**

1 In a large Dutch oven over medium heat, sauté sausage for 5 minutes or until browned. Set aside.

2. Add onion, celery, oregano, paprika, cayenne pepper and salt to pan and sauté for 3 minutes or until tender. Add broth, tomatoes and rice and bring to a boil. Cover, reduce heat and simmer for 18 to 20 minutes or until rice is tender and liquid is absorbed. Return sausage to Dutch oven and cook until heated through.

3. Place tortillas on a work surface. Divide filling equally among tortillas. Top with green onions. Fold both edges over filling. Roll up and serve immediately.

Variation

If you want to add some fiber, add 1 can (14 to 19 oz/398 to 540 mL) red kidney beans.

Vietnamese Pork Wraps

Serves 4

Using panko bread crumbs works great with the ground pork mixture, adding great flavor, texture and crunch.

¼ cup	unseasoned rice vinegar	60 mL
4 tbsp	vegetable oil, divided	60 mL
2 tbsp	granulated sugar	30 mL
1 tbsp	freshly squeezed lime juice	15 mL
1 tbsp	red chili sauce	15 mL
1 lb	ground pork	500 g
¼ cup	panko bread crumbs	60 mL
2	cloves garlic, minced	2
1 tsp	hot pepper flakes	5 mL
½ tsp	salt	2 mL
6	8-inch (20 cm) flour tortillas	6
1 cup	shredded napa cabbage	250 mL
½ cup	thinly sliced peeled cucumber	125 mL
½ cup	chopped fresh mint	125 mL

1. In a small bowl, whisk together vinegar, 1 tbsp (15 mL) of the oil, sugar, lime juice and red chili sauce until blended. Set aside.

2. In a large bowl, combine pork, panko, garlic, hot pepper flakes and salt. Form into 1½-inch (4 cm) balls. In a large nonstick skillet, heat remaining oil over medium-high heat. Fry meatballs, turning often, for 5 to 7 minutes per side until browned and no longer pink inside.

3. Place tortillas on a work surface. Place pork equally in center of each tortilla. Top with cabbage, cucumber and mint. Drizzle each tortilla with 1 tbsp (15 mL) of the dressing. Fold both edges over filling. Roll up and serve immediately.

Variation

You can also use ground beef, turkey or chicken in this recipe.

Chile-Spiced Pork Wraps with Yogurt Slaw

Serves 4

These wraps are amazing. The hint of spice with brown sugar on the pork pairs perfectly with the creamy yogurt slaw.

2 tbsp	light brown sugar	30 mL
2 tsp	chipotle seasoning	10 mL
2 tsp	chili powder	10 mL
1½ tsp	salt, divided	7 mL
½ tsp	hot pepper flakes	2 mL
1½ lbs	thinly sliced boneless pork loin chops	750 g
1	package (14 oz/400 g) shredded coleslaw mix	1
⅓ cup	Homemade Mayonnaise (page 321) or store-bought	75 mL
¼ cup	Greek yogurt	60 mL
¼ cup	chopped green onions	60 mL
1 tbsp	freshly squeezed lime juice	15 mL
2 tbsp	olive oil	30 mL
4	10-inch (25 cm) flour tortillas	4

1 In a small bowl, combine brown sugar, chipotle seasoning, chili powder, 1 tsp (5 mL) of the salt and hot pepper flakes. Rub over pork. Set aside.

2. In a large bowl, combine coleslaw, mayonnaise, yogurt, green onions, lime juice and remaining salt. Cover and set aside.

3. In a large nonstick skillet, heat oil over medium-high heat. Fry pork chops, turning once, for 4 minutes per side or until just a hint of pink remains inside. Cut pork into thin slices.

4. Place tortillas on a work surface. Place pork equally in center of each tortilla and top with slaw mixture. Fold both edges over filling. Roll up and serve immediately.

Tip: Substitute sour cream for the Greek yogurt.

Maple-Glazed Ham and Cheese Wraps

Serves 4

This simple ham and cheese sandwich gets an updated look with a mixture of apple butter and Dijon mustard served in a tortilla.

4	8-inch (20 cm) flour tortillas, warmed (see Tip, page 197)	4
2 tbsp	apple butter	30 mL
2 tbsp	Dijon mustard	30 mL
8 oz	thinly sliced deli-style maple-glazed ham	250 g
4	slices white Cheddar cheese	4

Toppings, optional

| | Bibb lettuce | |
| | Chopped fresh chives | |

- **Large baking sheet, lightly greased**
- **Preheat broiler**

1. Place tortillas on a work surface. Spread apple butter and Dijon mustard equally in center of each tortilla. Arrange ham and cheese over top. Place tortillas on prepared baking sheet. Broil in preheated oven for 2 minutes or until cheese is melted. Top with desired toppings. Fold both edges over filling. Roll up and serve immediately.

Variation

Serve this sandwich cold without baking in the oven.

Tip: If you can't find apple butter, you can substitute applesauce.

Tuna Caesar Wraps

Serves 4

This simple recipe is perfect for a weekend lunch sandwich. My kids request this sandwich often, and it's a great way to get kids to eat tuna.

2	cans (each 6 oz/170 g) water-packed tuna, preferably albacore, drained and flaked	2
½ cup	shredded carrot	125 mL
½ cup	diced green bell pepper	125 mL
⅓ cup	diced red onion	75 mL
¼ cup	Caesar dressing	60 mL
4	8-inch (20 cm) flour tortillas	4
8	romaine lettuce leaves	8
¼ cup	freshly grated Parmesan cheese	60 mL

1. In a large bowl, combine tuna, carrot, bell pepper, red onion and Caesar dressing. Cover and refrigerate for at least 2 hours to allow flavors to blend.

2. Place tortillas on a work surface. Top tortillas equally with lettuce leaves, tuna mixture and cheese. Fold both edges over filling. Roll up and wrap bottom half of each sandwich with plastic wrap. Serve immediately.

Shrimp and Mango Wraps

My family loves shrimp and mango. When I made this wrap sandwich, everyone went wild over it. This is really easy, fresh and light.

2 tbsp	Greek yogurt	30 mL
2 tbsp	Homemade Mayonnaise (page 321) or store-bought	30 mL
1 tbsp	freshly squeezed lime juice, divided	15 mL
1 tbsp	chopped fresh basil	15 mL
½ tsp	hot pepper flakes, divided	2 mL
1½ lbs	large cooked shrimp, peeled	750 g
1 cup	diced fresh mango	250 mL
4	8-inch (20 cm) sun-dried tomato flour tortillas, slightly toasted (see Tip, right)	4
1½ cups	baby spinach leaves	375 mL

1. In a small bowl, combine yogurt, mayonnaise, 1 tsp (5 mL) of the lime juice, basil and ¼ tsp (1 mL) of the hot pepper flakes. Set aside.

2. In a medium bowl, toss together shrimp, mango and remaining lime juice and hot pepper flakes.

3. Place tortillas on a work surface. Spread yogurt mixture equally in center of each tortilla. Arrange spinach leaves down center. Add shrimp mixture. Fold both edges over filling. Roll up and serve immediately.

Variation

You can use sour cream instead of Greek yogurt if you wish.

Tip: To toast tortillas: Place each tortilla in a large nonstick skillet for 30 seconds or until warmed.

Lime Shrimp Tacos

Serves 4

These tacos are light and refreshing and flavorful with a slight Southwestern or Argentinian flair. It's fun to serve these when you're entertaining outdoors.

1 lb	medium shrimp, peeled and deveined	500 g
¼ cup	freshly squeezed lime juice	60 mL
4 tsp	olive oil, divided	20 mL
2	cloves garlic, minced	2
1 tbsp	chopped fresh cilantro	15 mL
¼ tsp	salt	1 mL
¼ tsp	hot pepper flakes	1 mL
1	red onion, thinly sliced	1
½ cup	sliced green bell pepper	125 mL
½ cup	sliced red bell pepper	125 mL
4	8-inch (20 cm) flour tortillas, warmed (see Tip, page 197)	4

Toppings, optional

	Salsa
	Shredded cheese
	Sour cream
	Cilantro
	Lime juice

1. Place shrimp in a large resealable bag.

2. In a large bowl, combine lime juice, 2 tsp (10 mL) of the olive oil, garlic, cilantro, salt and hot pepper flakes. Pour over shrimp and marinate in the refrigerator for at least 30 minutes.

3. In a large skillet, heat remaining oil over medium heat. Sauté red onion and green and red bell peppers for 3 minutes or until tender. Add shrimp and sauté for 3 to 5 minutes or until shrimp are pink and opaque.

4. Place tortillas on a work surface. Spoon shrimp and bell pepper mixture equally in center of each tortilla. Top with desired toppings. Fold both edges over filling. Roll up and serve immediately.

Variation

This mixture is also fabulous served in a pita, on a crostini or on toasted French bread.

Mediterranean Tuna Wraps

This version of tuna is great in your favorite type of flavored tortilla wrap. These make a great picnic recipe idea.

2	cans (each 6 oz/170 g) water-packed tuna, preferably albacore	2
⅓ cup	diced red bell pepper	75 mL
⅓ cup	diced yellow bell pepper	75 mL
2 tbsp	chopped red onion	30 mL
2 tbsp	chopped green olives	30 mL
1 tbsp	chopped black olives	15 mL
4 tsp	drained capers, rinsed	20 mL
¼ cup	white wine vinegar	60 mL
2 tbsp	olive oil	30 mL
1 tsp	dried oregano	5 mL
¼ tsp	freshly ground black pepper	1 mL
4	8-inch (20 cm) flour tortillas	4
1 cup	baby spinach leaves	250 mL

1. In a large bowl, combine tuna, red and yellow bell peppers, red onions, green and black olives and capers. Stir in vinegar, olive oil, oregano and black pepper. Cover and refrigerate for at least 30 minutes.

2. Place tortillas on a work surface. Arrange spinach leaves and tuna mixture equally in center of tortillas. Fold both edges over filling. Roll up and serve immediately.

Tip: Feel free to make the tuna mixture 1 day ahead and assemble wraps when you're ready to serve.

Smoked Trout Wraps

Serves 4

Smoked trout is a great ingredient to use in sandwiches and dips. I like it in this wrap filled with avocados, tomato and basil.

8 oz	smoked trout	250 g
2 tbsp	Greek yogurt	30 mL
2 tbsp	Homemade Mayonnaise (page 321) or store-bought	30 mL
2 tbsp	freshly squeezed lemon juice	30 mL
2 tbsp	chopped fresh basil	30 mL
1/4 tsp	freshly ground black pepper	1 mL
4	8-inch (20 cm) flour tortillas	4
2	medium tomatoes, diced	2
2	avocados, thinly sliced	2
1 1/2 cups	Bibb lettuce	375 mL

1. In a small bowl, combine trout, yogurt, mayonnaise, lemon juice, basil and pepper.

2. Place tortillas on a work surface. Layer trout mixture, tomatoes, avocados and lettuce equally in center of each tortilla. Fold both edges over filling. Roll up and serve immediately.

Variation

You can substitute smoked salmon for the smoked trout.

Panko-Fried Fish Tacos

Serves 4 to 6

This is a great fish taco recipe. I like to use grouper, flounder or red snapper in this recipe.

1/2 cup	Homemade Mayonnaise (page 321) or store-bought	125 mL
1 tbsp	freshly squeezed lime juice	15 mL
1 tsp	jalapeño, seeded and diced	5 mL
1 tsp	Dijon mustard	5 mL
1	egg, beaten	1
1/2 cup	milk	125 mL
2 cups	panko bread crumbs	500 mL
1 lb	white fish fillets, cut into 3- by 1-inch (7.5 by 2.5 cm) strips	500 g
1/4 cup	vegetable oil	60 mL
4	8-inch (20 cm) flour or corn tortillas, warmed (see Tip, page 197)	4
1 cup	shredded cabbage or lettuce	250 mL
Pinch	salt	Pinch
Pinch	freshly ground black pepper	Pinch

- **Large sauté pan or skillet**

1. In a small bowl, combine mayonnaise, lime juice, jalapeño and mustard. Refrigerate until ready to serve.

2. In a shallow dish, combine egg and milk. Place bread crumbs on a shallow plate. Dredge each fish strip in egg mixture, then in panko, pressing crumbs to adhere.

3. In a large sauté pan or large skillet, heat oil over medium heat. Fry fish for 4 minutes per side or until golden brown or fish flakes easily when tested with a fork.

4. Place tortillas on a work surface. Spread mayonnaise mixture equally in center of each tortilla. Top with fish, slaw, salt and pepper. Fold both edges over filling. Roll up and serve immediately.

Tip: You can lighten this up by using skim milk, 1 egg white and reduced-fat mayonnaise.

Smoked Salmon and Caper Wraps

Serves 4

Smoked salmon is not just for breakfast, although this makes a great brunch recipe idea for showers or family get-togethers.

1	package (8 oz/250 g) cream cheese, softened	1
1 tbsp	prepared horseradish	15 mL
½ cup	chopped cucumber	125 mL
⅓ cup	chopped fresh dill	75 mL
¼ cup	chopped red onion	60 mL
¼ tsp	freshly ground black pepper	1 mL
¼ cup	drained capers, rinsed	60 mL
4	8-inch (20 cm) flour tortillas	4
6 oz	smoked salmon, cut into thin strips (see Tips, right)	175 g

1. In a small bowl, combine cream cheese, horseradish, cucumber, dill, red onion and pepper. Add capers and stir well.

2. Place tortillas on a work surface. Spread cream cheese mixture equally over each tortilla, leaving a 1-inch (2.5 cm) border around the edge. Add smoked salmon and fold both edges over filling. Roll up and serve immediately.

Tips: Smoked salmon can be kept in the freezer tightly packed for up to 3 months or, once it has been opened, in the refrigerator for 3 to 4 days.

I love to also serve this mixture on lavash or any sturdy cracker.

Shrimp Salad Wraps

Serves 4

Fresh dill, Dijon and white wine vinegar flavor this shrimp salad to perfection. I make these often for picnics or summer lunches.

½ cup	Homemade Mayonnaise (page 321) or store-bought	125 mL
2 tbsp	white wine vinegar	30 mL
2 tsp	Dijon mustard	10 mL
¼ cup	finely chopped fresh dill	60 mL
½ tsp	freshly ground black pepper	2 mL
2 lbs	large cooked shrimp, peeled	1 kg
1 cup	diced celery (about 2 stalks)	250 mL
⅓ cup	finely chopped red onion	75 mL
4	8-inch (20 cm) flour tortillas	4
4	lettuce leaves	4

1. In a medium bowl, whisk together mayonnaise, vinegar, mustard, dill and pepper. Add shrimp, celery and red onion. Toss gently. Cover and refrigerate for at least 1 hour or for up to 2 days.

2. Place tortillas on a work surface. Arrange shrimp and lettuce leaves equally in center of tortillas. Fold both edges over filing. Roll up and serve immediately.

Tip: If you don't have fresh dill on hand, feel free to substitute 1 tbsp (15 mL) dried dill.

Shrimp Caesar Wraps

Serves 4

This combines my son's two favorites: shrimp and Caesar salad. It's great to serve for a weeknight dinner.

½ cup	Homemade Mayonnaise (page 321) or store-bought	125 mL
2	cloves garlic, minced	2
⅓ cup	chopped flat-leaf Italian parsley	75 mL
1½ tsp	Dijon mustard	7 mL
1 tsp	grated lemon zest	5 mL
2 tbsp	freshly squeezed lemon juice	30 mL
1 lb	large cooked shrimp, peeled	500 g
¾ cup	freshly grated Parmesan cheese	175 mL
4	8-inch (20 cm) flour tortillas	4
½ cup	romaine lettuce leaves	125 mL

Toppings, optional

	Sliced tomatoes
	Red onion

1 In a large bowl, combine mayonnaise, garlic, parsley, mustard, lemon zest and lemon juice. Add shrimp and Parmesan cheese. Toss gently. Cover and refrigerate for at least 1 hour or for up to 8 hours.

2. Place tortillas on a work surface. Spread shrimp mixture, lettuce and desired toppings equally in center of each tortilla. Fold both edges over filling. Roll up and serve immediately.

Tips: Place shrimp on the grill for a few minutes (even though they are cooked) just to give them added grilled flavor.

If you are short on time, use your favorite store-bought Caesar dressing.

Blackened Catfish Wraps

Serves 4

This is a great way to serve fish, especially if you like something with a kick.

Slaw

2 cups	thinly sliced red or green cabbage	500 mL
2 tbsp	Homemade Mayonnaise (page 321) or store-bought	30 mL
1 tbsp	apple cider vinegar	15 mL
¼ tsp	granulated sugar	1 mL
2 tbsp	all-purpose flour	30 mL
2 tbsp	paprika	30 mL
2 tsp	dried oregano	10 mL
½ tsp	salt	2 mL
¼ tsp	cayenne pepper	1 mL
¼ tsp	freshly ground black pepper	1 mL
1½ lbs	skinless catfish fillets	750 g
2 tbsp	butter or margarine, melted	30 mL
4	8-inch (20 cm) flour tortillas, warmed (see Tip, page 197)	4

- **Preheat greased barbecue grill to medium-high**

1. *Slaw:* In a bowl, combine cabbage, mayonnaise, cider vinegar and sugar. Cover and refrigerate for at least 15 minutes.

2. In a shallow dish, combine flour, paprika, oregano, salt, cayenne and black pepper. Dredge fillets in flour mixture. Drizzle with melted butter.

3. Place fish on preheated grill, cover and grill, turning once, for 7 minutes per side or until fish flakes easily when tested with a fork.

4. Cut each catfish fillet lengthwise into 4 pieces. Place tortillas on a work surface. Arrange 4 fillet pieces equally in center of each tortilla. Top each serving with about ¾ cup (175 mL) of the slaw. Fold both edges over filling. Roll up and serve immediately.

Variation

Use any of your favorite white mild-flavored fish, such as grouper, cod or flounder.

Tip: Feel free to substitute 1 to 2 tbsp (15 to 30 mL) blackened seasoning for the homemade spice mixture.

Spring Roll Wraps

Serves 4

This twist on spring rolls is a really fun sandwich to serve, especially in the summertime when you want a cold sandwich.

1 lb	large shrimp, peeled and deveined	500 g
2 tbsp	sweet red chili sauce, divided	30 mL
2 tsp	vegetable oil	10 mL
1/4 cup	freshly squeezed lime juice	60 mL
2 tbsp	grated fresh gingerroot	30 mL
3 oz	dry rice noodles	90 g
3 cups	shredded iceberg lettuce	750 mL
1/2 cup	shredded carrots	125 mL
1/2 cup	chopped red bell pepper	125 mL
1/4 cup	chopped fresh mint	60 mL
4	8-inch (20 cm) flour tortillas, warmed	4
2 tbsp	chopped toasted peanuts, optional	30 mL

1 In a small bowl, toss together shrimp and 2 tsp (10 mL) of the sweet chili sauce to coat. In a large nonstick skillet, heat oil over medium-high heat. Fry shrimp, turning once, for 3 minutes per side or until shrimp are pink and opaque.

2. In another small bowl, whisk together lime juice, remaining sweet chili sauce and ginger.

3. In a large heatproof bowl, soak noodles in boiling water for 3 to 4 minutes or until softened. Drain and rinse in cold water.

4. In a medium bowl, combine lettuce, carrots, bell pepper, mint and noodles. Toss with dressing.

5. Place tortillas on a work surface. Top each tortilla equally with shrimp, noodle mixture and peanuts, if desired. Fold both edges over filling. Roll up and serve immediately or refrigerate until chilled, if desired.

Tip: To save time, purchase already peeled and cooked shrimp and omit sautéing in Step 1.

Tilapia Quesadillas

Serves 4 to 6

This creative quesadilla recipe is really flavorful. I like to serve these often for appetizers when company comes over.

1/4 tsp	salt	1 mL
1/4 tsp	freshly ground black pepper	1 mL
1 1/2 lbs	skinless tilapia fillets	750 g
3 tbsp	olive oil, divided	45 mL
6	8-inch (20 cm) flour tortillas	6
2 cups	shredded Monterey Jack cheese	500 mL

Toppings, optional

	Tomato slices
	Salsa
	Sour cream

1. Sprinkle salt and pepper over fish fillets. In a nonstick skillet, heat 1 tbsp (15 mL) of the oil over medium-high heat. Fry fish for 5 minutes per side or until fish flakes easily when tested with a fork. Flake fish and set aside.

2. Place tortillas on a work surface. Sprinkle cheese equally over 3 tortillas. Top with flaked fish. Cover equally with remaining 3 tortillas.

3. In a nonstick skillet, heat remaining oil over medium-heat. Fry quesadillas, one at a time, for 3 to 5 minutes per side or until golden. Cut into wedges and serve with desired toppings.

Tips: There are concerns about the sustainability of some fish and seafood so we recommend you check reliable sites such as www.seachoice.org for the latest information.

Use any of your favorite white fish, such as catfish, for this recipe.

Flounder Wraps with Avocado Poblano Salsa

Serves 6

This is a great way to be creative with fish. The Poblano Salsa is wonderful served on top.

12 oz	flounder fillets	375 g
2	cloves garlic, divided	2
½ tsp	salt, divided	2 mL
½ tsp	freshly ground black pepper, divided	2 mL
¼ cup	freshly squeezed lime juice, divided	60 mL
1	poblano pepper (see Tip, right)	1
1 cup	cherry tomatoes	250 mL
1	large ripe avocado, cut into bite-size pieces	1
2 tbsp	chopped fresh cilantro	30 mL
1 tbsp	chopped green onion	15 mL
6	8-inch (20 cm) corn tortillas, warmed	6

- **Preheat lightly greased barbecue grill to medium-high**
- **Grill rack, lightly greased**

1. Rub fish fillets evenly with 1 clove garlic, ¼ tsp (1 mL) each salt and pepper. Drizzle with 2 tbsp (30 mL) of the lime juice.

2. Cut poblano pepper in half. Remove and discard seeds. Place pepper, cut side down, on a lightly greased grill rack. Grill pepper over medium heat for 5 to 7 minutes or until skin looks charred and blistered. Remove pepper. Peel and discard skin. Chop pepper and place in a medium-size bowl. Add tomatoes, avocado, cilantro, green onion, remaining lime juice, remaining garlic and remaining salt and pepper. Toss gently.

3. Place fish on grill, cover and grill, turning once, for 4 to 6 minutes per side or until fish flakes easily when tested with a fork.

4. Place tortillas on a work surface. Top each tortilla equally with flounder and avocado poblano salsa. Fold both edges over filling. Roll up and serve immediately.

Tip: When cooking with poblanos, wash hands often and if cooking indoors, run the exhaust fan or open the door to get rid of the pepper fumes.

Lobster Tacos with Avocado Salsa

Serves 4

This is a special occasion recipe, but sometimes you just have to splurge.

1	large tomato, seeded and chopped	1
1	ripe avocado, chopped	1
¼ cup	finely chopped red onion	60 mL
2 tbsp	chopped fresh cilantro	30 mL
2	cloves garlic, minced	2
1 tbsp	minced jalapeño	15 mL
1 tbsp	freshly squeezed lime juice	15 mL
2 cups	chopped cooked lobster	500 mL
	Vegetable cooking spray	
1 tbsp	taco seasoning	15 mL
4	8-inch (20 cm) flour tortillas, warmed (see Tip, page 197)	4

Toppings, optional

	Shredded lettuce
	Shredded Mexican cheese blend
	Sour cream

1 In a medium bowl, combine tomato, avocado, red onion, cilantro, garlic, jalapeño and lime juice. Cover and refrigerate until ready to serve

2. Heat a large skillet coated with cooking spray over medium heat. Sauté lobster meat and taco seasoning for 3 minutes or until heated.

3. Place tortillas on a work surface. Arrange lobster mixture, avocado salsa and desired toppings equally in center of tortillas. Fold both edges over filling. Roll up and serve immediately.

Variation

Feel free to substitute shrimp or scallops for the lobster in this recipe.

International
Sandwiches

Bavarian Beef Sandwich

Serves 4

This Bavarian-style sandwich is super-easy and delicious. These are most often made with a pretzel-style bread or served with a homemade pretzel.

4 oz	cream cheese, softened	125 g
2 tbsp	sour cream	30 mL
2 tbsp	horseradish	30 mL
8	slices rye bread (½-inch/ 1 cm thick slices)	8
12 oz	thinly sliced roast beef	375 g

Toppings, optional

	Lettuce leaves	
	Sliced red onion	

1. In a small bowl, combine cream cheese, sour cream and horseradish.

2. Place bread on a work surface. Spread cream cheese mixture equally over one side of bread slices. Top 4 slices with roast beef, desired toppings, and remaining bread slices.

Tip: Feel free to substitute reduced-fat cream cheese and low-fat sour cream for the regular versions.

Spanish Turkey and Olives

Serves 4

Spanish olives, roasted red pepper spread and Manchego cheese replicate flavors of Spain.

2	cloves garlic, minced	2
1 cup	sliced Spanish olives	250 mL
2 tbsp	chopped flat-leaf parsley	30 mL
1 tbsp	drained capers, rinsed	15 mL
¼ tsp	ground oregano	1 mL
⅛ tsp	freshly ground black pepper	0.5 mL
4	baguettes, sliced horizontally, or 8 slices artisan bread (½-inch/1 cm thick slices)	4
½ cup	Roasted Red Pepper Aïoli (page 312)	125 mL
12 oz	thinly sliced turkey	375 g
½ cup	grated Manchego cheese	125 mL

1. In a small bowl, combine garlic, olives, parsley, capers, oregano and pepper.

2. Place baguette slices on a work surface. Spread both cut sides of baguettes with Red Pepper Aïoli and top 4 slices equally with turkey, olive mixture and Manchego cheese. Top with remaining bread halves and serve immediately.

Variation

If you don't have time to make the Roasted Red Pepper Aïoli, spread half of the bread slices with ¼ cup (60 mL) mayonnaise and top each sandwich evenly with 1 cup (250 mL) roasted red peppers.

Tip: Manchego cheese is a Spanish sheep's milk cheese. If you can't locate it, you can substitute Pecorino or Romano cheese.

Salmon Sandwich with Chermoula Sauce

Serves 4

Chermoula is a Moroccan condiment usually served with chicken, fish or vegetables. It flavors this salmon sandwich to perfection. This sauce gives the salmon a rich, beautiful color.

2	cloves garlic, minced	2
1/4 cup	chopped fresh cilantro	60 mL
2 tbsp	chopped Italian flat-leaf parsley	30 mL
1 tsp	ground paprika	5 mL
1 tsp	ground cumin	5 mL
1/8 to 1/4 tsp	cayenne pepper (see Tips, right)	0.5 mL to 1 mL
1/8 tsp	sea salt	0.5 mL
2 tbsp	olive oil	30 mL
2 tbsp	freshly squeezed lemon juice	30 mL
1 1/4 lbs	salmon fillet	625 g
8	slices sourdough (1/2-inch/ 1 cm thick slices), toasted	8

- **Preheat lightly greased barbecue grill to medium-high**

1. In a medium bowl, combine garlic, cilantro, parsley, paprika, cumin, cayenne to taste, salt, olive oil and lemon juice. Spread sauce equally over salmon fillets.

2. Grill salmon on preheated grill for 7 to 10 minutes or until fish flakes easily when tested with a fork. Cut into 4 equal pieces.

3. Place bread on a work surface. Top with salmon and top halves of bread. Serve immediately.

Tips: The chermoula is a wonderful mixture. If you like spicier foods, use 1/4 tsp (1 mL) cayenne pepper.

Cayenne pepper is ground dried chiles. Store in a closed container in the refrigerator to retain its color and flavor.

Grilled Crab-Cilantro Quesadillas

These quesadillas combine flavors of Mexico and the Caribbean. I love them made with flavored tortillas and cooked on the grill.

1 lb	lump crabmeat	500 g
1/2 cup	finely chopped cilantro	125 mL
2 tbsp	freshly squeezed lime juice	30 mL
1 tbsp	finely chopped jalapeño	15 mL
1 tbsp	white wine vinegar	15 mL
1/4 tsp	kosher salt	1 mL
1/4 tsp	freshly ground black pepper	1 mL
4	8-inch (20 cm) white or flavored tortillas	4
1 1/2 cups	shredded Monterey Jack cheese	375 mL
3	Roma (plum) tomatoes, thinly sliced	3
2	avocados, thinly sliced	2
2 tbsp	olive oil	30 mL

Toppings, optional

	Salsa
	Sour cream
	Chopped green onion

- **Preheat greased barbecue grill to medium**

1. In a medium bowl, combine crabmeat, cilantro, lime juice, jalapeño, vinegar, salt and pepper. Mix well.

2. Place tortillas on a work surface. Assemble quesadillas by spreading tortillas equally with cheese, crabmeat mixture, tomatoes and avocados. Fold over and brush with oil. Place quesadillas on preheated grill, close lid and grill for 1 to 2 minutes per side or until cheese is melted and tortillas are browned. Cut each quesadilla into 4 wedges. Top with salsa, sour cream and green onions, if desired.

Variation

You can substitute shrimp for the crabmeat in this recipe.

Tip: You can make these quesadillas in a nonstick skillet. Heat 2 tbsp (30 mL) oil over medium heat. Cook quesadillas for 5 minutes per side or until lightly browned.

Balsamic-Glazed Chicken with Peppers and Goat Cheese

Serves 4

The sweet, tangy flavor in this sandwich comes from the balsamic vinegar, which contributes to its Italian influence.

2 tbsp	olive oil, divided	30 mL
1½ lbs	chicken breast tenders	750 g
½ tsp	salt	2 mL
½ cup	balsamic vinegar, divided	125 mL
2 cups	thinly sliced red onion	500 mL
1 cup	red bell pepper strips (about 1 medium)	250 mL
1 cup	green bell pepper strips (about 1 medium)	250 mL
2	loaves (8 oz/250 g) focaccia bread, cut in half horizontally (see Tip, right)	2
4 oz	crumbled goat cheese	125 g

1. In a large skillet, heat 1 tbsp (15 mL) of the oil over medium heat. Add chicken and sprinkle both sides with salt. Sauté chicken for 2 minutes per side or until lightly browned. Add ¼ cup (60 mL) of the balsamic vinegar and sauté for 2 minutes more or until chicken is no longer pink inside. Remove chicken from pan and keep warm. Wipe pan clean.

2. Add remaining oil to pan. Sauté red onion and red and green bell peppers for 5 minutes or until tender. Add remaining balsamic vinegar and sauté for 2 minutes.

3. Place bread on a work surface. Arrange chicken on bottom halves. Top with bell pepper mixture, goat cheese and top halves of bread. Serve immediately

Tip: Look for flavored focaccia bread. I made this with rosemary focaccia, and it was wonderful.

Easy Tostadas

Tostadas, means "toasted" in Spanish. They are usually flat or bowl-shaped and filled with an array of Mexican ingredients.

4	8-inch (20 cm) corn tortillas	4
1 cup	refried beans	250 mL
1 cup	canned or cooked black beans, drained and rinsed	250 mL
1 cup	shredded Monterey Jack cheese	250 mL
1 cup	shredded iceberg lettuce	250 mL
1 cup	chopped avocado	250 mL
1 cup	chopped tomato	250 mL

Toppings, optional

	Salsa	
	Sour cream	
	Chopped jalapeños	

- **Preheat broiler**

1. Place tortillas on a baking sheet. Spread $1/4$ cup (60 mL) each refried beans, black beans and cheese over each tortilla. Broil for 2 minutes or until cheese is melted and edges are browned. Top equally with lettuce, avocado, tomato and desired toppings. Cut each tortilla into 4 wedges and serve immediately.

Variation

Feel free to add chopped cooked chicken, beef or shrimp to this recipe.

Tip: To cut calories, decrease the amount of refried beans, use low-fat sour cream, and use less cheese.

Sausage-Fontina Calzones

Serves 4

My kids loved making these calzones. Feel free to use your favorite toppings and cheeses when you make these. This is a great casual entertaining recipe idea.

1 lb	Italian sausage (bulk or removed from casings)	500 g
1 lb	store-bought pizza dough, at room temperature	500 g
1 cup	shredded fontina cheese	250 mL
1 cup	sliced roasted red peppers	250 mL
1/2 cup	sliced sun-dried tomatoes	125 mL
1/2 cup	shredded mozzarella cheese	125 mL
1/2 cup	chopped fresh basil	125 mL
2 tbsp	olive oil	30 mL

Tip: To make ahead, prepare recipe up to Step 3. Wrap in foil, place on a baking sheet and freeze until solid. Transfer to an airtight container or freezer bag and freeze for up to 3 months. To serve, return frozen calzones to baking sheet and bake at 375°F (190°C) for 30 minutes or until golden brown.

- **Preheat oven to 350°F (180°C)**

1. In a large skillet, cook sausage over medium heat, breaking up with a spoon, for about 8 minutes or until well browned and no longer pink inside. Drain off fat and let cool slightly.

2. On a lightly floured surface, divide dough into 4 equal pieces. Using a floured rolling pin, roll out each to a 6-inch (15 cm) circle. Spread sausage, fontina, red peppers, sun-dried tomatoes, mozzarella and basil equally over half of each calzone, leaving a 1/2-inch (1 cm) border.

3. Gently pull half of the dough over filling to make a half-moon shape. Fold bottom edge of dough over top edge and pinch firmly to seal. Brush tops of calzones with olive oil. Transfer to a large baking sheet.

4. Bake in preheated oven for 25 minutes or until golden brown. Let cool for 5 minutes.

Bondi Chicken Burger

Serves 4

This is very similar to a Portuguese Chicken Burger that originated in Bondi in Sydney. It has become popular in Australia and New Zealand. The chicken is marinated in a ginger, red pepper and lemon mixture and lightly fried.

3 tbsp	freshly squeezed lemon juice	45 mL
2 tsp	grated fresh gingerroot (see Tip, right)	10 mL
2	cloves garlic, minced	2
1 tsp	paprika	5 mL
1/4 tsp	hot pepper flakes	1 mL
4	chicken cutlets (about 1 1/2 lbs/750 g total)	4
1/2 cup	all-purpose flour	125 mL
1/4 tsp	salt	1 mL
1/4 tsp	freshly ground black pepper	1 mL
1/4 cup	olive or vegetable oil	60 mL
4	hamburger buns, spit	

Toppings, optional

	Mayonnaise
	Lettuce
	Tomato slices

1. In a small bowl, combine lemon juice, ginger, garlic, paprika and hot pepper flakes. Rub over chicken. Cover and refrigerate for at least 30 minutes.

2. On a small plate, combine flour, salt and pepper. Coat chicken in flour on both sides. In a large nonstick skillet, heat oil over medium heat. Cook chicken for 4 minutes per side or until no longer pink inside. Serve on buns with desired toppings.

Tip: When grating fresh ginger, be sure to remove any thin skin. I like to use a sharp knife or vegetable peeler. To store fresh ginger, place at room temperature in a cool, dark place or tightly sealed in the refrigerator in a plastic bag for up to 3 weeks.

Torta Ahogada

Serves 4

This popular sandwich from Mexico (usually in Guadalajara) is also called "Drowned Beef." It is submerged partially or totally in a spicy sauce. This is a less spicy version made with tomato sauce, but it has a fabulous kick.

1	can (10 oz/284 mL) chopped tomatoes with green chiles	
2 cups	tomato sauce	500 mL
2 tbsp	chopped chipotle chiles in adobo sauce (see Tips, right)	30 mL
1 tbsp	vegetable oil	15 mL
1 cup	thinly sliced onion	250 mL
2	cloves garlic, minced	2
1 tsp	jalapeño, seeded and diced	5 mL
2 tbsp	chopped fresh cilantro	30 mL
4	Bolillo rolls or crusty rolls, split and toasted (see Tips, right)	4
1 lb	deli roast beef, cut into strips	500 g
1 cup	refried beans, warmed, optional	250 mL
2	avocados, thinly sliced	2

1. In a medium saucepan over medium heat, combine tomatoes, tomato sauce and chipotles. Reduce heat to low. Bring to a simmer and cook, stirring occasionally, for 15 minutes.

2. In a large nonstick skillet, heat oil over medium heat. Sauté onion, garlic and jalapeño for 5 minutes or until tender. Add onion mixture to tomato sauce mixture, stirring well, and simmer for 5 minutes. Stir in cilantro.

3. Place rolls on a work surface. Arrange roast beef equally on bottom halves of rolls. Top with beans, if using, tomato sauce and avocado slices. Cover with top halves of rolls. Serve immediately.

Tips: Bolillo rolls are one of Mexico's most popular breads. They are made with a basic dough similar to a French baguette and have a crispy crust with a chewy, soft crumb. Substitute hoagie rolls or sourdough rolls if you can't locate them.

Serve the sauce on the side to dip the sandwiches in if you like less mess.

You can find chipotle chiles in adobo sauce in the international section of the grocery store where taco seasoning and salsas are found.

Caribbean Crab Sandwich

Serves 4

This is a summery fresh sandwich that makes you feel like you're in the islands. Serve with a tossed salad for a complete meal.

1 cup	diced avocado	250 mL
1 cup	diced mango	250 mL
½ cup	diced pineapple	125 mL
3 tbsp	freshly squeezed lime juice, divided	45 mL
12 oz	cooked lump crabmeat	375 g
2 tbsp	chopped fresh cilantro	30 mL
¼ tsp	hot pepper flakes	1 mL
4	hoagie rolls, split and toasted	4
½ cup	peanuts, toasted, optional	125 mL

1. In a small bowl, combine avocado, mango, pineapple and 1 tbsp (15 mL) of the lime juice. Set aside.

2. In a medium bowl, combine crab, remaining lime juice, cilantro and hot pepper flakes. Let stand for 10 minutes.

3. Place hoagies on a work surface. Spoon crab equally over cut sides of hoagies. Top with avocado mixture, and peanuts, if using. Serve immediately.

Tips: Use leftover mango mixture for an appetizer served on crackers or on top of a salad or chicken the next day.

Be sure to choose ripe mangos and avocados. To check if they are ripe, make sure they yield to palm pressure.

Steak Chimichurri Sandwich

Serves 4

Chimichurri is a condiment from Argentina. It pairs great with steak and makes a terrific dinnertime sandwich. Chimichurri is as common in Argentina as ketchup is in the United States.

1 lb	loaf ciabatta bread, cut into eight 1-inch (2.5 cm) slices, toasted	500 g
¼ cup	Homemade Mayonnaise (page 321) or store-bought	60 mL
1 lb	cooked beef flank steak or tenderloin, thinly sliced	500 g
2	large tomatoes, thinly sliced	2
1 cup	Chimichurri (page 319)	250 mL

1. Place bread slices on a work surface. Spread mayonnaise equally over one side of each 8 bread slices. Arrange steak, tomatoes and chimichurri equally over top. Serve open-faced. Serve 2 per person.

Tips: Use any of your favorite bread for this sandwich.

Chimichurri is great on meat, fish, poultry and pork.

Pan Bagnat

Serves 4

This sandwich, from Nice, France, is similar to a tuna niçoise salad. This is one of my favorite salads served in a sandwich.

3 tbsp	red wine vinegar, divided	45 mL
3 tbsp	olive oil, divided	45 mL
1 tbsp	freshly squeezed lemon juice	15 mL
1 tsp	Dijon mustard	5 mL
1/4 tsp	freshly ground black pepper	1 mL
1 lb	French loaf, cut in half lengthwise	500 g
1/2 cup	fresh basil leaves	125 mL
2	cans (each 6 oz/170 g) water-packed tuna, drained and crumbled	2
2	Roma (plum) tomatoes, diced	2
1	hard-boiled egg, sliced	1
1/2 cup	kalamata olives	125 mL
1/4 cup	chopped onion	60 mL

1. In a small bowl, combine 1 tbsp (15 mL) each of the vinegar and oil, and lemon juice, mustard and pepper. Set aside.

2. Place bread slices on a work surface. Brush cut sides of bread with remaining olive oil and line with basil leaves. Set aside.

3. In a medium bowl, combine tuna, tomatoes, egg, olives and onion. Drizzle with remaining red wine vinegar, tossing gently. Spoon equally over basil leaves. Drizzle with vinegar mixture and top with remaining bread half. Wrap tightly in plastic wrap so it holds its shape. Let stand at room temperature for 20 minutes.

4. Unwrap and cut into 1½-inch (4 cm) slices. Top with additional basil, if desired.

Tip: You can omit wrapping the sandwich in plastic wrap in Step 3 and instead let stand for 20 minutes at room temperature, if desired.

Shooter's Sandwich

Serves 4

This English favorite is so flavorful! Sometimes this sandwich is made with rib-eye steaks and is most often served in between crusty bread loaves. Usually the mushrooms are finely chopped, but I like them sliced.

1½ lbs	beef skirt steak or hanger steak	750 g
2	cloves garlic, minced	2
3 tbsp	chopped fresh thyme, divided	45 mL
2 tbsp	chopped chipotle chiles in adobo sauce	30 mL
2 tbsp	olive oil, divided	30 mL
1½ tsp	sea salt, divided	7 mL
½ tsp	freshly ground black pepper	2 mL
1½ cups	sliced button or shiitake mushrooms	375 mL
1	loaf ciabatta bread, cut into 4 wedges, split and toasted	1
	Chipotle Aïoli (page 311)	

- **Preheat lightly greased barbecue grill to medium-high**
- **Instant-read thermometer**

1. Season steak with garlic, 2 tbsp (30 mL) of the thyme, chipotle peppers, 1 tbsp (15 mL) of the olive oil, 1 tsp (15 mL) of the salt and pepper. Cover and marinate in the refrigerator for at least 1 hour or for up to 8 hours.

2. In a large skillet, heat remaining olive oil over medium heat. Sauté mushrooms for 4 minutes or until tender. Add remaining thyme and salt, mixing well. Set aside.

3. Place steak on preheated grill, close lid and grill for 6 minutes per side for medium or until desired doneness. Transfer to a cutting board, tent with foil and let stand for 5 to 10 minutes. Slice into thin strips.

4. Place bread on a work surface. Spread with Chipotle Aïoli equally on cut sides of bread. Top equally with steak, mushrooms and remaining bread halves. Serve immediately.

Tip: If you don't have time to prepare the Chipotle Aïoli, use Dijon or prepared mustard, which is traditionally served on this sandwich.

Vegetable Piadina

Serves 4

Piadina is part pizza, part salad and part sandwich. It is healthy and light and inspired by the Romagna region of Italy.

⅓ cup	balsamic vinegar	75 mL
¼ cup	olive oil, divided	60 mL
⅛ tsp	freshly ground black pepper	0.5 mL
14 oz	pizza dough (see Tip, below)	400 g
1 cup	marinara sauce	250 mL
2 cups	chopped romaine lettuce	500 mL
1 cup	chopped watercress	250 mL
1 cup	thinly sliced cucumber	250 mL
½ cup	thinly sliced radishes	125 mL
¼ cup	fresh basil leaves	60 mL
½ cup	shredded mozzarella cheese	125 mL
½ cup	crumbled feta cheese	125 mL

Tip: I purchase the pizza dough from the bakery section of my grocery store. It works great.

- **Preheat oven to 500°F (260°C)**
- **12-inch (30 cm) pizza pan or large baking sheet**

1. In a small bowl, whisk together balsamic vinegar, 3 tbsp (45 mL) of the olive oil and pepper. Set aside.

2. On a lightly floured surface, roll out pizza dough to a 12-inch (30 cm) circle, about ¼ inch (0.5 cm) thick. Place on a large pizza pan. Brush with remaining olive oil and spread with marinara, leaving a 1-inch (2.5 cm) border. Bake in preheated oven for 8 to 10 minutes.

3. In a large bowl, combine, romaine, watercress, cucumber, radishes, basil and mozzarella and feta cheeses. Add vinaigrette, tossing gently.

4. Remove pizza dough from oven. Arrange romaine mixture on top of crust and fold over. Cut into quarters and serve immediately.

Variation

Feel free to add chicken, shrimp or pepperoni.

Tuna and Sweet Corn

Serves 4

This traditional sandwich, served in England, is a great change of pace for the usual tuna sandwich. My kids loved it.

2	cans (each 6 oz/170 g) water-packed tuna, drained and crumbled	2
1/2 cup	thawed frozen or cooked fresh corn kernels	125 mL
1	clove garlic, minced	1
3 tbsp	chopped fresh cilantro	45 mL
2 tbsp	Homemade Mayonnaise (page 321) or store-bought	30 mL
2 tsp	freshly squeezed lime juice	10 mL
1/8 tsp	salt	0.5 mL
1/8 tsp	freshly ground black pepper	0.5 mL
8	slices multigrain bread (1/2-inch/1 cm thick slices)	8

Toppings, optional

Lettuce leaves	
Sliced cucumber	
Tomato slices	
Onion slices	
Cheese slices	

1. In a medium bowl, combine tuna, corn, garlic, cilantro, mayonnaise, lime juice, salt and pepper.

2. Place bread slices on a work surface. Spread tuna mixture equally on half of bread slices. Top with desired toppings and remaining bread, pressing together gently.

Tips: You can make the tuna ahead of time and refrigerate for up to 1 day.

This tuna is also great served over a bed of mixed greens.

Shawarma Sandwich

Often called the Middle Eastern taco, this sandwich originated in northwestern Turkey and was called the "doner kebab," meaning rotating roast. It is now found in a variety of forms around the world and also as the Middle Eastern version of a gyro.

2 lbs	boneless skinless chicken breast, cut into ½-inch (1 cm) slices (see Tip, right)	1 kg
2	cloves garlic, minced	2
1 tsp	salt	5 mL
1 tsp	freshly ground black pepper	5 mL
1 tsp	ground allspice	5 mL
1 tsp	ground cardamom	5 mL
½ tsp	ground nutmeg	2 mL
1 cup	plain nonfat yogurt	250 mL
¼ cup	freshly squeezed lemon juice	60 mL
4	6- to 8-inch (15 to 20 cm) pitas with pockets	4

Toppings, optional

	Shredded lettuce
	Chopped tomatoes
	Sliced cucumbers
	Hummus (page 313) or store-bought
	Cilantro-Yogurt Sauce (page 317) or Classic Tzatziki (page 315)

- **Preheat greased barbecue grill to medium-high**

1. In a large bowl, combine chicken, garlic, salt, pepper, allspice, cardamom, nutmeg, yogurt and lemon juice. Cover and marinate in the refrigerator for 1 hour or overnight.

2. Remove chicken from marinade, discarding excess marinade. Place chicken on preheated grill, close lid and grill, turning once, for 6 to 8 minutes per side for medium or until no longer pink inside. Serve inside of pita with desired toppings.

Variation

Replace chicken with roast beef.

Tip: You can broil the chicken instead of grilling. Place chicken on a large broiler pan, 4 to 6 inches (10 to 15 cm) away from heat and broil, turning once, for 6 minutes for medium or until chicken is no longer pink inside.

Camel Rider

This Middle Eastern sandwich is popular in many Greek and Lebanese restaurants in the United States. It is usually made with a vinaigrette dressing.

4	6- to 8-inch (15 to 20 cm) pitas with pockets	4
¼ cup	Homemade Mayonnaise (page 321) or store-bought	60 mL
6 oz	thinly sliced salami	175 g
6 oz	thinly sliced ham	175 g
4	slices provolone cheese	4
1⅓ cups	shredded lettuce	325 mL
2	large tomatoes, cut into 4 large slices each	2
2	pickles, cut into 8 slices	2
¾ cup	Italian vinaigrette	175 mL

1. Place pitas on a work surface. Spread mayonnaise equally in each pita. Arrange salami, ham, cheese, lettuce, tomato and pickles equally in each pita. Drizzle with dressing and serve immediately.

Variation

This sandwich is made many different ways with various meats and cheeses, such as bologna, roast beef, Swiss cheese or any of your favorites.

Tip: I used store-bought "light" Italian dressing.

Pork Carnitas

Carnita, Mexican for "little meats," is usually made from inexpensive pork simmered in liquid and served on tacos and burritos. Here I offer a simple version using shredded cooked pork.

4	8-inch (20 cm) corn tortillas, warmed	4
3 cups	shredded cooked pork	750 mL

Toppings, optional

	Pico De Gallo (page 328) or store-bought
	Diced tomatoes
	Chopped avocado
	Freshly squeezed lime juice

1. Place tortillas on a work surface. Arrange pork and desired toppings equally in enter of tortillas. Fold both ends over filling. Roll up and serve immediately.

Croque Monsieur

Serves 4

This French-style ham and cheese sandwich typically has Gruyère or Emmenthal cheese. It originated in France as a fast food snack in cafés and bars.

½ cup	milk	125 mL
2	eggs, lightly beaten	2
8	slices white or French bread (½-inch/1 cm thick slices)	8
⅓ cup	Dijon mustard	75 mL
8 oz	thinly sliced ham	250 g
8 oz	Gruyère cheese, thinly sliced	250 g
1 tbsp	butter	15 mL

Tip: This would also be great using an 8 oz (250 g) party bread loaf or any small bread for appetizers.

1. In a shallow dish, whisk together milk and eggs. Set aside.

2. Place bread slices on a work surface. Spread mustard equally over 4 bread slices. Arrange ham and cheese equally over mustard and top with remaining bread slices, pressing together gently. Dip sandwiches, one at a time, in milk mixture turning to coat.

3. In a large nonstick skillet, melt butter over medium heat. Fry sandwiches for 3 minutes per side or until golden. Repeat with remaining sandwiches.

Variation

To lighten, substitute low-fat milk for the milk and 2 egg whites for the eggs.

Peameal Bacon Sandwich

Serves 4

Peameal bacon, also called Canadian bacon and back bacon, is a variety of unsmoked bacon that is rolled in cornmeal or meal made from ground yellow peas.

12 oz	peameal bacon (see Tips, right)	375 g
8	slices white bread (½-inch/ 1 cm thick slices), toasted	8
¼ cup	Homemade Mayonnaise (page 321) or store-bought	60 mL
8	iceberg lettuce leaves	8
2	large tomatoes, each cut into 4 slices	2

1. In a large nonstick skillet, cook bacon for 2 minutes per side or until golden. Drain on paper towels.

2. Place toasted bread slices on a work surface. Spread 4 bread slices equally with mayonnaise. Arrange bacon, lettuce and tomatoes equally over mayonnaise. Cover with remaining bread slices and press together gently.

Tips: If you can't find peameal bacon, you can substitute your favorite bacon.

Also feel free to use any of your favorite sandwich breads in this recipe.

Jamaican Jerk Chicken Sandwich

Serves 4

All of the wonderful spices combined with orange juice make this chicken so juicy and flavorful. Jerk is a dry seasoning blend that originated in the Caribbean island after which it was named, and it is used most often on grilled meat.

¼ cup	chopped green onions	60 mL
2	cloves garlic, minced	2
2 tbsp	brown sugar	30 mL
1 tbsp	finely chopped jalapeño	15 mL
1 tbsp	ground allspice	15 mL
1 tbsp	dried thyme	15 mL
1 tsp	grated fresh gingerroot	5 mL
½ tsp	sea salt	2 mL
½ tsp	freshly ground black pepper	2 mL
¾ cup	white wine vinegar	175 mL
½ cup	freshly squeezed orange juice	125 mL
¼ cup	soy sauce	60 mL
¼ cup	vegetable oil	60 mL
1½ lbs	boneless skinless chicken breasts	750 g
4	slices French bread (½-inch/1 cm thick slices), toasted	4

Toppings, optional

	Tomato slices
	Sliced avocados
	Cheese
	Lettuce leaves
	Mayonnaise

- **Preheat greased barbecue grill to medium-high**

1. In a large bowl, combine green onions, garlic, brown sugar, jalapeño, allspice, thyme, ginger, salt and pepper. Stir in vinegar, orange juice, soy sauce and oil. Place chicken in resealable plastic bag and add marinade. Seal and marinate in the refrigerator for at least 30 minutes.

2. Remove breasts from marinade, reserving marinade (see Tips, below). Grill chicken on preheated grill for 6 to 8 minutes per side or until no longer pink inside Serve on cut sides of bread with desired toppings.

Tips: You can bring leftover marinade to a boil, then boil for 5 minutes, stirring occasionally, and serve on the side for dipping.

If you're short on time, purchase "jerk seasoning" in the spice aisle of the grocery store and combine with the liquid ingredients above.

Chicken Cordon Bleu Sandwich

Serves 4

The name of this French dish means "blue ribbon." There are many versions of this recipe, but this is a simple way to prepare it.

2 tbsp	white wine vinegar	30 mL
1 tbsp	Dijon mustard	15 mL
1 tbsp	liquid honey	15 mL
1 tbsp	freshly squeezed lemon juice, divided	15 mL
1/4 cup	olive oil, divided	60 mL
1 tbsp	finely chopped fresh thyme	15 mL
1 1/2 lbs	boneless skinless chicken breast cutlets (about 4)	750 g
1/2 tsp	salt	2 mL
1/2 tsp	freshly ground black pepper	2 mL
4 oz	thinly sliced prosciutto or deli ham	125 g
4	slices Swiss cheese	4
4	hamburger or Kaiser buns, split and toasted	4

- **Preheat greased barbecue grill to medium-high**

1. In a small bowl, combine vinegar, mustard, honey and 1 tsp (5 mL) of the lemon juice. Add 2 tbsp (30 mL) of the oil and fresh thyme.

2. Season chicken with salt and pepper. Drizzle with remaining lemon juice.

3. In a large skillet, heat remaining oil over medium-high heat. Cook chicken for 4 minutes per side or until chicken is no longer pink inside. Top chicken with ham slices and cook for 3 minutes more per side or until ham is lightly browned. Top with cheese and cook until slightly melted. Serve chicken in buns with Dijon sauce.

Tip: Serve the sauce as a spread on the buns or on top of the melted cheese. Either of these options work great.

Eggplant Parmesan Sandwich

Serves 4

This Southern Italian dish is always made with fried eggplant layered with tomato sauce. This is a comforting wintertime sandwich.

2 lbs	eggplant (about 2 medium), sliced into ¼-inch (0.5 cm) thick slices	1 kg
½ tsp	salt	2 mL
2	eggs	2
1 cup	Italian-seasoned bread crumbs (see Tips, below)	250 mL
½ cup	olive oil, divided	125 mL
8	slices Italian bread (½-inch/ 1 cm thick slices)	8
½ cup	marinara sauce	125 mL
4	slices mozzarella cheese	4
½ cup	freshly grated Parmesan cheese (see Tips, below)	125 mL
¼ cup	chopped fresh basil	60 mL

Toppings, optional

	Roasted red peppers
	Crumbled feta cheese

Tips: Alternate salting eggplant method: In a large bowl, dissolve 2 tbsp (30 mL) salt in 1 cup (250 mL) warm water. Add 3 quarts (3 L) cold water. Set aside. Trim eggplant and cut into ¼-inch (0.5 cm) thick slices. Put slices in salt water, weigh down with an upside-down plate, and let stand for 30 minutes. By adding a little salt it draws out the water and the bitterness and keeps eggplant firm for grilling or frying.

To make your own Italian-seasoned bread crumbs: In a bowl, combine 1 cup (250 mL) regular bread crumbs, ½ tsp (2 mL) each marjoram, garlic salt, parsley and dried oregano.

I love to use good-quality Parmesan cheese, such as Parmigiano-Reggiano. It makes a huge difference in flavor.

- **Preheat oven to 375°F (190°C)**
- **Panini grill or large skillet**
- **Preheat panini grill to medium, if using**

1. In a large baking dish, place eggplant slices and sprinkle with salt on both sides. Let stand for 30 minutes. Rinse eggplant well to remove salt and pat dry with paper towels. (Thorough drying is important. Squeezing out excess moisture will give you a less greasy result.)

2. In a shallow bowl, beat eggs with a fork. Place bread crumbs in another shallow bowl. Dip eggplant in egg mixture and then in bread crumbs, coating well on both sides. In a large skillet, heat ¼ cup (60 mL) of the oil over medium heat. Fry eggplant for 5 to 8 minutes per side or until golden brown and tender in center. Repeat with remaining eggplant. Transfer eggplant to a paper towel.

3. Brush one side of each bread slice equally with remaining olive oil. Place on work surface, oiled side down, and spread bottom halves equally with marinara sauce. Top bread equally with eggplant, mozzarella and Parmesan cheeses, basil and desired toppings. Cover with top halves and press together gently.

4. Place sandwiches on preheated panini pan or large skillet over medium heat and cook, turning once if using a skillet, for 3 to 4 minutes or until golden brown and cheese is melted. Serve immediately.

Antipasto Sandwich

Antipasto, meaning "before the meal," is an Italian term referring to hot or cold appetizers. This Italian classic becomes a sandwich and makes a great weekend or weeknight dinner option that is so flavorful and colorful.

¼ cup	red wine vinegar	60 mL
2 tbsp	olive oil	30 mL
2	cloves garlic, minced	2
¼ tsp	ground oregano	1 mL
⅛ tsp	salt	0.5 mL
⅛ tsp	freshly ground black pepper	0.5 mL
8	slices Italian bread (½-inch/ 1 cm thick slices), toasted	8
4 oz	Italian salami	125 g
4	slices provolone cheese	4
4	slices mozzarella cheese	4
1 cup	mixed lettuce leaves	250 mL
1 cup	quartered drained artichokes	250 mL
1 cup	roasted red peppers	250 mL
¾ cup	sun-dried tomatoes	175 mL
½ cup	chopped fresh basil	125 mL

1. In a small bowl, combine vinegar, oil, garlic, oregano, salt and pepper. Set aside.

2. Place toasted bread slices on a work surface. Arrange salami, provolone, mozzarella, lettuce, artichokes, red peppers, sun-dried tomatoes and basil equally over 4 bread slices. Drizzle equally with vinegar mixture. Cover with remaining bread slices and press together gently. Serve immediately.

Strawberry Cream Cheese Sandwich

Serves 4

This British tea sandwich is a light as a feather and pretty too. This makes a great sandwich to serve at baby showers.

12	slices thin white bread (½-inch/1 cm thick slices)	12
½ cup	cream cheese or mascarpone	125 mL
½ cup	liquid honey	125 mL
1½ cups	sliced fresh strawberries (see Tip, right)	375 mL

1. Place bread slices on a work surface. Spread 1 side of 4 bread slices equally with half of cream cheese. Drizzle with honey. Top with 4 more bread slices and remaining cream cheese and honey. Arrange strawberries on top and top with remaining 4 bread slices. Press slices together gently. Remove crusts and slice into triangles.

Tip: One pint of fresh strawberries equals 1½ to 2 cups (375 to 500 mL) sliced.

Mu Shu Chicken

Serves 4

This Chinese favorite is really simple to prepare. Usually it's made with pork, green onions, seasonings and scrambled eggs. It is usually served in thin pancakes, similar to crêpes, but this version works great in flour tortillas.

¼ cup	hoisin sauce	60 mL
2 tbsp	reduced-sodium soy sauce	30 mL
2 tsp	dark sesame oil (see Tip, right)	10 mL
2	cloves garlic, minced	2
1 tsp	liquid honey	5 mL
1 tbsp	vegetable oil	15 mL
2 lbs	boneless skinless chicken breasts or chicken tenders, cut into 1-inch (2.5 cm) pieces	1 kg
1 lb	shredded cabbage with carrots coleslaw mix	500 g
⅓ cup	lightly salted peanuts	75 mL
4	8-inch (20 cm) rice or flour tortillas, warmed	4

1. In a small bowl, whisk together hoisin sauce, soy sauce, sesame oil, garlic and honey.

2. In a large nonstick skillet, heat oil over medium-high heat. Stir-fry chicken for 3 minutes. Stir in sauce and bring to a simmer, stirring. Reduce heat and simmer, stirring, for 2 minutes or until chicken is no longer pink inside. Stir in cabbage mixture until well coated. Top with peanuts and serve over or in warmed tortillas, if desired.

Variation

Moo Shu Pork: Substitute 2 lbs (1 kg) thinly sliced pork tenderloins for the chicken in this recipe.

Tip: Dark sesame oil is made from toasted sesame seeds, whereas light-colored sesame oil is extracted from raw sesame seeds.

Moroccan Fish Wrap

Serves 4

This light and flavorful wrap is made with fish flavored with Moroccan spices, perfect for a weeknight spring or summertime dinner.

1 tsp	salt	5 mL
½ tsp	ground cinnamon	2 mL
½ tsp	paprika	2 mL
¼ tsp	cayenne pepper	1 mL
1½ lbs	halibut fillets	750 g
2 tbsp	olive oil	30 mL
1 cup	shredded carrots	250 mL
1 tsp	freshly grated lemon zest (see Tip, below)	5 mL
3 tbsp	freshly squeezed lemon juice, divided	45 mL
4	8-inch (20 cm) flour tortillas	4
4	leaf lettuce wedges	4
2 tbsp	chopped fresh mint	30 mL

Tip: One medium lemon usually yields 2 to 3 tbsp (30 to 45 mL) lemon zest.

- **Preheat oven to 375°F (190°C)**
- **Baking sheet, lined with foil and coated with cooking spray**

1. In a small bowl, combine salt, cinnamon, paprika and cayenne.

2. Drizzle halibut with olive oil and rub with cinnamon mixture. Place on prepared baking sheet. Top with carrots, lemon zest and 2 tbsp (30 mL) of the lemon juice.

3. Bake in preheated oven for 8 to 10 minutes or until fish flakes easily when tested with a fork.

4. Place tortillas on a work surface. Arrange fish fillets and lettuce equally in center of each tortilla. Top with fresh mint and drizzle with remaining lemon juice. Fold tortillas in half.

Variation

Substitute any white fish fillets for the halibut. Salmon also works great in this recipe.

Banh Mi

Serves 4

This Vietnamese sandwich is traditionally made with pickled carrots and daikon radishes, cucumbers and a filling of roasted or grilled pork, Vietnamese sausage, chicken or ham.

1/4 cup	white wine vinegar	60 mL
1 tsp	sesame oil	5 mL
2 tbsp	granulated sugar	30 mL
1/4 tsp	salt	1 mL
1/4 tsp	freshly ground black pepper	1 mL
1 lb	cooked pork loin or Vietnamese sliced pork, thinly sliced (see Tips, right)	500 g
1/2 cup	shredded carrots	125 mL
1/2 cup	daikon radish (see Tips, right)	125 mL
1/4 cup	thinly sliced cucumber	60 mL
2 tbsp	chopped fresh cilantro	30 mL
1 tsp	finely chopped jalapeño	5 mL
4	6-inch (15 cm) small French baguettes, split lengthwise	4
1/4 cup	Homemade Mayonnaise (page 321) or store-bought, optional	60 mL

1. In a large bowl, whisk together vinegar, sesame oil, sugar, salt and pepper Add pork and toss well. Cover and refrigerate until ready to serve.

2. In a medium bowl, combine carrots, radish, cucumber, cilantro and jalapeño.

3. Place baguette slices on a work surface. Spread mayonnaise, if using, equally on cut sides of baguette halves. Add pork and slaw mixture equally on top. Top with remaining bread halves. Serve immediately.

Tips: Daikon is a Japanese vegetable that is an Asian radish that has a sweet, fresh flavor. If you can't find these, substitute regular radishes.

I used a pre-marinated pork tenderloin and grill over medium-high heat for 10 minutes per side or until an instant-read thermometer registered 155°F (68°C).

To purchase Vietnamese sliced pork, visit a local Vietnamese store or restaurant in your area.

Falafel Sandwich

• **Food processor**

Serves 4

My three kids love this Middle Eastern favorite, made from ground chickpeas, served in a warm pita pocket with hummus.

2 cups	canned or cooked chickpeas, drained and rinsed	500 mL
1/2 cup	diced onion	125 mL
2 tbsp	chopped fresh cilantro	30 mL
2 tbsp	chopped Italian flat-leaf parsley	30 mL
2 tbsp	freshly squeezed lemon juice	30 mL
1 tsp	ground cumin	5 mL
1	clove garlic, minced	1
1/2 cup	olive oil	125 mL
4	6- to 8-inch (15 to 20 cm) pitas with pockets	4

Toppings, optional

	Arugula
	Tomato slices
	Chopped red onion
	Hummus (page 313) or store-bought

1. In a food processor, pulse chickpeas, onion, cilantro, parsley, lemon juice, cumin and garlic until blended. Shape into 8 equal patties, each 2 inches (5 cm) thick.

2. In a large skillet, heat oil over medium-high heat. Cook patties for 3 to 4 minutes per side or until golden brown. Place on paper towels to drain.

3. Place pita bread on skillet to warm. Place 2 falafels each and desired toppings in each pita.

Tip: You can make these lighter by using less oil and lightly sautéing the falafels.

Shrimp and Lime Sandwich

Serves 4

This New Zealand sandwich combination is light and flavorful and perfect for a weeknight spring or summertime dinner.

¼ cup	Homemade Mayonnaise (page 321) or store-bought	60 mL
2 tbsp	cocktail sauce	30 mL
¼ tsp	grated lime zest	1 mL
¼ cup	freshly squeezed lime juice, divided	60 mL
1½ lbs	large shrimp, peeled and deveined	750 g
¼ cup	finely chopped red onion	60 mL
¼ cup	chopped fresh cilantro (see Tips, right)	60 mL
2 tbsp	olive oil	30 mL
8	slices Brioche bread, toasted (see Tips, right)	8
1 cup	lettuce leaves	250 mL
2	avocados, thinly sliced	2

1. In a small bowl, combine mayonnaise, cocktail sauce, lime zest and 2 tbsp (30 mL) of the lime juice. Set aside.

2. In a large bowl, toss together shrimp, red onion, cilantro and remaining lime juice.

3. In a large skillet heat, heat oil over medium heat. Sauté shrimp for 2 minutes or until pink and opaque.

4. Place bread slices on a work surface. Spread cut sides of bread equally with mayonnaise mixture. Add shrimp mixture, lettuce and avocados, pressing bread halves together to seal.

Tips: Cilantro is widely used in Asian, Caribbean and Latin American cooking. It's found year round in supermarkets where parsley and fresh herbs are sold. Choose bunches with bright-colored leaves and store in a plastic bag in the refrigerator for up to 1 week.

Brioche is a light yeast bread that is rich in butter and eggs. If you can't find it, use any type of French or sourdough bread.

Jamaican Chicken Sandwich

Serves 4

I love the Jamaican flavors of rum, chili powder and pineapples in these sandwiches. The pineapple slaw and coconut tops it off just right.

4	fresh or canned pineapple slices, drained and juice reserved	4
1/3 cup	dark rum	75 mL
1 tbsp	liquid honey	15 mL
1 tbsp	chili powder	15 mL
1/4 tsp	hot pepper flakes	1 mL
4	boneless skinless chicken breasts	4

Pineapple Slaw

2 cups	shredded cabbage	500 mL
1 cup	diced red bell pepper	250 mL
1/4 cup	pineapple juice, divided	60 mL
2 tbsp	chopped green onions	30 mL
2 tbsp	white wine vinegar	30 mL
1 tbsp	olive oil	15 mL

4	sesame seed sandwich buns, split and toasted	4
4	lettuce leaves	4

1/4 cup	unsweetened flaked coconut, toasted, optional	60 mL

- **Preheat greased barbecue grill to medium-high**

1. In a shallow dish or resealable bag, combine 2 tbsp (30 mL) of the pineapple juice, rum, honey, chili powder and hot pepper flakes. Remove 1/4 cup (60 mL) and set aside. Add chicken. Cover and marinate in the refrigerator for at least 20 minutes or for up to 8 hours.

2. Remove chicken from marinade. Discard marinade. Place chicken on preheated grill, close lid and grill, brushing periodically with remaining rum mixture, for 5 minutes per side or until no longer pink inside. Grill pineapple for 2 minutes per side or until lightly browned.

3. *Pineapple Slaw:* Meanwhile, in a bowl, combine cabbage, bell pepper, 1/4 cup (60 mL) of the pineapple juice, green onions, vinegar and oil.

4. Place buns on a work surface. Place chicken and pineapple on bottom half of buns. Line with lettuce and top with pineapple slaw, and coconut, if using, and remaining buns.

Variation

Substitute pineapple juice for the rum in this recipe.

Tip: Hot pepper flakes, or crushed red pepper, are the seeds and flakes of fiery hot peppers. Refrigerate in a tightly covered container to preserve the flavor.

Bratwurst

Serves 4

This German sandwich is made with Bratwurst, which is a sausage composed of veal, pork or beef. It is served with German mustard in a bread roll or bun and sauerkraut.

4 cups	water or beef broth	1 L
4	bratwurst	4
4	brat buns, split (see Tip, right)	4

Toppings, optional

	German mustard	
	Sauerkraut	
	Grilled onions	

- **Preheat greased barbecue grill to medium-high**

1. In a large saucepan, bring water to a simmer over medium-high heat. Add bratwurst and cook for 10 minutes or until no longer pink inside. Drain.

2. Place sausages on preheated grill and grill, turning often, for 4 minutes or until slightly charred. Place on buns and serve with desired toppings.

Tip: If you can't find "brat buns," use hot dog buns.

The Cuban

Serves 4

My friend and fabulous cook, Nancy Bynon, gave me great pointers on how to make this sandwich better. She said this is "to die for." The Cuban originated as lunch food in Cuba for workers in cigar factories and sugar mills.

¼ cup	Dijon mustard	60 mL
⅛ tsp	ground oregano	0.5 mL
⅛ tsp	ground cumin	0.5 mL
4	hoagie rolls, split lengthwise	4
8	slices thinly sliced ham	8
8	slices thinly sliced roast beef or roasted pork	8
8	slices thinly sliced Swiss cheese	8
8	thinly sliced dill pickles	8
¼ cup	butter, softened	60 mL

Tip: If you have leftover pork, this is a great way to use it up.

- **Panini grill or large skillet**
- **Preheat panini grill to medium, if using**

1. In a small bowl, combine mustard, oregano and cumin. Place hoagie rolls on a work surface. Spread mustard mixture equally on cut sides of bread. Arrange 2 slices of ham, roast beef, cheese and pickles over each bottom half. Cover with top bread halves and press together gently.

2. Spread butter on outsides of bread. Place sandwiches on preheated panini grill or large skillet over medium heat and cook, turning once if using a skillet, for 3 to 4 minutes or until golden brown and cheese is melted. Serve immediately.

Red Chili Sandwich

Serves 4

Chili powder, brown sugar, salt and olive oil add great color and sweet-spicy flavor to the shrimp in this sandwich.

¼ cup	packed dark brown sugar	60 mL
2 tbsp	chili powder	30 mL
1	clove garlic, minced	1
1 tsp	kosher salt	5 mL
1 tbsp	olive oil	15 mL
2 tsp	freshly squeezed lime juice	10 mL
1¼ lbs	large peeled cooked shrimp (see Tips, right)	625 g
4	buns, split and toasted	4
¼ cup	chopped fresh basil	60 mL

1. In a small bowl, combine brown sugar, chili powder, garlic, salt, olive oil and lime juice. Rub over shrimp and let stand for 10 minutes. Serve in buns with lettuce and fresh basil.

Tips: Feel free to substitute any of your favorite breads in this recipe.

You can also purchase uncooked shrimp and marinate as in Step 1 and grill over medium heat for 2 minutes or until shrimp turn pink and opaque.

Scottish Smoked Salmon

Serves 4

A friend once told me they had a simple and fresh sandwich in Scotland. This is a replica of what they called a "Scottish Club."

4 oz	cream cheese, softened	125 g
2 tbsp	chopped fresh dill	30 mL
1 tsp	grated lemon zest	5 mL
¼ tsp	freshly ground black pepper	1 mL
8	slices white bread (½-inch/1 cm thick slices)	8
8 oz	smoked salmon	250 g
1 cup	thinly sliced cucumber (16 slices)	250 mL

1. In a small bowl, combine cream cheese, dill, lemon zest and pepper. Place bread on a work surface. Spread cream cheese mixture equally on one side of 4 slices of white bread. Top equally with salmon, cucumber and remaining bread halves. Remove crusts and cut into triangles.

Tips: Use any of your favorite soft bread for this sandwich.

The cream cheese mixture and smoked salmon also is fabulous served on crackers and bagels.

Feel free to substitute light cream cheese for the regular.

Lamb Gyros

Serves 4

This Greek specialty consists of spiced lamb that is molded around a spit and vertically roasted, and then the meat is shaved off. This is the next best step to classic Gyro meat. They were even a hit with my kids.

2	cloves garlic, minced	2
2 tbsp	chopped Italian flat-leaf parsley	30 mL
2 tbsp	chopped fresh mint	30 mL
2 tbsp	chopped fresh basil	30 mL
1 tbsp	grated lemon zest	15 mL
$\frac{1}{2}$ tsp	salt	2 mL
$\frac{1}{2}$ tsp	freshly ground black pepper	2 mL
8 oz	ground lamb	250 g
4	6- to 8-inch (15 to 20 cm) pitas with pockets, warmed	4

Toppings, optional

	Tomato slices
	Cucumber slices
	Lettuce leaves
	Crumbled feta
	Classic Tzatziki (page 315)

- **Preheat greased barbecue grill to medium-high**
- **Instant-read thermometer**

1. In a large bowl, combine garlic, parsley, mint, basil, lemon zest, salt and pepper. Add lamb to garlic mixture, mixing well. Shape lamb into 4 equal patties, each $\frac{1}{2}$ inch (1 cm) thick.

2. Place burgers on preheated grill, close lid and grill, turning once, for 6 minutes per side or until an instant-read thermometer registers 160°F (71°C). Serve in pita pockets with desired toppings.

Variation

To cook burgers in a skillet instead of the grill, heat a large skillet over medium-high heat. Add a thin layer of oil to coat skillet. Cook burgers, turning once, for about 6 minutes per side or until an instant-read thermometer registers 160°F (71°C).

Tip: Gyros can be made earlier in the day and refrigerated and cooked right before serving.

Kofta Gyro Sandwich

This Mediterranean classic can be made with lamb, chicken or beef. The panko adds texture and crunch to these burgers.

1 lb	ground lamb	500 g
¼ cup	chopped onion	60 mL
¼ cup	chopped Italian flat-leaf parsley	60 mL
1	clove garlic, minced	1
1 cup	panko bread crumbs	250 mL
¼ tsp	salt	1 mL
⅛ tsp	cayenne pepper	0.5 mL
4	6- to 8-inch (15 to 20 cm) pitas with pockets, warmed	4
1 cup	shredded iceberg lettuce	250 mL
	Cucumber-Yogurt Sauce (page 317)	

- **Preheat greased barbecue grill to medium-high**
- **Instant-read thermometer**

1. In a large bowl, combine lamb, onion, parsley and garlic. Add bread crumbs, salt and cayenne pepper. Shape into 4 equal patties, each ½ inch (1 cm) thick.

2. Place burgers on preheated grill, close lid and grill, turning once, for 6 minutes per side or until an instant-read thermometer registers 160°F (71°C). Place in warmed pitas and top with shredded lettuce and Cucumber-Yogurt Sauce. Serve immediately.

Variation

I also like to make these with ground sirloin or ground turkey.

Tip: You can also make this with 1½ lbs (750 g) lamb stew meat. Combine all ingredients in Step 1 in a food processor until it resembles ground lamb.

Fairy Bread

Serves 4

Commonly served at children's parties in Australia and New Zealand, this bread is covered with butter or margarine and colored sprinkles.

8	slices white bread (½-inch/ 1 cm thick slices), crusts trimmed	8
¾ cup	butter, softened	175 mL
1 cup	colored sprinkles	250 mL

1. Place bread slices on a work surface. Spread 1 slice bread with butter. Top with another slice and top with ¼ cup (60 mL) of the candy sprinkles. Cut into triangles. Repeat with remaining ingredients.

Tip: This is a great kid's party idea for birthdays, Easter or themed parties, such as fairy parties.

Shrimp Salad Tramezzini

Serves 4

This Italian sandwich is made with white bread with the crusts removed. The shrimp in this recipe are so light and flavorful with basil, lemon zest and hot pepper flakes.

1 lb	large shrimp, peeled and deveined	500 g
½ tsp	grated lemon zest (see Tip, right)	2 mL
2 tbsp	freshly squeezed lemon juice	30 mL
1 tsp	olive oil	5 mL
	Salt and freshly ground black pepper	
⅛ tsp	hot pepper flakes	0.5 mL
2 tbsp	Homemade Mayonnaise (page 321) or store-bought	30 mL
2 tbsp	chopped fresh basil	30 mL
8	slices white bread (½-inch/ 1 cm thick slices)	8
1 cup	baby arugula leaves	250 mL

- **Preheat oven to 400°F (200°C)**

1. In a medium bowl, combine shrimp, lemon juice, olive oil, ⅛ tsp (0.5 mL) salt, ¼ tsp (1 mL) black pepper and hot pepper flakes.

2. Spread shrimp on baking sheet and bake in preheated oven for 10 minutes or until shrimp turn pink and opaque. Let cool. Chop shrimp into chunks and place in a large bowl. Add mayonnaise, basil and lemon zest.

2. Place bread on a work surface. Top 4 bread slices with ½ cup (125 mL) of the shrimp salad and arugula leaves. Season with salt and pepper to taste. Top with remaining bread slices. Use a serrated knife to remove crusts and halve sandwich diagonally.

Tip: Be sure to wash and dry your lemon thoroughly before zesting.

Regional American
Sandwiches

Texas-Style Brisket

Serves 12

This Texas favorite is awesome when you taste the tender, melt-in-your mouth beef.

3 tbsp	onion powder	45 mL
2 tbsp	smoked paprika or chili powder	30 mL
4 tsp	brown sugar	20 mL
4 tsp	kosher salt	20 mL
1/2 cup	apple cider vinegar	125 mL
6 tbsp	Worcestershire sauce	90 mL
4 tsp	hot pepper sauce	20 mL
4 lbs	beef brisket, trimmed	2 kg
	Hamburger buns, split and toasted	
	Barbecue Sauce (page 325) or store-bought	
	Pickles	

Tips: While barbecuing the brisket, adjust heat or coals as necessary to maintain a temperature of 300°F (150°C). If your barbecue doesn't have a built-in thermometer, place an oven thermometer on the grill beside the brisket.

If you are looking for a leaner cut of brisket, look for "flat-cut" brisket.

• **Preheat greased barbecue grill to medium-low (see Tips, left)**

1. In a medium bowl, combine onion powder, paprika, brown sugar and salt. Stir in vinegar, Worcestershire sauce and hot pepper sauce. Place roast in a large bowl. Pour $1/3$ cup (75 mL) of the marinade mixture over roast and let stand for 10 minutes. Reserve remaining marinade.

2. Wrap brisket in heavy foil, leaving a hole in top of foil. Place brisket on preheated grill. Cover grill and open vent if there is one. Grill for $2\frac{1}{4}$ hours or until meat is very tender.

3. In a small saucepan, heat remaining marinade over low heat for 5 minutes or until heated.

4. Let brisket stand for 10 minutes. Transfer brisket to a platter and cut diagonally across the grain into thin slices. Serve beef in buns with barbecue sauce and pickles. Serve with reserved sauce.

Ancho Adobo Steak

Serves 4

The combination of apricot preserves, chipotle chiles and brown sugar flavor this steak sandwich with a taste of the Southwest.

1/3 cup	apricot preserves or jam	75 mL
1 tbsp	chopped chipotle chiles in adobo sauce (see Tip, right)	15 mL
1 tbsp	brown sugar	15 mL
1 tbsp	chili powder	15 mL
1 tsp	garlic powder	5 mL
1 tsp	kosher or sea salt	5 mL
1 tsp	freshly ground black pepper	5 mL
1 1/2 lbs	beef flank steak	750 g
4	hamburger buns, split and toasted	4

Toppings, optional

	Apricot preserves
	Lettuce leaves
	Tomato slices

- **Preheat lightly greased barbecue grill to medium-high**

1. In a small bowl, whisk together apricot preserves and chipotle chiles. Set aside.

2. In another bowl, combine brown sugar, chili powder, garlic powder, salt and pepper. Rub on both sides of steak. Brush with apricot mixture.

3. Place steak on preheated grill, close lid and grill, turning once, for 3 to 5 minutes per side for medium-rare or until desired degree of doneness, brushing with apricot mixture. Transfer to a cutting board, tent with foil and let stand for 5 minutes. Cut across the grain into thin slices.

4. Serve in hamburger buns with desired toppings.

Tip: If you can't find canned chipotle chiles, you can substitute 1 tsp (5 mL) ground chipotle seasoning. This can be found in the spice aisle and grocery stores. If you like more heat, add 2 tbsp (30 mL) chopped chipotle chiles.

Meatball Sandwich

Serves 6

This classic sandwich is popular in New York and Chicago. It's filled with provolone cheese and robust meatballs and made with a mixture of ground beef and sausage.

1 lb	extra-lean ground beef, preferably ground round	500 g
8 oz	ground sausage	250 g
1	jar (28 oz/769 mL) marinara sauce with peppers and mushrooms (see Tips, below)	1
1	clove garlic, minced	1
¼ tsp	hot pepper flakes	1 mL
1 lb	bread loaf, unsliced	500 g
6	slices provolone cheese	6

Tips: Feel free to use any of your favorite homemade or store-bought marinara sauce.

Hot pepper flakes have a pungent and smoky flavor. Store in a cool, dry place.

- **Preheat broiler**

1. In a large bowl, combine beef and sausage. Shape into 8 balls, each about 1 inch (2.5 cm).

2. In a large skillet over medium heat, sauté meatballs for 10 to 15 minutes or until browned. Drain and return to skillet. Add marinara, garlic and hot pepper flakes. Bring to a boil. Reduce heat and simmer, stirring occasionally, for 12 to 15 minutes or until meatballs are no longer pink inside.

3. Cut bread in half horizontally and scoop out bottom, leaving a ½-inch (1 cm) thick shell. Place, cut side up, on a baking sheet and broil for 1 to 2 minutes or until lightly toasted. Spoon meatball mixture into toasted shell. Top with provolone slices. Cover with bread top. Cut sandwiches into 6 slices and serve immediately.

Variations

Substitute ground turkey for the ground beef.

Substitute 6 hoagie rolls for the bread loaf.

New York Spiedies

Serves 4

This New York sandwich is a "skewered sandwich," created in Binghampton. It's a beef skewer wrapped in bread.

¹⁄₃ cup	white vinegar	75 mL
2 tbsp	olive oil	30 mL
1 tsp	freshly squeezed lemon juice	5 mL
1	clove garlic, minced (see Tips, below)	1
2 tbsp	finely chopped fresh mint	30 mL
½ tsp	dried basil	2 mL
½ tsp	dried oregano	2 mL
½ tsp	kosher salt	2 mL
½ tsp	freshly ground black pepper	2 mL
1 lb	boneless stewing beef, cut into 1½-inch (4 cm) thick cubes (see Tips, below)	500 g
4	slices French bread (½-inch/ 1 cm thick slices), toasted	4

Tips: Select heads of garlic that are firm to the touch and not discolored. Store them in a cool dry place or seal in a plastic bag and refrigerate.

For the beef, you can use your favorite beef cut.

- **Preheat greased barbecue grill to medium-high**
- **4 wooden skewers, soaked in water for 15 minutes**
- **Instant-read thermometer**

1. In a small bowl, combine vinegar, olive oil, lemon juice, garlic, mint, basil, oregano, salt and pepper.

2. Place beef in a resealable plastic bag. Add vinegar mixture, seal bag and marinate in the refrigerator for at least 4 hours or overnight.

3. Remove meat from marinade, discarding marinade. Thread beef onto 4 skewers. Place skewers on preheated grill, close lid and grill, turning once, for 6 to 8 minutes per side for medium or until desired doneness. Remove beef from skewers and place on bread. Serve immediately.

Variation

This recipe would also be great with chicken or pork.

Cheese Steak Sandwich

Sometimes people don't want to take the time to make a classic Philadelphia cheese steak sandwich, but this recipe is very easy and incredibly flavorful.

1 lb	top sirloin or New York strip steaks, cut into ¼-inch (0.5 cm) thick strips	500 g
1 tsp	garlic powder	5 mL
½ tsp	salt	2 mL
½ tsp	freshly ground black pepper	2 mL
2 tbsp	olive oil, divided	30 mL
1	green bell pepper, sliced	1
1	onion, sliced	1
4 oz	sliced fresh mushrooms	125 g
4	hoagie rolls, split	4
¾ cup	shredded Monterey Jack cheese	175 mL

- **Preheat broiler**

1. Place steaks in a shallow dish. Sprinkle with garlic powder, salt and pepper.

2. In a large skillet, heat oil over medium heat. Sauté steak slices for 5 minutes for medium-rare or until steak is desired degree of doneness. Set aside.

3. In same skillet, sauté green pepper, onion and mushrooms for 3 minutes or until vegetables are tender.

4. Place both halves of rolls on a broiler pan. Arrange steak and onions equally among bottom slices of bread halves. Add cheese. Broil for 2 minutes or until cheese is melted and bread is lightly toasted. Remove from oven and press two halves together.

Tips: These sandwiches are great also served with a topping of warm barbecue sauce.

You can also grill the steak on a preheated greased barbecue grill on medium-high heat. Grill for 4 minutes per side for medium-rare or until desired degree of doneness.

Chili Dogs

We often serve this all-American favorite on Halloween night, and the kids love them!

1 lb	extra-lean ground beef, preferably ground sirloin	500 g
1 cup	chopped onion	250 mL
2	cloves garlic, minced	2
2 cups	tomato sauce	500 mL
1 tsp	chili powder	5 mL
1/4 tsp	ground cumin	1 mL
1/4 tsp	salt	1 mL
4	wieners, grilled	4
4	hot dog buns	4

Toppings, optional

	Chopped onion
	Shredded Cheddar cheese

1. In a large skillet over medium-high heat, sauté beef, onion and garlic, breaking up beef with a spoon, for about 8 minutes or until meat is browned and no longer pink inside and onion is tender. Drain off any fat.

2. Stir in tomato sauce, chili powder, cumin and salt. Bring to a boil. Reduce heat, cover and simmer, stirring occasionally, for 15 minutes.

3. Place hot dog buns on a work surface. Place wieners in buns. Spoon beef mixture equally on top. Top with onion and Cheddar cheese, if desired.

Tip: You can make the chili mixture 1 or 2 days ahead.

Chicago Hot Dog

Chicago dogs have the most condiments of any hot dogs I have ever seen. Enjoy this simple, but delicious classic version.

4	wieners	4
4	hot dog buns, split	4

Toppings, optional

	Yellow mustard
	Pickle relish
	Diced tomatoes
	Diced onion
	Pickle spears
	Pickled peppers

• **Preheat greased barbecue grill to medium-high**

1. Place wieners on preheated grill, and grill, turning often, for 5 minutes or until heated through and slightly charred. Serve on buns with desired toppings.

Tip: It's fun to have a "hot dog bar" and serve hot dogs with all of the wonderful Chicago-style toppings. It makes a great casual party idea.

Classic Pastrami on Rye

Serves 4

This simple four-ingredient sandwich is popular at my house on big football game nights.

8	slices rye bread (½-inch/ 1 cm thick slices)	8
¼ cup	deli mustard	60 mL
8 oz	pastrami, slightly warmed (see Tip, right)	250 g
	Dill pickles, optional	

1. Place bread slices on a work surface. Spread mustard equally over one side of bread slice. Arrange warmed pastrami on top of 4 slices and cover with remaining bread slices, pressing together gently. Serve immediately with a side of dill pickles.

Variation

Add 4 oz (125 g) sliced Muenster or provolone cheese.

Tip: To warm pastrami, place on a large microwave-safe plate and heat in the microwave on High for about 30 seconds.

Black Forest Ham and Havarti with Chutney

Serves 4

Sweet fruit chutney gives these ham sandwiches new life. This sandwich is always highly requested by my friends.

8	slices pumpernickel bread (½-inch/1 cm thick slices)	4
12 oz	thinly sliced Black Forest ham	375 g
4	sliced Havarti cheese	4
4 tbsp	Mango or Plum Chutney (see Variations, pages 335) or store-bought	60 mL

1. Place bread slices on a work surface. Arrange ham and cheese equally on one side of bread slice. Spread equally with 1 tbsp (15 mL) of the chutney. Cover with remaining bread slices, pressing together gently. Serve immediately.

Variation

Substitute 4 oz (125 g) Muenster cheese for the Havarti and 8 oz (250 g) turkey for the ham.

Tip: If you want to add some crunch to this sandwich, add ¼ cup (60 mL) thinly sliced red onion.

Muffulettas

Serves 6

This hero-style sandwich is very famous in New Orleans, where meats and cheese are combined with an olive salad.

1 cup	finely chopped pitted black olives	250 mL
1 cup	finely chopped pimiento-stuffed olives	250 mL
3 tbsp	chopped Italian flat-leaf parsley	45 mL
2 tbsp	olive oil, divided	30 mL
4 tsp	freshly squeezed lemon juice	20 mL
2	cloves garlic, minced	2
1 tsp	dried oregano	5 mL
1/2 tsp	freshly ground black pepper	2 mL
1 lb	French bread, split lengthwise	500 g
6	lettuce leaves	6
4 oz	thinly sliced salami or pepperoni	125 g
4 oz	thinly sliced ham or turkey	125 g
4	slices provolone or Swiss cheese	4
2	medium tomatoes, thinly sliced	2

1. In a small bowl, combine black and pimiento olives, parsley, 1 tbsp (15 mL) of the olive oil, lemon juice, garlic, oregano and pepper. Cover and refrigerate for at least 1 hour.

2. Place bread on a work surface. Brush remaining olive oil on cut side of bread. Top with lettuce, salami, ham, cheese and tomato. Top with olive relish. To serve, cut into 6 portions.

Variations

Add pastrami on your muffuletta for an additional flavor.

Serve on a sesame seed buns. This is popular in the French Quarter of New Orleans.

Mini Muffulettas: Serve on 4 to 6 rolls. Warm on broil for 2 minutes or until cheese is melted.

Italian-Style Muffulettas: Prepare as above but omit green olive relish. Drain a 16-oz (500 mL) jar pickled mixed vegetables and chop vegetables, removing stems from pepperoncinis. Combine vegetables with 1/4 cup (60 mL) chopped pimiento olives, 1/2 tsp (2 mL) Italian seasoning and 1/4 tsp (1 mL) pepper. Assemble sandwich as above with pepperoni and mozzarella cheese.

Grilled Reubens

Serves 4

I have never been a huge "Reuben" person, but my kids love them! These are simple to prepare and taste like they were made at a New York deli.

8	slices rye bread (½-inch/ 1 cm thick slices)	8
½ cup	Thousand Island dressing	125 mL
1½ lbs	corned beef, thinly sliced	750 g
4	slices Swiss cheese	4
½ cup	canned sauerkraut, drained	125 mL
½ cup	butter, margarine or olive oil	125 mL

Tip: The key to making a great Reuben is using the highest quality corned beef, rye bread and sauerkraut. Don't skimp on those three ingredients.

- **Panini grill or large skillet**
- **Preheat panini grill to medium, if using**

1. Place bread on a work surface. Spread dressing equally on one side of each bread slice. Arrange corned beef, cheese and sauerkraut equally over 4 bread slices. Cover with remaining bread, pressing together gently.

2. Spread butter on each side of each sandwich. Place sandwiches, buttered side down, on preheated panini grill or in a skillet over medium heat and cook, turning once if using a skillet, for 3 to 4 minutes or until golden brown and cheese is melted. Serve immediately.

Variation

Turkey Reuben: Substitute 1 lb (500 g) sliced turkey for the corned beef and ½ cup (125 mL) Russian dressing for the Thousand Island.

Pulled Pork Sandwich

Serves 4

Pulled Pork is very Southern and an incredible sandwich when you're wanting to barbecue. I like to cook my pork butt in a slow cooker or in the oven on slow, low heat.

4	hamburger buns, split and warmed	4
2½ cups	pulled pork meat (see Tips, right)	625 mL
1 cup	Barbecue Sauce (page 325) or store-bought	250 mL
1 cup	small round pickle slices	250 mL
	Coleslaw, optional	

1. Place buns on a work surface. Arrange pork equally over bottom sides of bun. Top equally with barbecue sauce, pickles and coleslaw, if using. Top with buns. Serve immediately.

Tips: Slow cooker for pork: Place a 2-lb (1 kg) boneless pork shoulder blade (butt) in a 4-quart slow cooker with 1½ cups (375 mL) barbecue sauce. Cover and cook on Low for 8 hours or High for 4 hours or until pork is tender and falling apart. Remove pork and let stand for 15 minutes. Shred with two forks.

To cook pork in the oven: Preheat oven to 450°F (230°C). Place a 2-lb (1 kg) boneless pork shoulder blade (butt) in a roasting pan and pour 1½ cups (375 mL) barbecue sauce over top. Cover pan and roast pork for 30 minutes. Reduce oven temperature to 325°F (160°C) and roast for 2 hours more, basting every 30 minutes, until pork is fork-tender. Remove pork from oven and let stand for 15 minutes. Shred with two forks.

Cowboy-Spiced Pork Sandwich

Serves 4

This western-style sandwich has a touch of coffee in the chili powder rub mixture, adding a robust flavor.

2 tsp	ground expresso coffee granules	10 mL
2 tsp	chopped fresh thyme	10 mL
1 tsp	salt	5 mL
1 tsp	freshly ground black pepper	5 mL
1 tsp	ancho or other chili powder	5 mL
1 tsp	garlic powder	5 mL
1/4 tsp	ground coriander	1 mL
1 tbsp	olive oil	15 mL
1 1/4 lbs	pork tenderloin (about 2 small)	625 g
4	mini hamburger buns, split	4

Toppings, optional

	Lettuce
	Tomatoes slices
	Pickles

- **Preheat greased barbecue grill to medium-high**
- **Instant-read thermometer**

1. In a small bowl, combine coffee, thyme, salt, pepper, chili powder, garlic and coriander. Drizzle olive oil over tenderloin and rub with coffee mixture.

2. Place pork on preheated grill, cover with lid, and grill, turning twice, for 8 to 10 minutes per side or until an instant-read thermometer inserted into thickest portion registers 155°F (68°C). Transfer to a cutting board, tent with foil and let stand for 10 minutes. Cut crosswise into thin slices and serve in buns with desired toppings.

Tips: Letting the meat stand means wrapping in foil and standing at room temperature. This helps lock the juices into the meat.

If you're really short on time, use boneless skinless pork loin chops that are already sliced. These cook in a large lightly greased skillet for 2 to 3 minutes over medium-high heat per side or until a instant-read thermometer inserted into thickest portion registers 155°F (68°C).

Fried Green Tomato Sandwich

Serves 4

Fried green tomatoes are very Southern and very Alabamian, where I'm from. Everyone always loves this sandwich or just the tomatoes eaten alone as an appetizer.

½ cup	self-rising cornmeal	125 mL
¼ cup	all-purpose flour	60 mL
¼ cup	panko bread crumbs	60 mL
¼ tsp	salt	1 mL
¼ tsp	freshly ground black pepper	1 mL
2	eggs, lightly beaten	2
2	green tomatoes, thinly sliced	2
½ cup	olive oil	125 mL
8	slices sourdough bread (½-inch/1 cm thick slices)	8
¼ cup	Homemade Mayonnaise (page 321) or Rémoulade Sauce (page 333) or store-bought	60 mL
4	slices bacon, cooked	4
½ cup	arugula or watercress (see Tips, right)	125 mL

1. In a medium bowl, combine cornmeal, flour, panko, salt and pepper. Place eggs in a shallow dish. Dip tomatoes in egg and then in cornmeal mixture.

2. In a large nonstick skillet, heat oil over medium heat. Fry tomatoes for 4 minutes per side or until lightly browned.

3. Place bread slices on a work surface. Spread 4 bread slices equally with mayonnaise. Top equally with bacon, watercress and fried tomatoes. Top with remaining bread slices.

Tips: If you have any leftover green tomatoes, they are excellent broiled or added to relishes.

Arugula, also called roquette or rocket, has a spicy, pepper flavor. Place in a plastic bag and store in the refrigerator for up to 2 days.

Classic Barbecue Chicken Sandwich

Serves 4

This is a wonderful summertime sandwich, especially when you're in the mood for a barbecue.

4	boneless skinless chicken breasts (about 1½ lbs/750 g)	4
1 cup	Barbecue Sauce or White Barbecue Sauce (page 325) or store-bought	250 mL
4	hamburger buns, split	4
	Small round pickle slices	

Tip: I have two barbecue sauces to choose from. One is vinegar based and one has more citrus flavor. Both are wonderful!

- **Preheat greased barbecue grill to medium**

1. Place chicken in a large resealable plastic bag or shallow dish. Pour barbecue sauce over chicken and coat both sides. Cover and refrigerate for at least 2 hours.

2. Remove chicken from barbecue sauce, discarding sauce. Place chicken on grill, close lid and grill, turning once, for 4 to 6 minutes per side or until chicken is no longer pink inside. Let stand for 5 minutes. Serve chicken on buns with pickles.

Tip: Substitute 2 cups (500 mL) chopped cooked chicken for the chicken breasts. Place chicken in a microwave-safe dish, pour sauce over top and heat in the microwave on High for 1 or 2 minutes or until heated. Serve over buns.

Chicken-Avocado Dagwoods

Serves 4

This sandwich was named after Dagwood Bumstead, a character in the comic strip "Blondie," who made extremely large sandwiches.

8	slices white or multigrain bread (1/2-inch/1 cm thick slices), toasted	8
2 tbsp	Homemade Mayonnaise (page 321) or store-bought	30 mL
2 1/2 cups	sliced cooked chicken (see Tips, right)	625 mL
2	avocados, sliced (see Tips, right)	2
8	red onion slices	8
4	slices Monterey Jack or provolone cheese	4
8	bacon slices, cooked	8
8	lettuce leaves	8
8	tomato slices	8
1/8 tsp	kosher salt	0.5 mL
1/8 tsp	freshly ground black pepper	0.5 mL

1. Place bread slices on a work surface. Spread one side of bread slices equally with mayonnaise. Arrange chicken, avocados, red onion, cheese, bacon, lettuce and tomato equally over half of bread slices. Sprinkle with salt and pepper. Top with remaining bread slices, pressing together gently. Serve immediately.

Tips: I like to use leftover grilled chicken for this or baked chicken. I bake bone-in skin-on chicken breasts on a baking sheet in a 375°F (190°C) oven for 30 to 40 minutes or until an instant-read thermometer inserted in the thickest part registers 165°F (74°C).

You can use a rotisserie chicken for the chicken in this recipe.

To peel a ripe avocado, use a sharp knife to make a lengthwise cut down the middle of the skin. Open the two halves and remove the pit. Now cut into slices or make a cross-hatch pattern and scoop out.

Louisville Hot Browns

Serves 4

These sandwiches originated in Louisville, Kentucky, at The Brown Hotel. Early versions of this sandwich were made with country ham.

2 tbsp	butter or margarine	30 mL
2 tbsp	all-purpose flour	30 mL
1 cup	milk	250 mL
¾ cup	shredded Cheddar cheese	175 mL
½ cup	freshly grated Parmesan cheese	125 mL
4	slices sourdough or rustic bread (½-inch/1 cm thick slices), toasted	4
12 oz	sliced turkey	375 g
8	slices bacon, cooked	8
1	large tomato, sliced	1
⅛ tsp	freshly ground black pepper	0.5 mL

- **Preheat broiler**

1. In a small saucepan, melt butter over low heat. Add flour, stirring until smooth. Cook, stirring constantly, for 1 minute. Gradually add milk and stir for about 3 minutes or until slightly thickened. Add Cheddar and Parmesan cheeses and cook for 2 minutes more or until cheese is melted. Set aside.

2. Place bread slices on broiler pan. Arrange turkey, bacon, tomato and pepper equally over top. Top equally with cheese sauce. Broil 3 inches (7.5 cm) from heat for 4 minutes or until cheese sauce is golden. Serve immediately.

Tip: To lighten this sandwich, use skim milk and turkey bacon and decrease the cheese by half.

Californian

This is one of my favorite sandwiches. I love the simplicity of goat cheese and mayonnaise as the spread on this colorful vegetarian sandwich.

¹⁄₂ cup	Homemade Mayonnaise (page 321) or store-bought	125 mL
¹⁄₃ cup	crumbled goat cheese	75 mL
1¹⁄₄ cups	thinly sliced yellow squash (zucchini) (about 2 small)	300 mL
1¹⁄₄ cups	thinly sliced zucchini (about 1 large)	300 mL
3	Roma (plum) tomatoes, thinly sliced	3
¹⁄₄ tsp	salt	1 mL
¹⁄₄ tsp	freshly ground black pepper	1 mL
2 tbsp	olive oil	30 mL
8	slices multigrain bread (¹⁄₂-inch/1 cm thick slices)	8
2	avocados, thinly sliced	2
1 cup	alfalfa sprouts (see Tips, right)	250 mL

- **Preheat oven to 450°F (230°C)**

1. In a small bowl, combine mayonnaise and goat cheese. Cover and refrigerate until ready to serve.

2. Place squash, zucchini and tomatoes on a large baking sheet. Sprinkle with salt and pepper. Drizzle with olive oil. Place in preheated oven, tossing occasionally, for 20 to 25 minutes or until tender.

3. Spread mayonnaise mixture equally over one side of bread slices. Top 4 slices equally with roasted vegetables, avocados, sprouts and remaining bread slices, pressing together gently. Serve immediately.

Tips: If you can't find alfalfa sprouts, I love using broccoli sprouts, which are also widely available in grocery stories.

Choose zucchini that are firm with unbruised skin.

Oyster Bacon Po' Boys

Serves 4

This is New Orleans favorite sandwich, and when I want a taste of New Orleans, I make these.

8	slices bacon	8
1/3 cup	chopped onion	75 mL
1/4 cup	chopped green bell pepper	60 mL
1/4 cup	chopped celery	60 mL
1	tomato, seeded and chopped	1
2 tbsp	chopped fresh parsley	30 mL
1 tsp	garlic powder	5 mL
1/4 tsp	salt	1 mL
1/4 tsp	hot pepper sauce	1 mL
1/4 cup	Homemade Mayonnaise (page 321) or store-bought	60 mL
1 cup	panko bread crumbs	250 ml
1/2 cup	yellow cornmeal	125 mL
2	eggs, lightly beaten	2
12 oz	shucked fresh oysters, drained (see Tip, below)	375 g
	Vegetable oil	
4	6-inch (15 cm) French bread rolls, split and toasted	4
	Leaf lettuce leaves	

Tip: When purchasing oysters, they should be plump and uniform for their size and have a good color and smell. Refrigerate them for up to 2 days.

- **Candy/deep-fry thermometer**

1. In a large skillet, cook bacon until crisp. Remove bacon, reserving 1 tbsp (15 mL) drippings. Set bacon aside.

2. Add onion, bell pepper and celery to drippings in skillet, stirring constantly, until tender. Stir in tomato, parsley, garlic powder, salt and hot pepper sauce. Drain well. Stir in mayonnaise. Set aside.

3. In a medium bowl, combine panko and cornmeal. Place eggs in another bowl. Dip oysters first in egg, then dip in cornmeal mixture, pressing to coat. Place on a baking sheet. Discard any excess egg and cornmeal mixture.

4. In a Dutch oven or other deep pot, heat 2 inches (5 cm) of oil to 375°F (190°C). In batches of 3 or 4, fry oysters, turning once, for 1 1/2 to 2 minutes or until golden brown. Drain on paper towels.

5. Place rolls on a work surface. Spread mayonnaise mixture equally on cut surfaces of roll halves. Arrange bacon, lettuce and oysters equally on bottom halves of rolls. Cover with top bread halves, pressing together gently.

Variation

Substitute 12 oz (375 g) shrimp, peeled and deveined, for the oysters in this recipe.

Fish Po' Boys with Cocktail Sauce

Serves 4

We make these classic fish Po' Boys often at my house. They are great for a party sandwich in the summertime

4 tsp	Creole seasoning	20 mL
¼ cup	freshly squeezed lemon juice (see Tip, below)	60 mL
1 lb	catfish fillets	500 g
4	French rolls, split and toasted	4
½ cup	lettuce leaves	125 mL
1	large tomato, thinly sliced	1
½ cup	diced red onion	125 mL
	Cocktail Sauce (page 326) or store-bought	

Tip: To squeeze more juice from citrus fruits, bring lemon to room temperature or microwave chilled fruit for 20 seconds on High.

- **Preheat greased barbecue grill to medium-high**

1 Sprinkle Creole seasoning and lemon juice over both sides of catfish. Place fish on preheated grill or in a large skillet over medium-high heat and cook for 5 to 7 minutes per side or until fish flakes easily when tested with a fork.

2. Place rolls on a work surface. Arrange catfish, lettuce, tomato and red onion equally on bottom halves of rolls. Spread top halves equally with cocktail sauce and press slices together. Serve immediately.

Variation

Substitute any white fish fillets for the catfish in this recipe.

Top with crumbled bacon for added flavor and crunch.

Crab Louie Sandwich

Serves 4

This sandwich is a spin on the West Coast classic Crab Louie salad. In this sandwich, the crab mixture is piled high on iceberg lettuce and served on a hoagie bun.

¾ cup	chili sauce (see Tips, right)	175 mL
¾ cup	Homemade Mayonnaise (page 321) or store-bought	175 mL
¼ cup	chopped green bell pepper	60 mL
2	green onions, chopped	2
1 tsp	freshly squeezed lemon juice	5 mL
1 lb	cooked lump crabmeat	500 g
4	hoagie buns, split	4
1½ cups	iceberg lettuce	375 mL

1. In a large bowl, stir together chili sauce, mayonnaise, bell pepper, green onions, lemon juice and crabmeat.

2. Place buns on a work surface. Place lettuce equally on top. Spread crab mixture equally in center of hoagies over lettuce.

Variation

Substitute 1 lb (500 g) peeled cooked shrimp for the crab in this recipe.

Tips: Chili sauce is a blend of tomatoes, chiles, onions, peppers, vinegar, sugar and spices and can be found in the grocery where ketchup is located.

You can substitute reduced-fat mayonnaise for the regular.

Oven-Fried Fish Sandwich

Serves 4 to 6

I like the combination of cornmeal and panko in this oven-fried fish sandwich.

¼ cup	yellow cornmeal	60 mL
¼ cup	panko bread crumbs	60 mL
½ tsp	paprika	2 mL
½ tsp	sea salt	2 mL
½ tsp	freshly ground black pepper	2 mL
⅓ cup	milk	75 mL
1 lb	whitefish fillets, cut into 1-inch (2.5 cm) strips	500 g
2 tbsp	butter or margarine, melted	30 mL
4	kaiser rolls, split and toasted	4
	Tartar Sauce (page 333) or store-bought, optional	

- **Preheat oven to 450°F (230°C)**
- **13- by 9-inch (33 by 23 cm) glass baking dish, lightly greased**

1. In a shallow dish, combine cornmeal, panko, paprika, salt and pepper. Place milk in another shallow dish. Dip fish in milk and then dredge in cornmeal mixture. Place in a prepared baking dish. Drizzle with melted butter.

2. Bake in preheated oven for 10 minutes or until fish flakes easily when tested with a fork. Serve fish on rolls with Tartar Sauce, if using.

Variation

Use shrimp instead of whitefish.

Shrimp Rolls

Serves 4

New Englanders love their lobster rolls. If you want a less expensive version, these sandwiches filled with shrimp are great, too.

2 tbsp	olive oil	30 mL
¼ cup	finely chopped shallots	60 mL
2 tbsp + 2 tsp	freshly squeezed lemon juice	40 mL
¼ tsp	freshly ground black pepper	5 mL
1¼ lbs	medium shrimp, peeled and deveined (see Tips, right)	625 g
1 cup	Homemade Mayonnaise (page 321) or store-bought	250 mL
½ cup	chopped and peeled cucumber	125 mL
2 tbsp	finely chopped fresh chives (see Tips, right)	30 mL
1 tsp	grated lemon zest	5 mL
4	hot dog bun or hoagie buns, split	4
1 cup	shredded lettuce	250 mL

- **Preheat greased barbecue grill to medium-high**

1. In a small bowl, combine oil, shallots, 2 tbsp (30 mL) of the lemon juice and pepper. Pour over shrimp, tossing gently. Let stand for 10 minutes.

2. In another small bowl, combine mayonnaise, cucumber, chives, lemon zest and remaining 2 tsp (10 mL) lemon juice. Reserve ½ cup (125 mL) of the mixture.

3. On grill or in a skillet, grill or cook shrimp over medium-high heat for 1 to 2 minutes per side or until shrimp turns pink and opaque. Coarsely chop and stir in reserved mayonnaise.

4. Place buns on a work surface. Spread mayonnaise mixture on cut sides of bread. Place shrimp and lettuce in bread halves, pressing together gently.

Tips: I love to use peeled and deveined cooked frozen shrimp. It's not only quicker to use and cheaper, but also tastes great.

Chives are a member of the onion family and have a mild flavor. To store, wrap in paper towels and seal in a resealable bag in the refrigerator for up to 1 week.

Lobster Rolls with Creamy Dijon Sauce

Serves 4

This famous sandwich of Maine is so good and makes a nice special occasion sandwich to serve.

2	1½ to 1¾ lbs (750 to 875 g) live lobsters (see Tip, right)	2
⅓ cup	Homemade Mayonnaise (page 321) or store-bought	75 mL
2 tbsp	Dijon mustard	30 mL
⅓ cup	diced celery	75 mL
1 tbsp	minced onion	15 mL
1 tsp	lemon zest	5 mL
2 tsp	freshly squeezed lemon juice	10 mL
¼ tsp	cayenne pepper	1 mL
4	small hoagie rolls, split and toasted	4

1. In a large kettle or Dutch oven of boiling water, boil lobsters for 8 to 10 minutes until meat feels just firm when you move the tail. Drain and let cool.

2. Remove meat from lobster shell, tail and claws, and coarsely chop. Set aside.

3. In a large bowl, stir together mayonnaise, Dijon mustard, celery, onion, lemon zest, lemon juice and cayenne pepper. Add lobster meat, tossing gently. Spoon mixture equally into hoagie rolls.

Tip: If you're purchasing precooked, shelled lobster meat, you'll need about 1¼ lbs (625 g) for this recipe.

Light and Healthy
Sandwiches

Easy Beef Calzone

Serves 4

People usually think of calzones being high in calories and fat, but not these. These use lean beef, turkey pepperoni and reduced-fat cheese.

8 oz	lean ground beef	250 g
1/2 cup	turkey pepperoni slices, halved	125 mL
1/2 cup	chopped onion	125 mL
1	clove garlic, minced	1
1 tsp	Italian seasoning	5 mL
1/4 tsp	freshly ground black pepper	1 mL
1/8 tsp	salt	0.5 mL
14 oz	prepared pizza dough	400 g
1 cup	shredded reduced-fat mozzarella cheese	250 mL
1 cup	marinara sauce, warmed	250 mL

Tips: You can make these 1 day ahead and heat before serving the next day.

Lightly brush calzones with olive oil before placing in the oven for a nice golden color and crisp texture. These calzones keep well in the fridge for leftovers, too.

- **Preheat oven to 450°F (230°C)**
- **Baking sheet, coated with cooking spray**

1. In a large nonstick skillet over medium heat, sauté beef, pepperoni, onion and garlic, breaking up meat with a spoon until beef crumbles, for 5 minutes or until beef is no longer pink. Stir in Italian seasoning, pepper and salt. Drain and remove from heat.

2. Divide dough evenly into 4 pieces. Pat each dough piece into a 3-inch (7.5 cm) square. Spoon beef mixture equally over half of each square, leaving a 1/2-inch (1 cm) border. Top equally with cheese.

3. Fold dough over filling until edges almost meet. Bring bottom edge over top edge and crimp edges of dough with fingers to form a rim. Place on prepared baking sheet.

4. Bake in preheated oven for 10 to 12 minutes or until lightly browned. Serve topped with marinara sauce.

Greek Pita Pocket

This Greek-style sandwich is a delicious combination and is so easy to make. We love making these on busy weeknights.

1 cup	plain nonfat yogurt	250 mL
2 tbsp + 2 tsp	freshly squeezed lemon juice	40 mL
1 tbsp	chopped fresh dill (see Tips, right)	15 mL
1/2 tsp	lemon pepper, divided	2 mL
12 oz	lean ground beef	375 g
1/2 cup	diced onion	125 mL
2	cloves garlic, minced	2
1 cup	quartered cherry tomatoes	250 mL
1 tsp	Greek seasoning (see Tips, right)	5 mL
4	6- to 8-inch (15 to 20 cm) pitas with pockets	4
1 1/2 cups	chopped romaine lettuce	375 mL
4 tsp	reduced-fat crumbled feta cheese	20 mL

1. In a small bowl, combine yogurt, 2 tbsp (30 mL) of the lemon juice, dill and 1/4 tsp (1 mL) of the lemon pepper. Set aside.

2. In a large nonstick skillet over medium-high heat, sauté beef, onion and garlic, breaking up meat with a spoon until beef crumbles, for 5 minutes or until beef is no longer pink and onion is tender. Stir in tomatoes, Greek seasoning, remaining 2 tsp (10 mL) of lemon juice and remaining 1/4 tsp (1 mL) of lemon pepper. Cook for 5 minutes or until heated through.

3. Place pitas on a work surface. Spread yogurt sauce equally in each pita. Place lettuce, beef mixture and feta cheese equally in each pita.

Tips: Fresh dill can be kept for only about 2 days. It's wonderful in chicken salad, with seafood and as a garnish to many dishes.

To make your own Greek seasoning: In a small bowl, combine 1/4 tsp (1 mL) each dried oregano, dried parsley, dried garlic powder and salt.

Lean Ham and Cheese Sandwich

Low-fat ham and cheese? Yes, it's possible with this twist using white Cheddar and a sweet and savory mixture of apricot preserves and cream cheese.

2 tbsp	apricot preserves or jam	30 mL
2 tbsp	reduced-fat cream cheese, softened	30 mL
8	slices whole wheat bread	8
4 oz	lean ham	125 g
4	slices white Cheddar cheese	2
4 tsp	butter, melted	20 mL

Healthy Deli Meats

- When selecting deli meats look at the fat content by reading the labels.

- Watch for high levels of sodium particularly in bacon, sausage and salami. Some brands have reduced-sodium versions.

- Look for deli meats that are free of MSG, artificial colors, flavors and preservatives. There are even brands that are free of any nitrates or nitrates that are added as a color fixative.

- Check the vegetarian section at your grocery store for vegetarian versions of meats.

1. In a small bowl, combine preserves and cream cheese.

2. Place bread slices on a work surface. Spread apricot mixture equally over one side of each bread slice. Top 4 bread slices with ham, cheese and remaining bread slice. Brush melted butter on each side of sandwich.

3. Place sandwiches in a nonstick skillet over medium heat and cook for 2 minutes per side or until cheese is melted.

Variation

Substitute any of your favorite lean deli meats for the ham.

Tip: Let cream cheese soften slightly so it's easier to spread.

Mu Shu Chicken (page 252)

Californian (page 279)

Lobster Rolls with Creamy Dijon Sauce (page 284)

Greek Pita Pocket (page 287)

Salmon with Peach Salsa Sandwich (page 290)

Homemade Ice Cream Sandwich (page 341)

Chocolate Turtle Panini (page 343)

Warm Apple-Pecan Wrap (page 344)

Italian Sausage–Stuffed Portobello Mushrooms

Serves 4

Stuffing portobello mushrooms with Italian sausage is a great low carbohydrate main dish. This is a delicious summertime recipe. Serve with a side salad to round out the meal.

12 oz	Italian sausage, bulk or removed from casings	375 g
4	large portobello mushroom caps, stems removed (see Tip, below)	4
2	tomatoes, thinly sliced	2
1	medium red onion, thinly sliced	1
¼ cup	chopped fresh basil	60 mL
¼ cup	freshly grated Parmesan cheese, optional	60 mL

Tip: To clean mushrooms, wipe with a damp cloth or soft brush. Wash right before using.

- **Preheated lightly greased barbecue grill to medium heat, if using**

1. In a medium saucepan, cook sausage over medium heat, breaking up with a spoon, for about 7 minutes until browned and no longer pink inside. Fill portobello caps with sausage.

2. Place mushrooms on prepared grill or in a large greased skillet over medium heat. Top with tomatoes and red onion. Grill mushrooms for 2 minutes or until lightly charred. Top with basil and Parmesan, if using, and serve.

Variation

Ground Turkey–Stuffed Portobello Mushrooms: Substitute 12 oz (375 g) ground turkey for the Italian sausage.

Light Roast Beef Sandwich

Serves 4

Light mayonnaise combined with horseradish makes a flavorful spread for these simple sandwiches. Serve them open-faced to reduce the carbohydrates even more.

2 tbsp	light mayonnaise	30 mL
2 tbsp	horseradish sauce	30 mL
2 tsp	Dijon mustard	10 mL
8	slices rye bread	8
6 oz	thinly sliced deli roast beef	175 g
4	lettuce leaves	4
4	slices tomato	4

1. In a small bowl, combine mayonnaise, horseradish and mustard.

2. Place bread slices on a work surface. Spread mayonnaise mixture equally over each bread slice. Top 4 slices equally with roast beef, lettuce and tomato. Cover with remaining bread slice and press together gently.

Tip: If you don't have horseradish on hand just increase the Dijon mustard to 3 tbsp (45 mL).

Cornmeal-Crusted Fish Sandwich

Serves 4

Yellow cornmeal makes a wonderful flaky crust on these fish sandwiches. Serve with Pico de Gallo, Cocktail Sauce or Tartar Sauce using reduced-fat mayonnaise.

¾ cup	yellow cornmeal	175 mL
¼ tsp	hot pepper flakes	1 mL
3	egg whites, lightly beaten	3
4	white fish fillets, each 4 to 5 oz (125 to 150 g)	4
4	whole wheat buns, sliced	4
4	lettuce leaves	4
½ cup	Pico de Gallo (page 328) or store-bought	125 mL

- **Preheat oven to 400°F (200°C)**
- **13- by 9-inch (33 by 23 cm) metal baking pan or glass baking dish, lightly greased**

1. In a shallow plate, combine cornmeal and hot pepper flakes. Place egg whites in another shallow plate. Dip fillets in egg whites and then cornmeal, turning to coat. Place fillets in prepared baking dish.

2. Bake in preheated oven for 10 minutes or until fish flakes easily with a fork. Serve in buns with lettuce and Pico de Gallo.

Tip: When purchasing fish, look for fish that smells fresh. Skin should look vibrant.

Salmon with Peach Salsa Sandwich

Serves 4

This salmon dish is so easy to prepare. It's not only flavorful but also very colorful.

4	salmon fillets, each about 4 to 6 oz (125 to 175 g)	4
1 tsp	kosher salt	5 mL
¼ tsp	hot pepper flakes	1 mL
2 tbsp	freshly squeezed lime juice	30 mL
1 tbsp	olive oil	15 mL
4	slices sourdough bread, toasted	4
	Peach Salsa (page 335)	

- **Preheat lightly greased barbecue grill to medium-high**

1. Season salmon with salt and hot pepper flakes. Drizzle with lime juice and olive oil. Place salmon on grill, flesh side down, for 6 to 8 minutes. Turn fillets and grill for 2 to 4 minutes or until fish flakes easily when tested with a fork.

2. Place bread slices on a work surface. Arrange salmon over top. Serve open-faced and top with Peach Salsa.

Variations

This sandwich works great with any type of grilled fish.

Instead of Peach Salsa, use store-bought salsa or mango chutney.

Chicken, Artichoke and Arugula Sandwich

Serves 4

This is an easy light sandwich that is so quick and with very few ingredients.

2 tbsp	red wine vinegar	30 mL
1 tbsp	freshly squeezed lemon juice	15 mL
1/8 tsp	salt	0.5 mL
1/8 tsp	freshly ground pepper	0.5 mL
1 cup	diced tomatoes	250 mL
1 cup	canned artichoke hearts, rinsed, drained and chopped	250 mL
1 cup	diced cucumber	250 mL
4 cups	arugula	1 L
4	6- to 8-inch (15 to 20 cm) pitas with pockets	4
2 cups	chopped cooked chicken (see Tip, right)	500 mL

1. In a small bowl, whisk together vinegar, lemon juice, salt and pepper. Set aside.

2. In a large bowl, combine tomatoes, artichokes and cucumber. Add vinegar mixture and toss to coat.

3. Place pitas on a work surface. Place arugula equally in pita pockets. Arrange chicken over arugula and top with artichoke mixture. Serve immediately.

Variation

If you don't have arugula on hand, substitute spinach or lettuce leaves.

Tip: For the chicken, use leftover grilled chicken or chopped rotisserie chicken.

Greek Chicken Salad Pita with Lemon Vinaigrette

Serves 4

This chicken salad is one of my absolute favorites. I love using peppers, kalamata olives and feta in this because it adds fresh flavors.

¼ cup	freshly squeezed lemon juice	60 mL
2 tbsp	olive oil	30 mL
1	clove garlic, minced	1
⅛ tsp	freshly ground pepper	0.5 mL
2½ cups	chopped cooked chicken (see Tips, right)	625 mL
½ cup	red bell pepper	125 mL
½ cup	green bell pepper	125 mL
3 tbsp	sliced pitted kalamata olives (see Tips, right)	45 mL
3 tbsp	diced red onion	45 mL
¼ cup	crumbled feta cheese	60 mL
2 tbsp	chopped fresh Italian flat-leaf parsley	30 mL
4	6- to 8-inch (15 to 20 cm) pitas with pockets	4
4	lettuce leaves	4
8	thinly sliced tomatoes, optional	8

1. In a small bowl, whisk together lemon juice, olive oil, garlic and pepper. Set aside.

2. In a large bowl, combine chicken, red and green bell peppers, olives and red onion. Add feta and parsley and toss gently. Add dressing and toss to coat.

3. Place pitas on a work surface. Place lettuce leaves in pitas. Spoon chicken salad equally into pita pockets. Add tomatoes, if using.

Variation

Greek Shrimp Salad: Substitute 2½ cups (625 mL) chopped cooked peeled and deveined shrimp for the chicken in this dish and proceed as directed.

Tips: Use leftover grilled chicken or rotisserie chicken for this recipe.

Purchase the already-pitted kalamata olives, which can be found in the olive section of the grocery store. This saves time in having to slice and remove the pits.

Tomato, Basil and Feta Pita

Serves 4

This is similar to a sandwich a local restaurant, "Taziki's," serves. It's so light and delicious.

12	thinly sliced tomatoes (about 3 medium) (see Tips, right)	12
¼ cup	balsamic vinegar	60 mL
1 tbsp	olive oil	15 mL
1	clove garlic, minced	1
⅛ tsp	ground oregano (see Tips, right)	0.5 mL
⅛ tsp	ground thyme	0.5 mL
⅛ tsp	sea salt	0.5 mL
⅛ tsp	freshly ground black pepper	0.5 mL
1 cup	chopped fresh basil leaves	250 mL
½ cup	reduced-fat crumbled feta	125 mL
4	6- to 8-inch (15 to 20 cm) pitas with pockets, warmed	4

1. Place tomatoes on a shallow plate. Drizzle balsamic vinegar and olive oil over tomatoes. Sprinkle with garlic, oregano, thyme, sea salt and pepper and toss well. Let stand for at least 15 minutes. Add basil and feta and toss gently.

2. Place pitas on a work surface. Arrange tomato mixture equally in pitas. Serve immediately.

Variation

Add 1 cup (250 mL) grilled chicken or smoked turkey breast to pita with the other ingredients.

Tips: I love using Roma (plum) tomatoes in this sandwich.

If you can splurge, purchase fresh oregano and thyme and use 1 tsp (5 mL) of each.

Angus Burgers in Lettuce Wraps

Serves 4

Enjoy burgers without additional carbohydrates by using iceberg lettuce wedges to wrap your burger. These come out wonderfully.

1 lb	extra-lean ground beef, preferably ground sirloin (see Tip, below)	500 g
2 tbsp	finely chopped red onion	30 mL
2 tbsp	Worcestershire sauce	30 mL
1	clove garlic, minced	1
1/4 tsp	freshly ground black pepper	1 mL
4	large iceberg lettuce leaves	4
4	slices tomatoes	4

Tip: Use the ground beef of your choice. I prefer sirloin because it's leaner, and ground round is leaner than ground chuck.

- **Preheat lightly greased barbecue grill to medium-high**
- **Instant-read thermometer**

1. In a large bowl, combine beef, red onion, Worcestershire sauce, garlic and pepper. Divide mixture into 4 equal patties, each about 1/2 inch (1 cm) thick.

2. Place burgers on grill, close lid and grill, turning once, for 5 to 7 minutes per side until an instant-read thermometer inserted in the center registers 160°F (71°C).

3. Place lettuce on plates and top with patties and tomatoes. Serve immediately.

Variations

Stuffed Cheddar Burgers: Place 1 tbsp (15 mL) shredded Cheddar or crumbled blue cheese in the middle of the patties and shape. Proceed as directed.

Regular onion can be substituted for the red onion.

Dried Fruit, Almonds and Couscous Pita

Serves 4

Since I love dried fruit, nuts and couscous, I thought I would try it in a sandwich. This recipe is wonderful, and even my kids enjoyed it.

2 cups	reduced-salt fat-free chicken broth	500 mL
1 cup	couscous (see Tips, right)	250 mL
1/3 cup	chopped dried apricots	75 mL
1/4 cup	dried cranberries	60 mL
1/4 cup	almonds, toasted (see Tips, right)	60 mL
2 tbsp	chopped fresh basil	30 mL
1 tsp	grated orange zest	5 mL
4	6- to 8-inch (15 to 20 cm) pitas with pockets	4
2 cups	arugula	500 mL

1. In a medium saucepan over high heat, bring broth to a boil. Remove from heat. Stir in couscous, cover and let stand for 5 minutes. Uncover and fluff with a fork. Stir in apricots, cranberries, almonds, basil and orange zest.

2. Place pitas on a work surface. Arrange arugula leaves equally in pitas. Add couscous mixture and serve immediately.

Variation

Substitute pine nuts for the almonds if you wish.

Tips: Couscous can be found where the rice is sold in the grocery store. It is a grain made from semolina. It is quick and easy to prepare.

To toast almonds: Place almonds in a small dry skillet over medium-high heat, stirring frequently, for about 2 minutes or until golden and toasted.

Oven-Fried Panko-Crusted Chicken Sandwich

Serves 4

The combination of panko and Parmesan provides great crunchy texture and wonderful flavor on these "oven-fried" chicken cutlets.

½ cup	panko bread crumbs	125 mL
¼ cup	freshly grated Parmesan cheese	60 mL
¾ tsp	lemon pepper	3 mL
¼ tsp	paprika	1 mL
3 tbsp	olive oil	45 mL
2 tbsp	freshly squeezed lemon juice	30 mL
1½ lbs	boneless skinless chicken cutlets (see Tip, right)	750 g
4	whole wheat sandwich bun halves	4
4	lettuce leaves	4
4	thinly sliced tomatoes	4

- **Preheat oven to 400°F (200°C)**
- **Baking sheet, lightly greased**

1. In a shallow dish, combine panko, Parmesan, lemon pepper and paprika.

2. Drizzle olive oil and lemon juice over chicken breasts. Dredge chicken in panko mixture, pressing firmly to coat. Place chicken on prepared baking sheet.

3. Bake in preheated oven for 12 minutes or until chicken is lightly browned, crispy and no longer pink inside.

4. Place buns on a work surface. Place lettuce and tomatoes on buns and top with chicken. Serve open-faced.

Tip: Using chicken cutlets work great in this recipe because they take less time to cook.

Grilled Pepper Salad Flatbread

Serves 4

This is a wonderful spring or summertime recipe, but it can be made anytime during the year.

1/3 cup	red wine vinegar	75 mL
2 tbsp	olive oil, divided	30 mL
2	cloves garlic, minced	2
2 tbsp	chopped fresh basil	30 mL
1/2 tsp	kosher salt, divided	2 mL
1/2 tsp	freshly ground black pepper, divided	2 mL
4	large bell peppers, a variety of colors	4
4	6- to 8-inch (15 to 20 cm) pitas with pockets	4
2 cups	mixed baby greens	500 mL
1/4 cup	pitted kalamata olives (see Tip, below)	60 mL
2 tbsp	drained capers, rinsed	30 mL

Tip: Look for pitted kalamata olives in the olive section of your grocery store.

- **Preheat lightly greased barbecue grill to medium-high**

1. In a small bowl, whisk together vinegar, 1 tbsp (15 mL) of the oil, garlic, basil and 1/4 tsp (1 mL) each of the salt and pepper.

2. Place bell peppers on a grill, turning occasionally, for 10 minutes or until peppers look blistered. Let cool and place in a resealable plastic bag. Seal and let stand for 10 minutes. Peel peppers. Remove seeds and slice into thin strips.

3. Place pitas on a work surface. Brush pitas with remaining olive oil, salt and pepper. Place on grill for 2 minutes or until lightly browned.

4. Place pitas on 4 servings plates. Arrange greens, peppers, olives and capers equally in pitas. Drizzle with dressing. Serve immediately.

Variation

If you're short on time, omit the vinegar mixture and use a commercial reduced-fat Italian or balsamic vinaigrette instead.

Cuban-Style Tofu Sandwich

Serves 4

Tofu is a wonderful protein source that is high in vitamins and minerals and low in calories and saturated fat. Grilling brings out its great flavor.

1/3 cup	freshly squeezed orange juice	75 mL
2 tbsp	freshly squeezed lime juice	30 mL
2	cloves garlic, minced	2
2 tbsp	chopped fresh cilantro	30 mL
1 tsp	ground cumin	5 mL
1/4 tsp	salt	1 mL
1/4 tsp	freshly ground black pepper	1 mL
1 lb	extra-firm tofu, drained (see Tip, right)	500 g
8	slices Italian bread	8
1 tbsp	butter	15 mL
4	lettuce leaves	4
4	tomato slices	4
	Low-fat mayonnaise, optional	

- **Preheat lightly greased barbecue grill to medium-high**

1. In a small bowl, combine orange juice, lime juice, garlic, cilantro, cumin, salt and pepper. Cut tofu horizontally into four 1/2 inch (1 cm) thick slices. Pour orange juice mixture over tofu and refrigerate for 30 minutes.

2. Place tofu on grill for 5 minutes per side or until thoroughly heated.

3. Place bread slices on a work surface. Brush one side of each bread slice with butter. Place bread on grill, buttered side down, for 1 to 2 minutes or until toasted. Serve tofu on bread with lettuce, tomato and mayonnaise, if using. Serve immediately.

Tip: Feel free to freeze firm or extra-firm tofu. To use, just thaw and squeeze dry.

Salmon Sandwich with Sour Cream Dill Sauce

Serves 4

This is a great way to use salmon fillets, and it is such an easy main dish dinner. Serve with a salad or fresh vegetable for a complete meal.

1½ lbs	salmon fillets	750 g
¼ tsp	salt	1 mL
¼ tsp	freshly ground pepper	1 mL
2 tbsp	freshly squeezed lemon juice	30 mL
1 tbsp	olive oil	15 mL
8	slices sourdough bread (½-inch/1 cm thick slices)	8
4	turkey bacon slices, cooked	4
4	lettuce leaves	4
4	tomato slices	4
	Sour Cream Dill Sauce (page 327) or store-bought reduced-fat mayonnaise	

- **Preheat lightly greased barbecue grill to medium**

1. Season salmon with salt and pepper and drizzle with lemon juice and olive oil. Place skin side down on preheated grill, close lid and grill for 5 to 7 minutes or until fish flakes easily when tested with a fork.

2. Place bread slices on a work surface. Place salmon on 4 bread slices and top equally with bacon, lettuce, tomato and dill sauce. Top with remaining bread slice, pressing together gently. Serve immediately.

Tip: If you have any salmon leftover, use it in a hot or cold pasta dish or on top of a salad.

Roasted Vegetable Sandwich

Serves 4

This seasonal summer sandwich is fabulous to make when you have ripe avocados. The roasted vegetables pair well with fresh basil and goat cheese.

1½ cups	yellow summer squash (zucchini), cut lengthwise	375 mL
1 cup	sliced onion (about 1 small)	250 mL
1 cup	diced red bell pepper (about 1)	250 mL
¼ tsp	salt	1 mL
¼ tsp	freshly ground black pepper	1 mL
1 tbsp	olive oil	15 mL
8 oz	French bread loaf, cut into 8 slices	250 g
4 oz	crumbled goat cheese (see Tip, right)	125 g
1	large avocado, diced	1
¼ cup	chopped fresh basil	60 mL
1 tbsp	balsamic vinegar	15 mL

Wise Cheese Choices

Goat cheese is lower in saturated fat and calories than almost any other cheese.

Cheddar is a great cheese filled with 200 mg of calcium per ounce.

Swiss is the lowest-sodium choice of cheeses.

Part-skim mozzarella has only 3.5 g saturated fat per ounce.

When choosing feta, purchase reduced-fat.

- **Preheat oven to 400°F (200°C)**
- **Baking sheet, lined with parchment paper**

1. Arrange squash, onion and bell pepper on prepared baking sheet. Season with salt and pepper. Drizzle with oil. Roast in preheated oven for 25 to 30 minutes or until vegetables are lightly browned and softened.

2. Place bread slices on a work surface. Spread 1 tbsp (15 mL) of the goat cheese on one side of each bread half. Layer roasted vegetables, avocado and basil equally on top. Drizzle with balsamic vinegar. Top with remaining bread slice.

Tip: Goat cheese (chèvre in French) is made from goat's milk and is sold plain or coated with herbs. Once opened, wrap in plastic and store in the refrigerator for up to 1 week.

Oven-Fried Beef and Bean Chimichangas

Serves 4

These oven-fried chimichangas are just as tasty as the full-fat version. These are simple to prepare, and kids love them.

1 lb	lean ground beef	500 g
1	can (16 oz/500 g) fat-free refried beans	1
1 cup	shredded reduced-fat sharp (aged) Cheddar cheese	250 mL
1	can (4$\frac{1}{2}$ oz/127 mL) chopped green chiles, drained	1
$\frac{1}{4}$ cup	mild salsa	60 mL
8	9-inch (23 cm) reduced-fat flour tortillas, warmed (see Tip, right)	8

Toppings, optional

	Shredded lettuce
	Nonfat sour cream or Greek yogurt
	Pico de Gallo (page 328) or store-bought

- **Preheat oven to 350°F (180°C)**
- **Baking sheet, coated with cooking spray**

1. In a large skillet, brown beef for 4 minutes or until meat is no longer pink inside.

2. In a large bowl, combine beef, refried beans, cheese, green chiles and salsa.

3. Place warmed tortillas on a work surface. Place $\frac{1}{3}$ cup (75 mL) of the bean mixture just below center of each tortilla. Fold opposite sides of tortillas over filling, forming rectangles. Secure with wooden toothpicks. Place on prepared baking sheet.

4. Bake in preheated oven for 8 minutes. Turn and bake for 5 minutes more or until lightly browned. Remove toothpicks, and serve with desired toppings.

Variation

Chicken Chimichangas: Omit beef, add 1$\frac{1}{2}$ cups (375 mL) chopped cooked chicken with the beans in Step 2 and proceed as directed.

Tip: To warm tortillas, place on a plate, layered with paper towels, alternating paper towels and tortillas covering top layer with a towel. Microwave on High for 10 to 20 seconds or until warm.

Pepper Jack, Avocado and Sprouts Sandwich

Serves 4

This vegetarian sandwich is a breeze to prepare. It's made with the freshest ingredients, including avocados and sprouts.

8	slices multigrain bread	8
¾ cup	Hummus (page 313) or store-bought	175 mL
4	slices pepper Jack cheese	4
2	avocados, thinly sliced (see Tip, right)	2
½ cup	baby spinach leaves	125 mL
½ cup	shredded carrots	125 mL
½ cup	alfalfa sprouts	125 mL
⅛ tsp	freshly ground black pepper	0.5 mL

1. Place bread slices on a work surface. Spread hummus equally over one side of bread slices. Top equally with cheese, avocados, spinach, carrots and sprouts. Sprinkle with pepper. Top with remaining bread slices, pressing together gently. Serve immediately

Variation

Turkey Hummus Pitas: Add 8 oz (250 g) deli sliced turkey to this recipe.

Tip: To speed the ripening of avocados, place them in a paper bag with an apple. Pierce the bag in several places and store at room temperature for up to 3 days.

Field Greens Salad and Chicken in Pita

Serves 4

I'm not sure how I came up with this idea, but maybe it came from taking all my favorite ingredients and putting it into one sandwich. It's as good as it sounds.

¼ cup	freshly squeezed orange juice	60 mL
1 tsp	liquid honey	5 mL
1 tsp	Dijon mustard	5 mL
1 tsp	soy sauce	5 mL
1 tsp	olive oil	5 mL
⅛ tsp	hot pepper flakes	0.5 mL
4 cups	mixed salad greens	1 L
1	navel orange, sectioned and each sliced in half	1
½ cup	chopped pecans, toasted (see Tip, below)	125 mL
¼ cup	dried cranberries	60 mL
2 cups	chopped cooked chicken (see Tip, right)	500 mL
4	6- to 8-inch (15 to 20 cm) pitas with pockets	4

Tip: To toast pecans, spread in a single layer on a baking sheet. Bake in a 350°F (180°C) oven, stirring occasionally, for 10 to 15 minutes.

1. In a small bowl, whisk together orange juice, honey, mustard, soy sauce, olive oil and hot pepper flakes. Set aside.

2. In a large bowl, combine mixed greens, orange, pecans and cranberries. Add chicken and dressing and toss well.

3. Place pitas on a work surface. Spread chicken salad mixture equally in pita pockets. Serve immediately.

Tip: I purchase rotisserie chicken for this recipe or when I grill chicken, I grill extra.

Healthy Breads

Half of a 6-inch (15 cm) pita is among the lowest calorie of breads along with tortillas.

Using 100% whole-grain bread is your best source of nutrition and fiber. Be careful with rye bread because many varieties are high in sodium.

When selecting healthy breads consider the following:

Be label conscious. Look for breads with 1 to 7 grams of fat and zero grams of saturated fat.

Look for high fiber, such as 3 to 5 grams of fiber per serving.

Buy whole wheat. Check the label and make sure it's the first ingredient in the ingredient list.

Multigrain doesn't necessarily mean healthy. Look at the label and make sure whole wheat is the first ingredient.

Try sprouted bread. It's made from whole grains that have been allowed to sprout. These breads have a low glycemic index, are low in saturated fat and have more nutrients.

Balsamic Chicken Sandwich

Serves 4

Balsamic vinegar, fresh basil and parsley make a wonderful marinade for the chicken in this sandwich. It's one of my children's top requests.

2 cups	chopped Italian flat-leaf parsley	500 mL
2 cups	chopped fresh basil	500 mL
1 tbsp	balsamic vinegar (see Tips, right)	15 mL
1 tbsp	olive oil	15 mL
1	clove garlic, minced	1
1/4 tsp	freshly ground black pepper	1 mL
1 1/2 lbs	boneless skinless chicken breasts	750 g
4	6- to 8-inch (15 to 20 cm) pitas with pockets, warmed	4

Toppings, optional

	Spinach leaves
	Sliced tomatoes
	Crumbled reduced-fat feta cheese
	Balsamic vinegar

- **Preheat lightly greased barbecue grill to medium-high**

1. In a resealable plastic bag, combine parsley, basil, balsamic vinegar, olive oil, garlic and pepper. Add chicken and cover and refrigerate for at least 2 hours.

2. Remove chicken from marinade, discarding marinade. Place chicken on preheated grill, close lid and grill, for 6 minutes or until chicken is no longer pink inside. Let cool slightly and cut into thin strips.

3. Place warmed pitas on a work surface. Place chicken filling in center of pitas with desired toppings.

Tips: Selecting balsamic vinegar can be like buying fine wine. Some stores allow you to sample bottles because many different varieties vary in flavor. The most refined have been aged in wooden barrels and have an intense woody flavor. Drizzle balsamic vinegar over salads, vegetables, fruit and prosciutto.

Feel free to use leftover sliced cooked chicken if you like.

Mahi with Chipotle Slaw

Serves 4

Chipotle seasoning is the perfect combination of smoky yet spicy flavors. It is fabulous in the slaw, which is great on the mahi mahi in this recipe.

3 cups	thinly sliced green and purple cabbage (see Tip, below)	750 mL
1/4 cup	chopped fresh cilantro	60 mL
1/4 cup	reduced-fat mayonnaise	60 mL
1/4 cup	freshly squeezed lime juice, divided	60 mL
1 tsp	chipotle seasoning, divided	5 mL
1 1/2 lbs	mahi mahi fillets	750 g
1/4 tsp	kosher salt	1 mL
4	8-inch (20 cm) whole wheat reduced-fat flour tortillas, warmed (see Tip, page 301)	8

Tip: Purchase pre-shredded cabbage or slaw mix to save you time.

- **Preheat lightly greased barbecue grill to medium-high**

1. In a large bowl, combine cabbage, cilantro, mayonnaise, 2 tbsp (30 mL) of the lime juice and 1/2 tsp (2 mL) of the chipotle seasoning. Set aside.

2. Season mahi mahi with salt, remaining lime juice and chipotle seasoning

3. Place fish on preheated grill, close lid and grill, for 4 minutes or until fish flakes easily when tested with a fork.

4. Place warmed tortillas on a work surface. Place fillets and slaw equally in center of tortillas. Fold both ends over filling. Roll up tortilla and serve immediately.

Variation

Feel free to substitute any white fish fillets in this recipe.

Italian Steak Sandwich

Serves 4 to 6

I make this recipe all of the time. The combination of Worcestershire sauce and balsamic vinegar makes a tangy marinade that flavors the steak to perfection.

¼ cup	Worcestershire sauce	60 mL
¼ cup	balsamic vinegar	60 mL
1 lb	boneless beef rib-eye steaks, about 1 inch (2.5 cm) thick	500 g
⅓ cup	reduced-fat mayonnaise	75 mL
2 tbsp	chopped sun-dried tomatoes	30 mL
8	slices Italian bread (½-inch/ 1 cm thick slices)	8
1 cup	chopped lettuce	250 mL
2	tomatoes, thinly sliced	2
1 tbsp	crumbled blue cheese	15 mL

Tip: If you incorporate blue cheese into the mayonnaise mixture, it will keep the topping from falling off.

- **Preheat lightly greased barbecue grill to medium-high**

1. In a shallow dish or resealable plastic bag, combine Worcestershire sauce and vinegar. Add steaks. Cover and seal and refrigerate for at least 30 minutes.

2. Place steaks on preheated grill, close lid and grill, turning once, for 6 to 8 minutes per side for medium or to desired degree of doneness. Slice across the grain into thin slices.

3. In a small bowl, combine mayonnaise and sun-dried tomatoes. Place bread slices on a work surface. Spread mayonnaise mixture on 4 bread slices. Layer steak, lettuce, tomatoes and blue cheese equally over bread and top with remaining bread slices, pressing together gently.

Variation

Add chopped red onion to the mayonnaise mixture for added flavor.

Tuna Melt Sandwich

Serves 4

This tuna is so light and fresh. It works wonderfully served open-faced with melted Gruyère cheese.

2	cans (6 oz/170 g) water-packed white tuna, drained	2
¼ cup	chopped red bell pepper	60 mL
2 tbsp	chopped fresh basil	30 mL
2 tbsp	white wine vinegar	30 mL
1 tbsp	freshly squeezed lemon juice	15 mL
2 tbsp	olive oil	30 mL
¼ tsp	salt	1 mL
¼ tsp	freshly ground black pepper	1 mL
4	whole wheat English muffin halves (see Tip, right)	4
4 oz	Gruyère cheese, thinly sliced	125 g

- **Preheat broiler**

1. In a large bowl, combine tuna, bell pepper, basil, vinegar, lemon juice, oil, salt and pepper.

2. Place English muffins on a work surface. Spread tuna mixture equally among English muffin halves. Top with cheese and broil for 3 minutes or until cheese is melted.

Variation

Use Parmesan cheese instead of the Gruyère.

Tip: English muffins are low in calories, carbohydrates and fat. One English muffin has about 120 calories, 23 carbohydrates and 1 gram of fat.

Dijon Peppercorn Steak Wraps

Serves 4

The Dijon peppercorn mixture is so good on this sandwich. It's equally good served with either chicken or pork.

¼ cup	Dijon mustard, divided	60 mL
1 tbsp	whole black peppercorns, crushed and divided	15 mL
1 lb	boneless beef rib-eye or strip loin steaks, about 1 inch (2.5 cm) thick	500 g
⅓ cup	light mayonnaise	75 mL
1 tsp	grated lemon zest	5 mL
1 tbsp	freshly squeezed lemon juice	15 mL
4	8-inch (20 cm) reduced-fat flour tortillas, warmed (see Tip, page 301)	4
3	Roma (plum) tomatoes, chopped	3
½ cup	finely chopped red onion	125 mL
½ cup	thinly sliced cucumber	125 mL

Tip: You may substitute cracked pepper if you don't have peppercorns on hand.

- **Preheat lightly greased barbecue grill to medium-high**

1. In small bowl, stir together 2 tbsp (30 mL) of the mustard and two-thirds of the crushed peppercorns. Rub evenly over beef. Cover and refrigerate for 2 hours.

2. Place beef on preheated grill, close lid and grill for 5 minutes per side for medium depending on thickness or to desired degree of doneness. Let stand for 10 minutes. Cut steak across the grain into thin slices.

3. In a bowl, stir together mayonnaise, lemon zest, lemon juice, remaining mustard and crushed peppercorns.

4. Place tortillas on a work surface. Arrange beef slices equally in center of each tortilla. Top equally with tomatoes, red onion and cucumber. Top equally with mayonnaise mixture and roll up.

Condiments

Classic Aïoli

Makes about 1 cup (250 mL)

Aïoli is a garlic mayonnaise that goes well with all types of seafood and vegetables.

2	egg yolks (see Tip, right)	2
1½ cups	extra virgin olive oil, divided	375 mL
1	clove garlic, coarsely chopped	1
1 tbsp	freshly squeezed fresh lemon juice	15 mL
1 tsp	Dijon mustard	5 mL
¼ tsp	kosher salt	1 mL
¼ tsp	freshly ground black pepper	1 mL

Ways to Serve Aïoli

- On asparagus
- With french fries or sweet potato fries
- On any burger imaginable
- With prosciutto
- On any sandwich calling for "mayonnaise"
- With avocado, fresh carrots and celery as a dip
- Stir into shrimp, chicken or tuna salad

- **Food processor**

1. In a food processor, process egg yolks for 2 minutes. With processor running, slowly drizzle ½ cup (125 mL) of the olive oil through the feed tube, until slightly thickened. (This must be done very slowly or the oil will not emulsify and your sauce will not thicken.) While processor is still running, add garlic, lemon juice and mustard and blend well.

2. Slowly add remaining olive oil until creamy and slightly thick. If too thick, turn processor back on and add 1 to 4 tsp (5 to 20 mL) water. Season with salt and pepper. Cover and refrigerate for 30 minutes. Store in refrigerator for up to 3 days.

Tip: This recipe contains raw egg yolks. If you are concerned about the safety of using raw eggs, use pasteurized eggs in the shell or ¼ cup (60 mL) pasteurized liquid whole eggs.

Chipotle Aïoli

This sauce is great on burgers, steak, pork or chicken. It has a kick but also a hint of fresh lime.

½ cup	Homemade Mayonnaise (page 321) or store-bought	125 mL
2 tbsp	chopped chipotle chiles in adobo sauce (see Tips, right)	30 mL
1 tbsp	chopped fresh cilantro	15 mL
1 tsp	freshly grated lime zest	5 mL
1 tsp	freshly squeezed lime juice	5 mL

1. In a small bowl, combine mayonnaise, chipotle chiles, cilantro, lime zest and lime juice. Cover and refrigerate for up to 2 days.

Tips: Reduced-fat mayonnaise may be substituted for regular.

You can find chipotle chile peppers in adobo sauce in a can in the international section of the grocery store.

Fresh Basil Aïoli

Serve basil aïoli on top of any type of sandwich or served with vegetables and crackers.

1	clove garlic, coarsely chopped	1
¼ tsp	kosher salt	1 mL
1 cup	fresh basil leaves	250 mL
1 cup	Homemade Mayonnaise (page 321) or store-bought	250 mL
1 tbsp	Dijon mustard	15 mL
½ tsp	grated lemon zest	2 mL
½ tsp	freshly squeezed lemon juice	2 mL
1 tbsp	extra virgin olive oil	15 mL

• **Food processor or blender**

1. In a food processor or blender, process garlic, salt, basil, mayonnaise, mustard, lemon zest and lemon juice until smooth. With processor running, slowly drizzle oil through the feed tube, until slightly thickened. (This must be done very slowly or the oil will not emulsify and your sauce will not thicken.) Use immediately or cover and refrigerate for up to 3 days.

Tips: Reduced-fat mayonnaise can be substituted for regular.

A key to success in making aïoli is to add the oil very slowly.

Basil-Lemon Aïoli

Makes about 1 cup (250 mL)

This aïoli has a hint of lemon, basil and Greek yogurt. It's great served with any sandwich and as an appetizer on crackers or with vegetables.

1/3 cup	fresh basil leaves	75 mL
3	cloves garlic, coarsely chopped	3
1 tsp	freshly grated lemon zest	5 mL
3 tbsp	freshly squeezed lemon juice	45 mL
1/4 cup	Homemade Mayonnaise (page 321) or store-bought	60 mL
1 tbsp	nonfat Greek yogurt	15 mL
2 tbsp	extra virgin olive oil (see Tip, right)	30 mL

- **Food processor**

1. In a food processor, process basil, garlic, lemon zest, lemon juice, mayonnaise and yogurt until basil is chopped. With processor running, slowly drizzle olive oil through the feed tube until combined. Use immediately or cover and refrigerate for up to 2 days.

Tip: I prefer extra virgin olive oil, derived from the first pressing of the olives, because it has the most delicate flavor and the most antioxidant benefits.

Roasted Red Pepper Aïoli

Makes 1/2 cup (125 mL)

I love using this aïoli on any sandwich with protein and crusty bread. The roasted red peppers and basil give it a wonderful flavor.

1/3 cup	Homemade Mayonnaise (page 321) or store-bought	75 mL
1/2 cup	chopped roasted red peppers	125 mL
2	cloves garlic, minced	2
2 tbsp	chopped fresh basil leaves	30 mL
1 tbsp	drained capers, rinsed	15 mL
1/4 tsp	salt	1 mL

- **Food processor**

1. In a food processor, pulse mayonnaise, peppers, garlic, basil, capers and salt until well blended. Use immediately or cover and refrigerate for up to 2 days.

Hummus

When I make homemade hummus, my family loves it. I try to lighten it up a bit by omitting the olive oil and adding the liquid from the chickpeas.

4	cloves garlic, coarsely chopped	4
2 cups	canned chickpeas, drained, liquid reserved	500 mL
⅓ cup	tahini (sesame paste)	75 mL
6 tbsp	freshly squeezed lemon juice (about 2 lemons)	90 mL
2 tbsp	water or liquid from the chickpeas	30 mL
1½ tsp	kosher salt	7 mL
1 tsp	hot pepper sauce	5 mL

Toppings, optional

	Cayenne pepper
	Paprika
	Olive oil

- **Food processor**

1. In a food processor, purée garlic, chickpeas, tahini, lemon juice, water or chickpea liquid, salt and hot pepper sauce. Top with desired toppings, if using.

Variation

Substitute 2 tbsp (30 mL) extra virgin olive oil if you want a stronger olive flavor.

Red Pepper Hummus

Makes 1½ cups (375 mL)

This hummus is a twist on regular hummus but gives all sandwiches a wonderful kick. It also works great as an appetizer served with pita triangles and crudités.

1	can (14 to 19 oz/398 to 540 mL) chickpeas, drained and rinsed	1
⅓ cup	roasted red peppers from a jar, drained	75 mL
2	cloves garlic, coarsely chopped	2
¼ cup	tahini (see Tip, right)	60 mL
2 tbsp	minced Italian flat-leaf parsley	30 mL
2 tbsp	freshly squeezed lemon juice	30 mL
1½ tsp	ground cumin	7 mL
¼ tsp	kosher salt	1 mL
¼ tsp	cayenne pepper	1 mL

- Food processor

1. In a food processor, purée chickpeas, roasted peppers, garlic, tahini, parsley, lemon juice, cumin, salt and cayenne until smooth. Use immediately or cover and refrigerate for up to 2 days.

Variation

Cannellini or white beans may be substituted for chickpeas in this recipe.

Tip: Tahini is a thick paste made of ground sesame seeds and is found in Middle Eastern cooking. Look for it in the international section of the grocery stores.

Condiments and Health

When thinking of condiments but also thinking healthy, less is more and some deliver huge flavors in small amount. Here are some of my favorite choices:

Hummus is rich in flavor and fiber and usually a quarter of the calories of mayonnaise.

Tapenade is low in calories but high in sodium so just a small amount is all you need.

Mustards are great with virtually no calories but 1 tsp (5 mL) usually has around 50 mg of sodium.

Pesto is so flavorful and is full of fresh herbs and all the good fats. It usually has fewer calories than mayonnaise.

Classic Tzatziki

Makes 1¼ cups (300 mL)

This Greek or Turkish sauce is also known as an appetizer usually made from sheep's or goat's milk with cucumber, garlic and fresh herbs. It's great served on many sandwiches or as dip with pita bread.

1 cup	plain nonfat yogurt	250 mL
½ cup	diced cucumber	125 mL
1	clove garlic, minced	1
1 tbsp	chopped fresh mint	15 mL
1 tbsp	chopped fresh dill	15 mL
1 tsp	freshly squeezed lemon juice	5 mL
1 tsp	extra virgin olive oil	5 mL
⅛ tsp	salt	0.5 mL

1. In a small bowl, combine yogurt, cucumber, garlic, mint, dill, lemon juice, olive oil and salt. Cover and refrigerate until ready to serve or for up to 1 day.

Tip: Serve tzatziki over chicken, lamb or pork. It also is great as a dip on crackers.

Tapenade

Makes 1 cup (250 mL)

Tapenade comes from France's Provence region and is a thick paste usually made from capers, olives, anchovies, olive oil, lemon juice and seasonings. Since so many people aren't fond of anchovies, I usually leave them out of my version.

1 lb	pitted mixed olives	500 g
3 tbsp	olive oil	45 mL
1 tbsp	freshly squeezed lemon juice	15 mL
2 tbsp	chopped fresh basil	30 mL
2	cloves garlic, coarsely chopped	2

- **Food processor**

1. In a food processor, process olives, olive oil, lemon juice, basil and garlic until smooth, stopping once to scrape down the sides. Spoon into a serving dish or cover and refrigerate for up to 3 days.

Cucumber Tzatziki Sauce

Makes 1 cup (250 mL)

This cucumber sauce is wonderful with turkey or chicken or any Mediterranean dish. I love to serve it alongside warm pita bread.

1 cup	Greek yogurt	250 mL
1	medium cucumber, peeled, seeded and diced	1
1 tsp	chopped fresh mint	5 mL
1	clove garlic, minced	1
1/2 tsp	kosher salt	2 mL
1/4 tsp	freshly ground black pepper	1 mL

1. In a small bowl, combine yogurt, cucumber, mint, garlic, salt and pepper. Cover and refrigerate until ready to serve or for up to 2 days.

Greek Cucumber Sauce

Makes about 1/2 cup (125 mL)

This spread is made with Greek yogurt, which adds a rich creamy texture. I love this served on any Greek-style or Mediterranean sandwich.

1/4 cup	Greek yogurt	60 mL
1/3 cup	diced cucumber	75 mL
1	clove garlic, minced	1
2 tbsp	crumbled feta	30 mL
1 tbsp	chopped fresh mint or cilantro	15 mL
1/2 tsp	freshly grated lemon zest	5 mL
1/8 tsp	sea salt	0.5 mL

1. In a small bowl, combine yogurt, cucumber, garlic, feta, cilantro, lemon zest and salt. Use immediately or cover and refrigerate for up to 2 days.

Cucumber-Mango Raita

Makes 1¹⁄₂ cups (375 mL)

This recipe is Indian-inspired, and I first tasted it at Birmingham Bake and Cook, a local cooking store, on a sandwich with Mango-Avocado Relish (page 323) and chicken on naan bread.

2	medium cucumbers, peeled, seeded and grated	2
1	medium mango, peeled and chopped	1
2 tbsp	freshly chopped mint (see Tip, right)	30 mL
2 tbsp	freshly chopped cilantro	30 mL
2 cups	plain Greek yogurt	500 mL
¹⁄₂ tsp	kosher salt	2 mL

1. In a large bowl, combine cucumber, mango, mint and cilantro. Stir in yogurt and salt and mix well. Use immediately or cover and refrigerate for up to 2 days.

Tip: When substituting fresh mint for dried, use 3 times as much fresh for the dried.

Cilantro-Yogurt Sauce

Makes about 1 cup (250 mL)

This cilantro sauce is wonderful on many sandwiches, especially ones with a little heat.

³⁄₄ cup	plain yogurt	175 mL
¹⁄₂ cup	chopped cucumber	125 mL
2 tbsp	chopped Italian flat-leaf parsley	30 mL
2 tbsp	chopped fresh cilantro	30 mL
1 tsp	freshly grated lemon zest	5 mL
¹⁄₄ tsp	salt	1 mL
¹⁄₄ tsp	freshly ground black pepper	1 mL

1. In a small bowl, whisk together yogurt, cucumber, parsley, cilantro, lemon zest, salt and pepper. Use immediately or cover and refrigerate for up to 2 days.

Basil Oil Spread

Makes about 1 cup (250 mL)

This spread is great on almost any sandwich drizzled on tomatoes or on a salad.

2 cups	packed fresh basil leaves	500 mL
1/3 cup	extra virgin olive oil	75 mL
1 tsp	freshly squeezed lemon juice	5 mL
1/2 tsp	salt	2 mL
1	clove garlic, coarsely chopped	1

- **Food processor or blender**

1. In a food processor or blender, process basil, olive oil, lemon juice, salt and garlic until smooth.

Light Horseradish Sauce

Makes 1 1/3 cups (325 mL)

This light horseradish tastes like the full-fat version and is wonderful on almost any sandwich.

1 cup	reduced-fat sour cream	250 mL
2 tbsp	prepared horseradish	30 mL
1 tbsp	Worcestershire sauce	15 mL
1 tbsp	chopped fresh chives	15 mL

1. In a small bowl, combine sour cream, horseradish, Worcestershire sauce and chives. Use immediately or cover and refrigerate for up to 2 days.

Chimichurri

Chimichurri is a garlicky condiment from Argentina. It is great spooned over beef or chicken. It is used much like ketchup is in North America. Chimichurri sauce is also great as an appetizer, served with chunks of crusty bread that can be dipped into the sauce.

1 cup	Italian flat-leaf parsley, trimmed	250 mL
¼ cup	tightly packed fresh cilantro, trimmed	60 mL
2	cloves garlic, coarsely chopped	2
1 tsp	kosher salt	5 mL
½ tsp	ground cumin	2 mL
½ tsp	ground oregano	2 mL
¼ tsp	hot pepper flakes	1 mL
½ cup	extra virgin olive oil	125 mL
¼ cup	red wine vinegar	60 mL
1 tsp	freshly squeezed lemon juice	5 mL

- **Food processor**

1. In a food processor, process parsley, cilantro, garlic, salt, cumin, oregano, hot pepper flakes, olive oil, vinegar and lemon juice until finely chopped. Transfer to a bowl. Let stand for 30 minutes before serving to allow flavors to develop.

Tip: You can make this ahead and store, covered, in the refrigerator for up to 3 days.

Caponata Spread

Makes 1 cup (250 mL)

This spread is wonderful on hamburgers, fish and chicken as well as perfect served as an appetizer.

1	medium eggplant, thinly sliced	1
2 tbsp	olive oil	30 mL
1	clove garlic, minced	1
½ tsp	salt	2 mL
¼ tsp	freshly ground black pepper	1 mL
4	Roma (plum) tomatoes, thinly sliced	4
1	small red onion, thinly sliced	1
2 tbsp	chopped kalamata olives	30 mL
2 tbsp	drained capers, rinsed	30 mL
2 tbsp	pine nuts, toasted (see Tips, right)	30 mL
3 tbsp	red wine or balsamic vinegar	45 mL
1 tsp	liquid honey	5 mL
2 tbsp	chopped Italian flat-leaf parsley	30 mL

- **Preheat oven to 450°F (230°C)**

1. On a large baking sheet, place eggplant in a single layer. Drizzle with olive oil and season with garlic, salt and pepper. Bake in preheated oven for 15 minutes. Add tomatoes and red onion and bake for 15 minutes more. Let cool slightly.

2. In a large bowl, combine eggplant mixture, olives, capers, pine nuts, vinegar, honey and parsley. Use immediately or cover and refrigerate for up to 2 days.

Tips: Pine nuts, also called, pignoli, are the seeds from the cone of certain pine tress. They turn rancid quickly and should be refrigerated for no more than 1 month.

To toast pine nuts: Place pine nuts in a hot dry skillet over medium heat, stirring occasionally, for 4 minutes or until lightly browned. Or place nuts in a single layer on a baking sheet in a preheated 375°F (190°C) oven, stirring once or twice, for 5 minutes or until fragrant and golden.

Homemade Mayonnaise

Makes about 1 cup (250 mL)

If you ever want to make homemade mayonnaise, this recipe is for you. It's as easy as can be and wonderful served on anything.

1	egg (see Tip, right)	1
1 tbsp	freshly squeezed lemon juice	15 mL
1 tsp	Dijon mustard	5 mL
¾ cup	extra virgin olive oil	175 mL
	Salt and freshly ground black pepper	

- **Food processor or blender**

1. In a food processor or blender, process egg, lemon juice and mustard until smooth. With motor running, add oil in a slow steady stream through the feed tube until mixture thickens and emulsifies. Season with salt and pepper to taste. Use immediately or cover and refrigerate for up to 2 days.

Tip: This recipe contains raw eggs. If you are concerned about the safety of using raw eggs, use pasteurized eggs in the shell or ¼ cup (60 mL) pasteurized liquid whole eggs.

Lemon Dill Mayonnaise

Makes about 1¼ cups (300 mL)

I love the combination of fresh lemon and dill. This works as a great spread on all types of burgers and wraps, especially ones with fish and chicken.

½ cup	Homemade Mayonnaise (above) or store-bought	125 mL
1½ tsp	freshly grated lemon zest	7 mL
2 tbsp	freshly squeezed lemon juice	30 mL
2 tbsp	chopped fresh dill	30 mL

1. In a small bowl, combine mayonnaise, lemon zest, lemon juice and dill. Use immediately or cover and refrigerate for up to 2 days.

Tip: Reduced-fat mayonnaise may be substituted for regular.

Nectarine Relish

Makes 1 cup (250 mL)

This fresh combination is one of my favorites. I make it all the time when nectarines are in season to top burgers, seafood and sandwiches.

2	nectarines, diced	2
1/2 cup	diced red bell pepper	125 mL
1/2 cup	diced red onion	125 mL
1 tsp	diced seeded jalapeño	5 mL
1/4 cup	chopped fresh cilantro	60 mL
2 tbsp	chopped fresh mint	30 mL
1 tbsp	liquid honey	15 mL
1 tbsp	freshly squeezed lime juice	15 mL
1/4 tsp	hot pepper flakes	1 mL
1/4 tsp	kosher salt	1 mL

1. In a medium bowl, combine nectarines, bell pepper, red onion, jalapeño, cilantro, mint, honey, lime juice, hot pepper flakes and salt. Use immediately or cover and refrigerate for up to 2 days.

Variation

Substitute peaches or plums for the nectarines in this recipe.

Cherry Tomato Relish

Makes about 3 cups (750 mL)

This relish is perfect for any summertime sandwich. It is also wonderful on top of Brie, crackers or crostini.

2 1/2 cups	halved cherry tomatoes (see Tip, right)	625 mL
1/4 cup	sliced black olives	60 mL
2	green onions, chopped	2
2 tbsp	balsamic vinegar	30 mL
1 tbsp	extra virgin olive oil	15 mL
2 tsp	chopped fresh oregano	10 mL
1/4 tsp	salt	1 mL
1/4 tsp	freshly ground black pepper	1 mL

1. In a small bowl, combine cherry tomatoes, olives, green onions, vinegar, oil, oregano, salt and pepper. Use immediately or cover and refrigerate for up to 2 days.

Tip: I like to store fresh tomatoes at room temperature away from direct sunlight. Cold temperatures destroy the fresh flavors of the tomatoes.

Mango-Avocado Relish

Makes 2 cups (500 mL)

This relish is incredible on too many sandwiches to mention. It really works well with Indian-spiced sandwiches or dishes.

3	mangos, chopped	3
3	avocados, chopped	3
1	jalapeño, seeded and chopped	1
1/2 cup	chopped fresh cilantro	125 mL
1/4 cup	chopped red onion	50 mL
1/4 cup	freshly squeezed lime juice	50 mL
1/8 tsp	ground cumin	0.5 mL
1/8 tsp	sea or kosher salt	0.5 mL

1. In a large bowl, combine mangos, avocados, jalapeño, cilantro, red onion, lime juice, cumin and salt. Use immediately or cover and refrigerate for up to 2 days.

Sweet Pepper Relish

Makes 2 1/2 cups (625 mL)

This relish is great on crostini, bagel chips, crackers, turkey, beef, fish or poultry.

1	red bell pepper, diced	1
1	yellow bell pepper, diced	1
1	small onion, diced	1
2	cloves garlic, minced	2
1 tbsp	olive oil	15 mL
1 tbsp	balsamic vinegar	15 mL
1/2 tsp	sea salt	2 mL
1/2 tsp	dried Italian seasoning	2 mL
	Vegetable cooking spray	

- **Preheat oven to 400°F (200°C)**
- **Large baking dish, coated with cooking spray**

1. In a medium bowl, stir together red and yellow bell peppers, onion, garlic, olive oil, vinegar, salt and Italian seasoning. Transfer to prepared baking dish. Bake in preheated oven for 45 minutes or until vegetables are softened.

2. Transfer to a bowl and let cool for at least 30 minutes. Use immediately or cover and refrigerate for up to 2 days.

Tip: You could also roast the peppers in a preheated 500°F (260°C) oven for 10 minutes or until tender.

Pineapple Relish

This relish is particularly good on pork and beef burgers, but it's also incredible with seafood.

1 cup	diced fresh pineapple (see Tip, right)	250 mL
¼ cup	diced red bell pepper	60 mL
¼ cup	diced green bell pepper	60 mL
2 tbsp	finely chopped jalapeño	30 mL
2 tbsp	chopped fresh cilantro	30 mL
1 tbsp	finely chopped red onion	15 mL
2 tbsp	freshly squeezed lime juice	30 mL
1 tsp	light brown sugar	5 mL

1. In a medium bowl, combine pineapple, red and green bell peppers, jalapeño, cilantro, red onion, lime juice and brown sugar. Use immediately or cover and refrigerate for up to 3 days. For fresher flavor, refrigerate for at least 2 hours before serving.

Tip: I purchase already cored pineapple to save extra time.

Creole Honey Mustard

This three-ingredient recipe is fabulous served on any sandwich. It's also great served alongside chicken fingers.

⅓ cup	Dijon mustard	75 mL
2 tbsp	Creole mustard (see Tips, page 333)	30 mL
4 tsp	liquid honey	20 mL

1. In a small bowl, combine Dijon mustard, Creole mustard and honey. Use immediately or cover and refrigerate for up to 3 days.

Variations

Substitute 2 tbsp (30 mL) coarse-grain mustard for the Creole mustard.

Honey Mustard: Omit the Creole mustard and prepare as directed.

Barbecue Sauce

Make about 1 cup (250 mL)

This simple barbecue sauce is so easy and is wonderful anytime you want a hearty classic barbecue sandwich.

¾ cup	apple cider vinegar	175 mL
½ cup	ketchup	125 mL
⅓ cup	chili sauce	75 mL
2 tbsp	Worcestershire sauce	30 mL
1	clove garlic, minced	1
⅛ tsp	cayenne pepper	0.5 mL

1. In a medium saucepan over medium heat, combine cider vinegar, ketchup, chili sauce, Worcestershire sauce, garlic and cayenne. Bring to a boil. Reduce heat and simmer, stirring occasionally, for 30 minutes. Use immediately or cover and refrigerate for up to 3 days.

White Barbecue Sauce

Makes 1¼ cups (300 mL)

In the Southern United States, White Barbecue Sauce is popular on any barbecue chicken or pork sandwich.

1 cup	Homemade Mayonnaise (page 321) or store-bought	250 mL
¼ cup	apple cider vinegar	60 mL
2 tbsp	freshly squeezed lemon juice	30 mL
2 tbsp	white wine Worcestershire sauce (see Tips, right)	30 mL
1 tbsp	freshly ground black pepper (see Tips, right)	15 mL
⅛ tsp	cayenne pepper	0.5 mL

1. In a small bowl, whisk together mayonnaise, cider vinegar, lemon juice, Worcestershire sauce, black pepper and cayenne until blended. Use immediately or cover and refrigerate for up to 2 days.

Tips: If you can't find white wine Worcestershire sauce, make your own by combining 2 tbsp (30 mL) Worcestershire sauce and 1 tsp (5 mL) white wine.

I know this looks like a lot of pepper in this recipe, but I promise, it tastes great.

Orange-Soy Barbecue Sauce

Makes 2 cups (500 mL)

This barbecue sauce has a thinner consistency than regular barbecue sauce and is salty and sweet. I love it on so many sandwiches because it adds just the right heat.

1 tbsp	dark brown sugar	15 mL
1	clove garlic, minced	1
¾ cup	freshly squeezed orange juice	175 mL
¾ cup	chili sauce	175 mL
⅓ cup	molasses	75 mL
2 tbsp	soy sauce	30 mL
2 tbsp	freshly squeezed lemon juice	30 mL
1 tbsp	hot pepper sauce	15 mL
1 tsp	Worcestershire sauce	5 mL
2 tbsp	apple cider vinegar	30 mL

1. In a large saucepan, combine brown sugar, garlic, orange juice, chili sauce, molasses, soy sauce, lemon juice, hot pepper sauce and Worcestershire sauce and heat for 20 minutes over low heat. Add apple cider vinegar and heat for 15 minutes more. Use immediately or cover and refrigerate for up to 2 days.

Cocktail Sauce

Makes 1¼ cups (300 mL)

This classic cocktail sauce is a staple for any seafood dish, sandwich or appetizer. My kids love to dip crackers into it.

1 cup	ketchup	250 mL
3 tbsp	prepared horseradish	30 mL
1 tsp	freshly grated lemon zest	5 mL
2 tbsp	freshly squeezed lemon juice	30 mL

1. In a small bowl, combine ketchup, horseradish, lemon zest and lemon juice. Cover and refrigerate for 30 minutes before using or for up to 3 days.

Variation

Tarragon Cocktail Sauce: Add 1 tbsp (15 mL) chopped fresh tarragon to the mixture.

Wasabi Ketchup

Makes about ⅔ cup (150 mL)

This ketchup is flavored with a touch of wasabi powder. I love it on fresh tuna sandwiches.

1 tsp	wasabi powder (see Tip, right)	5 mL
½ cup	ketchup	125 mL
2 tsp	freshly squeezed lemon juice	10 mL
⅛ tsp	hot pepper sauce	0.5 mL

1. In a small bowl, combine wasabi powder and 1 tsp (5 mL) water, stirring to form a paste.

2. In another small bowl, combine ketchup, lemon juice, wasabi mixture and hot pepper sauce. Use immediately or cover and refrigerate for up to 3 days.

Variation

You may substitute 1 tbsp (15 mL) horseradish for wasabi powder.

Tip: Wasabi is a variety of green horseradish grown only in Japan. It has a sharp flavor slightly more bitter than horseradish. You can find it in the powdered form in the grocery store in the Asian section.

Sour Cream Dill Sauce

Makes ¾ cup (175 mL)

This sauce works great on fish recipes, especially with smoked salmon or with fresh cold shrimp.

½ cup	sour cream	125 mL
¼ cup	chopped fresh dill	60 mL
2	cloves garlic, minced	2
¼ tsp	salt	1 mL
¼ tsp	freshly ground black pepper	1 mL

1. In a small bowl, combine sour cream, dill, garlic, salt and pepper. Cover and refrigerate for 30 minutes before using or for up to 3 days.

Variation

You can substitute reduced-fat sour cream or nonfat or reduced-fat Greek yogurt for regular sour cream.

Pico de Gallo

Makes 1½ cups (375 mL)

I love this salsa-type of spread. It's great on any Southwestern sandwiches, tacos and fajitas or served with tortilla chips.

4	large tomatoes, peeled, seeded and chopped	4
⅓ cup	diced red onion	75 mL
1 tsp	jalapeño pepper, seeded and diced	5 mL
½ cup	chopped fresh cilantro	125 mL
2 tbsp	freshly squeezed lime juice	30 mL
½ tsp	ground cumin	2 mL
¼ tsp	chili powder	1 mL

1. In a medium bowl, combine tomatoes, red onion, jalapeño, cilantro, lime juice, cumin and chili powder. Cover and refrigerate until ready to use or for up to 2 days.

Horseradish Sauce

Makes about ⅓ cup (75 mL)

This is my favorite version of horseradish sauce. I use it for fish and chicken sandwiches as well as on burgers.

1 cup	Homemade Mayonnaise (page 321) or store-bought	250 mL
1 tbsp	Dijon mustard	15 mL
1 tbsp	coarse-grain mustard	15 mL
1 tbsp	prepared horseradish	15 mL
¼ cup	sour cream or nonfat Greek yogurt	60 mL
⅛ tsp	sea salt	0.5 mL

1. In a small bowl, whisk together mayonnaise, Dijon, coarse-grain mustard, horseradish, sour cream and salt. Use immediately or cover and refrigerate for up to 2 days.

Tip: Using Greek yogurt adds protein and thickness to this sauce. Even the nonfat version works wonderfully.

Horseradish-Chili Spread

Makes about ⅔ cup (150 mL)

This mixture of horseradish and chili sauce is wonderful on burgers, pork, steak, chicken and fish sandwiches. I like it as a dipping sauce as well.

½ cup	Homemade Mayonnaise (page 321) or store-bought	125 mL
2 tbsp	chili sauce	30 mL
2 tbsp	prepared horseradish (see Tips, right)	30 mL
2	green onions, chopped	2
1	clove garlic, minced	1

1. In a small bowl, combine mayonnaise, chili sauce, horseradish, green onions and garlic. Use immediately or cover and refrigerate for up to 2 days.

Tips: You can substitute reduced-fat mayonnaise for regular.

Find horseradish on the shelves near the mayonnaise in the grocery store.

Basil Pesto

Makes 2 cups (500 mL)

Fresh Basil Pesto makes any sandwich taste better. I love it on vegetarian sandwiches because it gives them such a depth of flavor.

½ cup	packed fresh basil leaves	125 mL
½ cup	freshly grated Parmesan cheese	125 mL
¼ cup	pine nuts, toasted (see Tip, page 320)	60 mL
¼ cup	walnuts, toasted	60 mL
⅔ cup	extra virgin olive oil (see Tip, right)	150 mL
2	cloves garlic, coarsely chopped	2
1 tbsp	freshly squeezed lemon juice	15 mL
½ tsp	salt	2 mL
½ tsp	freshly ground black pepper	2 mL

- **Food processor or blender**

1. In a food processor or blender, process basil, Parmesan, pine nuts, walnuts, oil, garlic, lemon juice, salt and pepper until smooth, stopping once to scrape down sides. Use immediately or cover and refrigerate for up to 3 days.

Tip: I prefer extra virgin olive oil, derived from the first pressing of the olives because it has the most delicate flavor and the most antioxidant benefits.

Sun-Dried Tomato Pesto

This pesto is one of my favorites. I lather it on so many sandwiches and also serve it as an appetizer with vegetables and crackers.

2	cloves garlic, minced	2
½ cup	sun-dried tomatoes, undrained	125 mL
2 tbsp	chopped fresh basil	30 mL
⅛ tsp	salt	0.5 mL
⅛ tsp	freshly ground black pepper	0.5 mL
2 tbsp	freshly grated Parmesan cheese	30 mL

- **Food processor**

1. In a food processor, process garlic, sun-dried tomatoes, basil, salt and pepper until smooth. Stir in cheese and process again until smooth. Use immediately or cover and refrigerate for up to 3 days.

Cilantro Pesto

This pesto, made with cilantro, adds unique flavor to burgers, wraps and even on top of crostini.

½ cup	loosely packed fresh cilantro leaves	125 mL
½ cup	freshly grated Parmesan cheese (see Tip, right)	125 mL
¼ cup	pine nuts	60 mL
3	cloves garlic, coarsely chopped	3
2 tbsp	olive oil	30 mL
1 tbsp	freshly squeezed lime juice	15 mL
½ tsp	salt	2 mL
¼ tsp	ground cumin	1 mL

- **Food processor or blender**

1. In a food processor or blender, process cilantro, Parmesan, pine nuts, garlic, oil, lime juice, salt and cumin until smooth, stopping once to scrape down sides. Use immediately or cover and refrigerate for up to 3 days.

Tip: I used Parmigiana-Reggiano Parmesan cheese, but if you can't find it or don't have it on hand, the regular version is fine.

Roasted Asparagus Pesto

Makes 1½ cups (375 mL)

This pesto is perfect on any vegetarian sandwich as well as steak, chicken and turkey sandwiches.

1 lb	asparagus, cut into ½-inch (1 cm) pieces	500 g
¼ cup + 2 tbsp	olive oil, divided	90 mL
2 tbsp	grated lemon zest	30 mL
	Kosher salt and freshly ground black pepper	
¾ cup	freshly grated Parmesan cheese	175 mL
¼ cup	chopped pine nuts, toasted	50 mL
1	clove garlic, minced	1
2 tbsp	freshly squeezed lemon juice	30 mL

- **Preheat oven to 400°F (200°C)**
- **Large baking sheet, lined with parchment paper**
- **Food processor**

1. Place asparagus in a single layer on prepared baking sheet. Drizzle with 2 tbsp (30 mL) of the olive oil. Sprinkle with lemon zest, ½ tsp (2 mL) salt and ¼ tsp (1 mL) pepper. Bake in preheated oven for 8 to 10 minutes or until tender. Let cool slightly.

2. In a food processor, process asparagus, cheese, pine nuts, garlic and lemon juice until combined. With processor running, slowly add remaining oil through the feed tube. Season with ¼ tsp (1 mL) each salt and pepper. Use immediately or cover and refrigerate for up to 2 days.

Variation

Walnuts or almonds can be substituted for the pine nuts.

Kalamata and Black Olive Pesto

Makes 1¼ cups (300 mL)

Using both olives in this pesto gives it a wonderful flavor. Try this on a baguette with goat or feta cheese or even on its own with warm toasted bread.

½ cup	pitted kalamata olives	125 mL
4 oz	black olives	125 g
2 tbsp	drained capers, rinsed (see Tip, right)	30 mL
1	clove garlic, minced	1
⅛ tsp	hot pepper flakes	0.5 mL
⅓ cup	freshly grated Parmesan cheese	75 mL
2 tbsp	extra virgin olive oil	30 mL

• **Food processor**

1. In a food processor, process kalamata and black olives, capers, garlic, hot pepper flakes and Parmesan until smooth. With motor running, add oil through the feed tube until combined. Use immediately or cover and refrigerate for up to 3 days.

Tip: Capers are wonderful in condiments, sauces and as a garnish on meat, seafood and vegetable dishes.

Herb Sauce

Makes 3½ cups (875 mL)

This double herb sauce is almost as good as a dip with vegetables or crackers as it is on a sandwich.

2 cups	light sour cream	500 mL
1 cup	Homemade Mayonnaise (page 321) or store-bought	250 mL
2	cloves garlic, coarsely chopped	2
3 tbsp	chopped fresh basil	45 mL
3 tbsp	chopped fresh dill	45 mL
¼ tsp	kosher salt	1 mL
¼ tsp	freshly ground black pepper	1 mL

• **Food processor**

1. In a food processor, pulse sour cream, mayonnaise, garlic, basil, dill, salt and pepper until combined. Use immediately or cover and refrigerate for up to 3 days.

Rémoulade Sauce

This French sauce, which is also very Southern New Orleans, is very popular served with shrimp, oysters and crabs. I love it spread on seafood sandwiches or as a dip with cold shrimp.

¼ cup	extra virgin olive oil	60 mL
2 tbsp	freshly squeezed lemon juice	30 mL
2 tbsp	Creole whole-grain mustard (see Tips, right)	30 mL
2 tbsp	chopped green onions	30 mL
1 tbsp	prepared horseradish	15 mL
1 tbsp	ketchup	15 mL
1 tbsp	chopped Italian flat-leaf parsley	15 mL
¼ tsp	hot pepper sauce	1 mL
1	clove garlic, minced	1

1. In a small bowl, combine olive oil, lemon juice, mustard, green onions, horseradish, ketchup, parsley, hot pepper sauce and garlic. Use immediately or cover and refrigerate for up to 2 days.

Tips: This sauce is usually made with mayonnaise, mustard, capers, herbs and even anchovies. It is great served with meats, shellfish and seafood.

Creole mustard is a variation of whole-grain mustard in which the seeds are slightly crushed. It is often found in the South at local grocery stores, usually produced in New Orleans. To make your own, add horseradish or hot sauce to regular mustard. You can substitute brown or deli mustard for Creole whole-grain if you can't find it or don't have time to make your own.

Tartar Sauce

This classic version of tartar sauce is my favorite. I love it on top of any seafood sandwich or as dipping sauce.

¾ cup	Homemade Mayonnaise (page 321) or store-bought	175 mL
¼ cup	freshly squeezed lime juice	60 mL
2 tbsp	chopped pickles	30 mL
2 tbsp	chopped red onion	30 mL
2 tbsp	chopped Italian flat-leaf parsley	30 mL
1 tsp	chopped jalapeño (see Tip, right)	5 mL

1. In a medium bowl, combine mayonnaise, lime juice, pickles, red onion, parsley and jalapeño. Cover and refrigerate until serving for up to 2 days.

Tip: Be careful when chopping jalapeños. Make sure you wash your hands well before touching your eyes.

Tomatillo Tartar Sauce

This tartar sauce gets it kick from fresh tomatillos and is wonderful on fish sandwiches, fish tacos and any seafood sandwiches.

1 lb	tomatillos, husks removed	500 g
1 cup	Homemade Mayonnaise (page 321) or store-bought	250 mL
2 tbsp	freshly squeezed lime juice	30 mL
1 tsp	hot pepper sauce	5 mL
1 tsp	salt	5 mL

- **Food processor**

1. Thoroughly wash tomatillos after removing husks. In a large saucepan, cover tomatillos with water and bring to a boil over medium-high heat. Cook for 15 minutes. Drain and let cool.

2. In a food processor, pulse tomatillos until chopped. Spoon into a bowl. Stir in mayonnaise, lime juice, hot pepper sauce and salt. Use immediately or cover and refrigerate for up to 3 days.

Tip: Tomatillos are easy to cook with because they don't need to be peeled or seeded. Be sure to wash thoroughly though to remove the sticky substance on the skin.

Southwestern Corn Salsa

Most people think of corn salsa as an appetizer, but I love it topped on grilled chicken or fish sandwiches as well as burgers.

2	cans (14 to 19 oz/398 to 540 mL) black beans, drained and rinsed	2
1½ cups	drained canned or frozen corn kernels (thawed if frozen) (see Tips, right)	375 mL
½ cup	chopped red bell pepper	125 mL
¼ cup	chopped red onion	60 mL
2 tbsp	chopped fresh cilantro	30 mL
½ tsp	ground cumin	2 mL
⅓ cup	freshly squeezed lime juice	75 mL

1. In a large bowl, combine black beans, corn, bell pepper, red onion, cilantro, cumin and lime juice. Use immediately or cover and refrigerate for up to 3 days.

Tips: Use fresh grilled corn instead of canned for this recipe.

Use leftover Southwestern Corn Salsa as an appetizer served with tortilla chips, on top of salads, or served with meats, poultry and seafood. You can also cut this recipe in half, if desired.

Peach Salsa

Makes 1¼ cups (300 mL)

This summery salsa is best with ripe peaches. It complements fish, chicken, beef or pork dishes, especially when they're grilled.

2	ripe peaches, peeled and diced	2
1	medium red bell pepper, diced	1
1	jalapeño pepper, seeded and diced	1
½	red onion, chopped	½
¼ cup	chopped fresh cilantro	60 mL
2 tbsp	chopped fresh mint	30 mL
2 tbsp	freshly squeezed lime juice	30 mL
1 tbsp	liquid honey	15 mL
¼ tsp	cayenne pepper, divided	1 mL
¼ tsp	salt	1 mL

1. In a medium bowl, combine peaches, bell pepper, jalapeño, red onion, cilantro, mint, lime juice, honey, cayenne and salt. Cover and refrigerate for at least 30 minutes or for up to 3 days.

Variation

Nectarine Salsa: Substitute 2 nectarines for the peaches.

Peach-Ginger Chutney

Makes 2½ cups (625 mL)

This chutney is delicious served on top of cold sandwiches and hot sandwiches, including burgers.

2	peaches, chopped (about 2 cups/500 mL)	2
3 tbsp	peach preserves or jam	45 mL
2 tbsp	rice wine vinegar	30 mL
1 tbsp	grated fresh gingerroot	15 mL
¼ tsp	kosher salt	1 mL
2 tbsp	chopped green onions	30 mL

1. In a small saucepan over medium heat, simmer peaches, preserves, rice wine vinegar, ginger and salt, stirring occasionally, for 10 to 15 minutes or until liquid has evaporated. Stir in green onions. Use immediately or cover and refrigerate for up to 3 days.

Variations

Plum Chutney: Substitute 2 cups (500 mL) plums for the peaches and omit the ginger.

Mango Chutney: Substitute 2 cups (500 mL) chopped mango for the peaches.

Sun-Dried Tomato Spread

Makes 1½ cups (375 mL)

This lower-fat combination is a winner served on steak sandwiches, crostini and even with vegetables and crackers.

1 cup	low-fat cream cheese, softened	250 mL
½ cup	low-fat mayonnaise	125 mL
2	cloves garlic, coarsely chopped	2
½ cup	sun-dried tomatoes	125 mL
1 tbsp	chopped fresh basil	15 mL

- **Food processor**

1. In a food processor, process cream cheese, mayonnaise, garlic, sun-dried tomatoes and basil until combined. Use immediately or cover and refrigerate for up to 2 days.

Guacamole

Makes 1½ cups (375 mL)

This guacamole is wonderful on any sandwich or also perfect for an appetizer with tortilla chips.

4	ripe Hass avocados, diced (see Tips, right)	4
½ cup	diced red onion (1 small onion)	125 mL
1	large clove garlic, minced	1
3 tbsp	freshly squeezed lemon juice (1 lemon)	45 mL
½ tsp	hot pepper sauce	2 mL
1	medium tomato, seeded and diced	1
1 tsp	freshly ground black pepper	5 mL
½ tsp	kosher salt	2 mL

1. In a medium bowl, combine avocados, red onion, garlic, lemon juice and hot pepper sauce. Gently stir in tomato, pepper and salt. Use immediately or cover and refrigerate for up to 2 days.

Tips: The most important thing when making guacamole is starting with ripe avocados. I also like my guacamole chunky so I try to coarsely mash them.

I prefer using Hass avocados. When selecting avocados, look for ones that are heavy for their size and unblemished. Store unripe avocados at room temperature, and once they are ripe, in the refrigerator for up to 5 days.

Desserts

Dessert Crêpes

Serves 4

My best friend, Lisa, from Nashville, makes these for company all of the time, and she always receives rave reviews. I was so excited for her to share this recipe in my book.

1 cup	all-purpose flour	250 mL
2	eggs	2
½ cup	milk	125 mL
2 tbsp	butter, melted	30 mL
½ tsp	vanilla extract	2 mL
¼ tsp	salt	1 mL
1 tbsp	vegetable oil	15 mL

Cream Cheese Snow Filling

1	package (8 oz/250 g) cream cheese, softened	1
2 cups	confectioner's (icing) sugar	500 mL
2 tbsp	grated lemon zest	30 mL
1 cup	heavy or whipping (35%) cream	250 mL
	Sliced strawberries or blueberries	

1. In a large bowl, whisk together flour and eggs. Gradually add milk and ½ cup (125 mL) water, stirring to combine. Beat in butter, vanilla and salt until smooth.

2. In large skillet, heat oil over medium heat. Pour ¼ cup (60 mL) of the batter into skillet for each crêpe. Tilt pan in a circular motion so that batter covers the surface of pan. Cook crêpes for 2 minutes or until bottom is golden brown. Loosen with a spatula.

3. *Cream Cheese Snow Filling:* In a medium bowl, using an electric mixer, beat cream cheese until soft. Blend in sugar and beat until creamy. Add lemon zest.

4. In a separate bowl, whip cream until slightly thickened. Fold into cream cheese mixture. Serve over warm crêpes with berries.

Tips: You can make the crêpe batter ahead of time and refrigerate for up to 8 hours.

Don't flip crêpes too early. Wait until the edges begin to brown.

Banana and Honey Wraps with Mascarpone

Serves 4

This is an incredible flavor combination and is an absolute breeze to make.

½ cup	mascarpone cheese	125 mL
¼ cup	liquid honey	60 mL
½ tsp	ground cinnamon	2 mL
4	8-inch (20 cm) flour tortillas	4
3	bananas, thinly sliced	3
½ cup	chopped pecans, toasted	125 mL

1. In a small bowl, combine mascarpone, honey and cinnamon.

2. Place tortillas on a work surface. Spread marscapone mixture equally down center of each tortilla. Top with sliced bananas and nuts. Fold both ends over filling. Roll up and serve immediately.

Tip: These wraps are great cold or warmed. In a skillet, melt 2 tbsp (30 mL) butter over low heat. Heat wraps for 3 minutes per side or until lightly browned.

Coffee and Hot Fudge Ice Cream Wraps

Serves 4

This wrap is wonderful for kids and adults. This is a fun summertime party idea.

4	8-inch (20 cm) flour tortillas	4
2 cups	coffee ice cream	500 mL
¼ cup	chocolate fudge sauce	60 mL
½ cup	mini chocolate chips	125 mL

Tip: You can roll the wrap so that it's cone-shaped.

1. Place tortillas on a work surface. Arrange ice cream and chocolate sauce equally in center of each tortilla. Sprinkle with chocolate chips. Fold both ends over filling. Roll up and serve immediately or freeze for 1 hour.

Variations

Ice Cream Wrap with Caramel and Pecans: Substitute vanilla ice cream for the coffee, caramel sauce for the hot fudge and pecans for the mini chocolate chips.

Use 2 cups (500 mL) vanilla ice cream instead of the coffee ice cream and substitute ½ cup (125 mL) chocolate sprinkles for the chocolate chips.

Strawberry and Mascarpone Sandwich

Serves 4

Spring is the perfect time to make this breakfast sandwich. Top with fresh mint for added color.

4	slices Italian bread (½-inch/ 1 cm thick slices)	4
2 tbsp	butter, softened	30 mL
½ cup	mascarpone cheese	125 mL
2 tbsp	liquid honey	30 mL
2½ cups	thinly sliced strawberries	625 mL
¼ cup	confectioner's (icing) sugar	60 mL

What to Do with Mascarpone

- Serve with cantaloupe
- Stir it into pasta
- Serve with poached pears or baked apples
- Mix with Gorgonzola and spread on crackers
- Stir into cheesecake mixtures
- Serve on top of toasted bread
- Eat with a spoon
- Use in parfaits
- Use a spread in panini sandwiches

- **Preheat oven or toaster oven to 350°F (180°C)**

1. Place bread slices on a work surface. Spread butter over one side of bread slices. Toast in an electric toaster or preheated oven for 2 minutes or until lightly browned.

2. In a small bowl, combine mascarpone and honey. Spread mascarpone mixture equally over bread slices. Top with strawberries and sift confectioner's sugar over strawberries. Serve open-faced.

Variations

Feel free to substitute cream cheese or melted chocolate for the mascarpone cheese.

Substitute four 8-inch (20 cm) tortilla wraps for the bread slices.

Mascarpone and Brie–Stuffed Raisin Bread

Serves 4

I love this simple combination of mascarpone and Brie with a mix of honey. It's a great dessert and also works well as a sweet appetizer.

¼ cup	mascarpone, at room temperature	60 mL
¼ cup	liquid honey	60 mL
8	slices raisin bread (½-inch/ 1 cm thick slices)	8
¼ cup	butter or margarine	60 mL
4 oz	Brie, thinly sliced (see Tip, below)	125 g

Tip: When using Brie, let it come to room temperature before using. The rind of the Brie is edible, but feel free to trim it off if you wish.

- **Preheat panini grill to medium heat, if using**

1. In a small bowl, stir together mascarpone and honey. Brush one side of each bread slice with butter. Place on work surface, buttered side down, and spread 4 slices with mascarpone mixture. Top equally with Brie. Cover with top halves of bread and press together gently.

2. Place sandwiches on preheated panini grill or in a large skillet over medium heat and cook, turning once if using a skillet, for 3 to 4 minutes or until golden brown and cheese is melted. Serve immediately.

Homemade Ice Cream Sandwich

Serves 4

Sometimes it's the little things in life that are so wonderful. These are easy to make, adorable and taste delicious.

2 cups	vanilla ice cream	500 mL
16	chocolate chip cookies (see Tip, right)	16

Toppings, optional

	Sprinkles	
	Chopped nuts	
	Mini chocolate chips	

1. Let ice cream stand at room temperature for 10 minutes to soften.

2. Place ¼ cup (60 mL) of the ice cream on 8 cookies. Place remaining cookies on top of ice cream, pressing gently to seal. Roll edges in desired toppings. Serve immediately or wrap in plastic wrap and freeze for up to 3 days.

Tip: Use your favorite chocolate chip recipe for these cookies or store-bought cookies.

Coffee Ice Cream Sandwich

Serves 4

Since Oreo cookies and coffee ice cream are my favorite (and my three kids), I had to put this simple dessert cookie sandwich in the book.

8	cream-filled chocolate sandwich cookies, such as Oreo	8
1 cup	coffee ice cream	250 mL

- **Large baking sheet, lined with waxed paper**

1. Remove filling from cookies and separate cookie rounds into 2 pieces. Spoon 2 tbsp (30 mL) coffee ice cream onto 4 cookie rounds and top with remaining half. Place rounds on prepared baking sheet. Freeze for at least 1 hour.

Tip: Feel free to substitute your favorite ice cream. These make a great kid's party dessert.

Chocolate and Raspberry Panini

Serves 4

Chocolate and raspberry pair well together in this simple dessert.

8	slices baguette or French bread (½-inch/1 cm thick slices)	8
½ cup	butter, softened	125 mL
½ cup	raspberry preserves or jam	125 mL
1 cup	semisweet chocolate chips, melted (see Tip, below)	250 mL

Tip: To melt chocolate: Place chocolate chips in microwave on High for 1 minute or until chocolate is melted.

- **Preheat panini grill to medium heat, if using**

1. Brush one side of 4 bread slices with butter. Place on a work surface, buttered side down, and spread other side with 2 tbsp (30 mL) of the raspberry preserves. Top equally with melted chocolate. Cover with remaining bread and press together gently. Spread bread tops with butter.

2. Place sandwiches on preheated panini grill or in a large skillet and cook, turning once if using a skillet, for 3 to 4 minutes or until golden brown and cheese is melted. Serve immediately.

Variation

Substitute bittersweet (dark) chocolate for the semisweet chocolate.

Chocolate Turtle Panini

Serves 4

These are "to die for" as one person said when I served these for dessert. They are simple to make.

5 tbsp	butter or margarine, melted and divided	75 mL
12	caramel squares	12
1 cup	semisweet chocolate chips	250 mL
8	slices challah or French bread (½-inch/1 cm thick slices) (see Tips, below)	8
⅓ cup	chopped pecans	75 mL

Tips: Use leftover challah bread for French toast and bread pudding recipes. It works great.

If you can't find challah bread, any soft ½-inch (1 cm) thick white bread will work.

- **Preheat panini grill to medium heat, if using**

1. In a small saucepan, heat 3 tbsp (45 mL) of the butter and caramels over low heat for 5 minutes or until melted. Remove from heat.

2. Melt chocolate chips in a microwave-safe bowl on High for 1 minute or until melted.

3. Butter half of the bread slices. Place bread slices, buttered side down, on a work surface. Spread melted chocolate equally over one side of 4 bread slices. Top with caramel mixture, nuts and remaining bread slices. Spread remaining butter equally over top sides of bread.

4. Place sandwiches on preheated panini grill or in a large skillet and cook, turning once if using a skillet, for 3 to 4 minutes or until golden brown and cheese is melted. Serve immediately.

Variation

Peanut Butter Panini: You can add ¼ cup (60 mL) peanut butter with 1 tbsp (15 mL) butter instead of caramels and chocolate.

Warm Apple-Pecan Wraps

Serves 4

This twist on an apple turnover dessert is great served in a warm wrap.

¼ cup	butter, divided	60 mL
3½ cups	diced apples (about 2) (see Tip, below and right)	875 mL
¼ cup	pure maple syrup	60 mL
1 tsp	ground cinnamon	5 mL
¼ tsp	kosher salt	1 mL
½ cup	pecan halves	125 mL
4	6- or 8-inch (15 or 20 cm) flour tortillas	4
	Vanilla ice cream, optional	

Tip: I used Braeburn apples, but Granny Smith or Gala apples work great, too.

1. In a large skillet, heat 2 tbsp (30 mL) of the butter over medium heat until melted. Add apples, maple syrup, cinnamon and salt. Reduce heat to low and cook, stirring occasionally, for 10 minutes or until tender. Stir in pecans and cook for 2 minutes more or until heated through.

2. In a separate skillet, heat remaining butter over low heat. Add tortillas, one a time, and heat, turning once, for 2 minutes or until lightly browned.

3. Place tortillas on a work surface. Divide apple mixture equally in center of tortillas. Top with ice cream, if using. Fold ends over filling and roll up.

Tip: When selecting apples for recipes, 2 large or 3 medium apples yield about 3½ cups (875 mL) chopped apples.

S'Mores Cookie

Serves 4

These classic indoor s'mores are a hit.

16	graham crackers	16
4 oz	semisweet chocolate, melted	125 g
1 cup	mini marshmallows	250 mL

Tips: Make sure you watch these carefully in the oven because they cook very fast.

You can also easily place these on foil and make these on a grill.

- **Preheat broiler**
- **Large baking sheet, lined with foil**

1. Place 8 graham crackers on prepared baking sheet. Arrange chocolate and marshmallows equally on top of graham crackers. Place under preheated broiler with door partially opened for 1 minute or until marshmallows look golden and roasted. Top with remaining graham cracker and press down lightly.

Variations

Italian S'mores: Substitute hazelnut spread for the chocolate.

Use a French baguette instead of the crackers and top with chopped hazelnuts.

Hazelnut and Banana Panini

Serves 4

Hazelnut spread is fabulous with the roasted bananas in this recipe, making a wonderful dessert panini.

8	slices challah (½-inch/1 cm thick slices) (see Tips, below)	8
¼ cup	butter or margarine	60 mL
½ cup	hazelnut spread, such as Nutella	125 mL
2	bananas, thinly sliced	2

Tips: Challah bread is a special bread rich with eggs. You can find it at many bakeries, especially on Fridays or look for "French white bread."

Look for hazelnut spread in your grocery store where peanut butter is sold.

- **Preheat panini grill to medium heat, if using**

1. Brush one side of each bread slice with butter. Place on a work surface, buttered side down, and spread 4 bread slices with hazelnut spread. Top equally with banana slices and remaining bread slice, pressing together gently

2. Place sandwiches on preheated panini grill or in a large skillet and cook, turning once if using a skillet, for 3 to 4 minutes or until golden brown and cheese is melted. Serve immediately.

Variations

You can use melted chocolate or almond butter instead of the hazelnut spread.

If you don't have time to roast bananas, raw ones are also fabulous on this.

Grilled Dark Chocolate and Almond Butter Sandwich

Serves 4

I love using almond butter on just about anything, and it works great here combined with any type of chocolate.

2 tbsp	butter	30 mL
8	slices white bread (½-inch/ 1 cm thick slices), crusts removed	8
¼ cup	almond butter (see Tip, below)	60 mL
4 oz	bittersweet (dark) chocolate squares, chopped	125 g
	Confectioner's (icing) sugar, optional	
	Fresh berries, optional	

Tip: Look for almond butter in the specialty section of your grocery store where peanut butter is sold. You can grind it yourself, which is my preferred way.

- **Preheat panini grill to medium heat, if using**

1. Brush one side of each bread slice with butter. Place on work surface, buttered side down, and spread 1 tbsp (15 mL) of the almond butter over 4 bread slices. Sprinkle chopped chocolate equally over almond butter, pressing gently to adhere. Top with remaining bread slices, pressing gently.

2. Place sandwiches on preheated panini grill or in a large skillet and cook, turning once if using a skillet, for 3 to 4 minutes or until golden brown and chocolate is melted. Serve immediately. Dust with confectioner's sugar and top with berries, if desired.

Variations

Peanut butter may be substituted for the almond butter.

Challah or multigrain bread may be substituted for the white bread.

Bananas Foster Wraps

Serves 4

Bananas Foster was first made in the 1950s at Brennan's Restaurant in New Orleans, named for Richard Foster, a favorite customer. It is still one of their most requested desserts and very popular at Southern restaurants. It's one of my family's favorite desserts. It is delicious and fun served in a wrap. Ice cream melts the warm glaze of bananas along with their buttery rum sauce.

⅓ cup + 1 tbsp	butter, divided	90 mL
4	medium ripe bananas, cut in half lengthwise	4
½ cup	firmly packed dark brown sugar	125 mL
¼ tsp	ground cinnamon	1 mL
¼ tsp	ground nutmeg	1 mL
½ cup	dark rum	125 mL
¼ cup	banana liqueur	60 mL
4	8-inch (20 cm) flour tortillas, warmed	4
	Vanilla ice cream or yogurt	

1. In a large nonstick skillet, heat 1 tbsp (15 mL) of the butter over medium-high heat. Add bananas and cook for 2 to 3 minutes or until lightly browned. Set aside.

2. Add remaining butter and heat until melted. Add brown sugar, cinnamon and nutmeg and cook, stirring constantly, for about 2 minutes or until bubbling. Stir in rum and banana liqueur and cook for 2 minutes more.

3. Ignite rum with a long match. Let flames die down. Return bananas to skillet and cook over medium heat for 2 to 3 minutes or until curled slightly.

4. Place warmed tortillas on a work surface. Spoon banana mixture over tortillas and top with vanilla ice cream or yogurt. Fold tortillas in half.

Tip: Be very careful when igniting the rum and liqueur and move any children away from the stove area. I like to tip the pan away from myself.

Blueberry Bread Sandwich

Serves 8

I love the idea of using a quick bread that is so incredible as this as the base for a dessert sandwich. This recipe is one of my favorites.

⅓ cup	butter or margarine	75 mL
1 cup	granulated sugar	250 mL
2	eggs	2
1½ cups	all-purpose flour	375 mL
1 tsp	baking powder	5 mL
1 tsp	ground cinnamon	5 mL
½ tsp	salt	2 mL
½ cup	milk	125 mL
3 tbsp	grated orange zest, divided	45 mL
2½ cups	fresh or frozen blueberries, divided	625 mL
1 cup	blueberry preserves or jam	250 mL
4 oz	cream cheese, softened	125 g

Tip: Serve leftover blueberry bread toasted with cream cheese, mascarpone cheese, melted butter or just as is.

- **Preheat oven to 350°F (180°C)**
- **8- by 4-inch (20 by 10 cm) loaf pan, greased**

1. In a bowl, beat together butter, sugar and eggs.

2. In another bowl, combine flour, baking powder, cinnamon and salt. Stir into egg mixture, alternating with milk. Fold in 1 tbsp (15 mL) of the orange zest and 1½ cups (375 mL) of the blueberries. Pour into prepared pan.

3. Bake in preheated oven for 55 to 60 minutes or until a toothpick inserted in center comes out clean. Let cool in pan for 10 minutes. Cut into eight ½-inch (1 cm) thick slices.

4. Meanwhile, in a saucepan over low heat, stir together remaining 1 cup (250 mL) of blueberries and preserves for 5 minutes or until warm. Set aside.

5. In a small bowl, combine cream cheese and remaining orange zest. Set aside.

6. On a serving plate, spread cream cheese mixture over 4 slices of blueberry bread. Top with remaining piece and drizzle with blueberry sauce. Serve immediately.

Variation

Lemon zest can be substituted for the orange zest.

Library and Archives Canada Cataloguing in Publication

Lewis, Alison, 1967–
    400 best sandwich recipes : from classics & burgers to wraps & condiments / Alison Lewis.

Includes index.
ISBN 978-0-7788-0265-5

    1. Sandwiches. I. Title. II. Title: Four hundred best sandwich recipes.

TX818.L48 2011   641.8'4   C2010-907387-8

Index

v = variation

A

aïolis, 310–12

alfalfa sprouts
California Grilled Cheese, 122
Californian, 279
Crunchy Vegetable Wraps, 190
Egg, Avocado and Sprout Wraps, 18
Pepper Jack, Avocado and Sprouts Sandwich, 302
Smoked Turkey Hummus Wraps, 50
Veggie and Goat Cheese Wraps, 187

almond butter
Almond Butter, Honey and Banana Chips Wraps, 192
Almond Butter, Honey and Banana Sandwich, 56
Grilled Dark Chocolate and Almond Butter Sandwich, 346
Hazelnut and Banana Panini (v), 345

almonds
Caribbean Chicken Wraps, 202
Dried Fruit, Almonds and Couscous Pita, 295
Grilled Applewood Smoked Bacon and Almonds, 91
Roasted Asparagus Pesto (v), 331
Thai Chicken Curry Wraps, 201
Trail Mix Wraps, 190
Veggie and Goat Cheese Wraps, 187

Antipasto Sandwich, 251

apples
Chicken, Apple and Smoked Gouda, 85
Chicken Waldorf Sandwich, 71
Grilled Apple Blue Cheese Sandwich, 131
Grilled Apple Cheddar Sandwich, 96
Grilled Brie, Apple and Thyme Sandwich, 95
Grilled Turkey and Brie with Apricot, 115
Turkey, Apple and Brie Sandwich, 54
Warm Apple-Pecan Wraps, 344

apricot preserves/jam
Ancho Adobo Steak, 265
Grilled Goat Cheese and Figs (v), 93
Grilled Turkey and Brie with Apricot, 115
Peach-Glazed Hot Roast Beef Sandwich (v), 32
Trail Mix Wraps, 190

apricots (dried)
Almond Butter, Honey and Banana Chips Wraps, 192
Apricot, Walnut and Blue Cheese Sandwich, 45
Dried Fruit, Almonds and Couscous Pita, 295
Grilled Apricot Blues, 99
Trail Mix Wraps, 190

artichokes
Antipasto Sandwich, 251
Chicken, Artichoke and Arugula Sandwich, 291
Eggs Sardou Sandwich, 16
Grilled Swiss, Artichokes, Tomato and Olives, 138
Mini Broccoli Quiche Sandwich (v), 26

arugula
Chicken, Artichoke and Arugula Sandwich, 291
Dried Fruit, Almonds and Couscous Pita, 295
Roast Beef and Fontina Focaccia Panini, 126
Smoked Mozzarella, Arugula and Tomato, 97
Smoked Turkey Wraps, 204
Thanksgiving Turkey Wraps, 206
Tomato Tea Sandwich with Arugula and Basil, 42
Turkey Hummus Wraps, 204

Asian-Style Turkey Burgers, 164

asparagus
Chicken and Asparagus Wraps, 197
Grilled Asparagus Swiss Pesto, 100
Roasted Asparagus Pesto, 331

Aussie Burgers, 148

avocado
Beef Tenderloin and Watercress Wraps, 209
BLT Grilled Cheese with Avocado, 92
California Grilled Cheese, 122
Californian, 279
Chicken-Avocado Dagwoods, 277
Chicken Thai Wraps, 202
Egg, Avocado and Sprout Wraps, 18
Flounder Wraps with Avocado Poblano Salsa, 229
Grilled Crab, Mango and Avocado, 86
Grilled Crab-Cilantro Quesadillas, 234
Grilled Guacomento, 77
Guacamole, 336
Ham, Turkey and Muenster Sandwich, 58

Huevos Rancheros Wraps, 17
Lobster Tacos with Avocado Salsa, 230
Mango-Avocado Relish, 323
Nacho Wraps, 189
Pepper Jack, Avocado and Sprouts Sandwich, 302
Roast Beef and Pepper Jack Sandwich (v), 57
Shrimp and Lime Sandwich, 256
Shrimp-Avocado Grilled Cheese, 108
Smoked Trout Wraps, 222
Southwestern Grilled Cheese, 120
Tomato, Avocado and Boursin, 32
Torta Ahogada, 239
Turkey Guacamole Burgers, 167
Turkey-Pesto Roll-Up, 53
Turkey Spinach Cobb Wraps, 205

B

bacon and pancetta
Bacon, Figs and Brie Crostini, 35
Bacon, Mushroom and Swiss Croissant, 25
Bacon and Cheese–Stuffed Burgers, 160
BLT and Pimiento Cheese Sliders, 159
BLT Breakfast Sandwich, 24
BLT Grilled Cheese with Avocado, 92
BLT Sandwich, Classic, 61
Breakfast Tacos, 15
Chicken-Avocado Dagwoods, 277
Club Sandwich, Classic, 74
Egg Salad with Smoked Paprika (v), 73
Eggs Benedict Sandwich, 14
Grilled Applewood Smoked Bacon and Almonds, 91
Grilled Bacon and Fried Green Tomatoes, 116
Grilled Pimiento Cheese BLT, 113
Grilled Pimiento Cheese with Bacon and Pickles, 115
Grilled Spinach, Pepper Jack and Bacon, 94
Grilled Turkey Cobb, 112
Louisville Hot Browns, 278
Oyster Bacon Po' Boys, 280
Peameal Bacon Sandwich, 247
Salmon BLT Sandwich, 62
Smoked Turkey Wraps, 204
Spinach Salad Wraps, Classic, 188
Turkey Hummus Wraps, 204

350